Kawsay Vida

Kawsay Vida

A MULTIMEDIA QUECHUA COURSE FOR BEGINNERS AND BEYOND

By ROSALEEN HOWARD

With contributions by
Phil Jimmieson,
Pedro Plaza,
Julieta Zurita,
Rufino Chuquimamani,
Carmen Alosilla,
and Phil Russell

Course Book
and Interactive Multimedia DVD

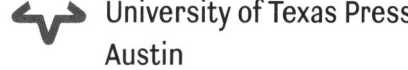
University of Texas Press
Austin

This book is published as part of the Recovering Languages and Literacies of the Americas initiative. Recovering Languages and Literacies is generously supported by the Andrew W. Mellon Foundation.

The royalties from the sale of *Kawsay Vida* will be used to fund educational and linguistic initiatives among the communities in Bolivia and Peru who collaborated in the project.

The Interactive Multimedia DVD enclosed with this book was produced by the author. The University of Texas Press is not responsible for its contents.

Copyright © 2013 by the University of Texas Press
All rights reserved
Printed in the United States of America
First edition, 2013

Requests for permission to reproduce material from this work should be sent to:
    Permissions
    University of Texas Press
    P.O. Box 7819
    Austin, TX 78713-7819
    http://utpress.utexas.edu/index.php/rp-form

♾ The paper used in this book meets the minimum requirements of ANSI/NISO Z39.48-1992 (R1997) (Permanence of Paper).

Library of Congress Cataloging-in-Publication Data
Howard, Rosaleen.
  Kawsay Vida : a multimedia Quechua course for beginners and beyond : course book and interactive multimedia dvd / By Rosaleen Howard ; With contributions by Phil Jimmieson, Pedro Plaza, Julieta Zurita, Rufino Chuquimamani, Carmen Alosilla, and Phil Russell. — 1st ed.
    audio disc: digital,CD audio; 4 ¾ in.
  Includes bibliographical references and index.
  ISBN 978-0-292-75624-3 (cloth : alk. paper) — ISBN 978-0-292-75444-7 (pbk. : alk. paper)
  1. Quechua language—Textbooks for foreign speakers. 2. Quechua language—Grammar. 3. Quechua language—Sound recordings for foreign speakers. I. Title.
  PM6303.H69 2014
  498'.32382421—dc23
                                                            2013013477

doi:10.7560/754447

This work is dedicated to the many people
who have shared their knowledge of the Quechua language
with me over many years; and to my family and friends

Qhichwa yachachiqniykunapaqpis ayllu masiykunapaqpis

CONTENTS

Acknowledgments xi

Introduction / About *Kawsay Vida* 1

PART I

1 / Juk ⌘ Napaykuna / Greetings 11
Kawsay / Andean Life: The Quechua Language

Greeting people and inquiring after their health; verb **kay** 'to be,' singular forms; personal pronouns, singular forms; suffix **-chka-** with **kay** indicating temporary state; interrogative pronouns **imayna** 'how?' and **imataq** 'what?'; suffix **-rí** in questions; suffixes **-pis, -lla, -taq** and their combination.

2 / Iskay ⌘ Runakuna / People 21
Kawsay / Andean Life: Identities

Talking about different members of groups in Bolivian society; making simple statements using suffix **-qa**; asking questions using suffix **-chu**; emphatic suffix **-puni**.

3 / Kimsa ⌘ P'acha / Clothing 30
Kawsay / Andean Life: Clothing

Talking about typical items of clothing in Bolivia; interrogative pronoun **ima** 'what?'; use of **-taq** in interrogatives; use of demonstratives **kay, chay, jaqay**; making negative assertions using **mana . . .-chu**.

4 / Tawa ⌘ Ruwana / Daily Tasks 39
Kawsay / Andean Life: Technologies

Talking to doña Elisa about daily activities; verbs in the singular unmarked tense; use of **-chka-** to show action in progress; **-ta** direct-object marker.

5 / Phichqa ⌘ Maymantataq jamunki? / Where Do You Come From? 48

Kawsay / Andean Life: The Fiesta Cycle

> Talking to don Máximo about where people are from; verb **kay** 'to be,' plural forms; personal pronouns, plural forms; suffix **-manta** marking point of origin; interrogative pronoun **machkha** 'how many'/ 'how much?'; further use of **-pis**; contrastive use of **-taq**; numbers 1–10.

6 / Suqta ⌘ Maymantaq richkanki? / Where Are You Going? 58

Kawsay / Andean Life: Geography and Travel

> Talking to people from Coacarí as they arrive in San Pedro for the fiesta; noun suffix **-man** indicating movement toward a place; verb suffix **-mu-** marking direction of action; nominalizing suffix **-q** marking "doer" of action; **-q** with verbs of movement indicating purpose; noun suffix **-pi** to mark location.

7 / Qanchis ⌘ Yuyarina / Review 68

PART II

8 / Pusaq ⌘ Allin kay / Health 75

Kawsay / Andean Life: Health and Sickness

> Talking about your health and parts of the body; interrogative form **imayki**? 'what of yours?'; possessive suffixes, singular forms; the basics of person/object-marking in verb phrases.

9 / Jisq'un ⌘ Chhiqa / Places 82

Kawsay / Andean Life: Music

> Talking to a charango player about musical beliefs; reflexive suffix **-ku-**; **-ku-** combined with -mu- as -kamu-; plurals of nouns; causative suffix **-chi-** marking delegated action; further use of interrogative marker -chu; further use of -ta.

10 / Chunka ⌘ Away / Weaving 92

Kawsay / Andean Life: Weaving

> Talking to doña Imigdia about weaving techniques; suffix **-wan** 'with'; interrogative form **imawan** 'what with?'; further uses of -**manta**; possessive suffixes, singular and plural; the genitive suffix in possessive constructions; noun + noun construction.

11 / Chunka jukniyuq ⌘ Simikuna / Languages 103

Kawsay / Andean Life: Languages

> Talking to don Vitalio about the languages people speak; indirect past tense **-sqa-**; further uses of -**manta** and –**ta**; class-free suffixes -**ña** 'already' and -**raq** 'still'; attributive suffix -**yuq**.

12 / Chunka iskayniyuq ⌘ P'achamanta / Clothing Styles   113

Kawsay / Andean Life: Social Change

> Talking to doña Filomena about changes in clothing styles over time; direct past tense -**rqa**-; habitual past tense -**q ka**-; more about the suffix -**yuq**; suffix -**tawan** in forming lists; suffix -**spa** marking secondary verb in complex sentences.

13 / Chunka kimsayuq ⌘ Yuyarina / Review   123

PART III

14 / Chunka tawayuq ⌘ Awayta yachay / Learning to Weave   129

Kawsay / Andean Life: Learning Skills for Life

> Talking to doña Filomena about learning how to weave; describing sequences of actions using -**spataq**; interrogative **jayk'aq** 'when?'; -**y** nominalizing suffix; "infinitive as object" construction; suffix -**paq** "purposive"; further use of -**pis**; emphatic -**pacha**; diminutive -**itu**.

15 / Chunka phichqayuq ⌘ Fiesta ruwana tiyan / Having to Sponsor a Fiesta   139

Kawsay / Andean Life: Fiesta Sponsorship

> Talking to doña Primitiva about the custom of fiesta sponsorship; expressing obligation and talking about getting things done; -**na** nominalizing suffix; -**na tiyan** construction to express obligation; "-**na**- + -**paq**" construction to express purpose; use of **ima** to close a list; further practice of causative suffix -**chi**- expressing delegated action.

16 / Chunka suqtayuq ⌘ Unquy / Illness   147

Kawsay / Andean Life: Sickness and Cosmovision

> Talking about causes and symptoms of ill health; talking about the weather; use of impersonal verbs; the future tense; object marking on verbs, 1st- and 2nd-persons plural; conjectural suffix -**chá**.

17 / Chunka qanchisniyuq ⌘ Feriaman riy / Going to Market   159

Kawsay / Andean Life: Trade and Markets

> Negotiating a purchase in the market in San Pedro. How to talk about prices and personal taste in clothing. Imperative forms of the verb; expressions of courtesy and respect; interrogative forms **mayqintaq** 'which?' and **machkhapitaq** 'how much is it?' Verb suffix -**ri**- inceptive action; verb suffix -**yku**-, movement and politeness marker.

18 / Chunka pusaqniyuq ⌘ Mikhunata ruway / Preparing Food   167

Kawsay / Andean Life: Foods

> Talking to doña Roberta about the technique of preparing pelado (peeled corn); describing processes; forming complex sentences using the subordinating suffixes -**pti**- and -**spa**; more practice of verb suffixes -**ri**- and -**yku**-.

19 / Chunka jisq'unniyuq ⌘ Inkamanta / About the Incas   173
Kawsay / Andean Life: The Conquest of the Incas

> Talking to don Celestino about the popular Quechua drama *Tragedia del fin de Atahuallpa*; talking about socioeconomic differences and natural resources; **kay** as an abstract noun 'being'; uses of verb suffix **-pu-** as benefactive, with verbs of movement, and indicating decisive action; **-pu-** compared with **-mu-** and **-ku-**.

20 / Iskay chunka ⌘ Kamachiqmanta / About the President   182
Kawsay / Andean Life: Indigenous Political Revival

> In this unit we discuss the social and political situation in Bolivia since January 2006, when the indigenous leader Evo Morales was elected president; use of the suffix **-sqa**, the noun suffix **-kama**; and the verb suffix **-naku-**.

21 / Iskay chunka jukniyuq ⌘ Yuyarina / Review   188

22 / Iskay chunka iskayniyuq ⌘ Jallp'amanta Parlarisun / Let's Talk about the Earth   195

Vocabulary Checklist   199
References   209

ACKNOWLEDGMENTS

Many people have contributed to the development of the *Kawsay Vida* program (course book and multimedia DVD) at different stages over a number of years.

The cultural information and Quechua language content are based on live conversations and interviews with people in the cantón of San Pedro de Buenavista, province of Charcas, Northern Potosí, Bolivia; and with people in the community of Parpacalla, San Salvador district, department of Cuzco, Peru.

The following people contributed to the collection, design, and writing of the program materials:

Native language proficiency and linguistic expertise:

    Bolivian Quechua: Rosaleen Howard, Pedro Plaza, Julieta Zurita

    Peruvian Quechua: Rufino Chuquimamani, Carmen Alosilla Morales

Multimedia programming: Phil Jimmieson

Multimedia courseware design: Phil Russell

Video camerawork: Mary Jo Dudley, Renato Flores

Still photography: Andrew Canessa, Mary Jo Dudley, Rosaleen Howard

    Photo p. 76, Felicity Nock, courtesy of Gwennie and Simon Fraser

    Photo p. 104, from Howard-Malverde, Rosaleen. 1995. "Pachamama is a Spanish word: linguistic tension between Aymara, Quechua and Spanish in Northern Potosí (Bolivia)." *Anthropological Linguistics*, 37 (2): 141–168.

    Photo p. 176, Ximena Córdova

Anthropological expertise: Andrew Canessa, Rosaleen Howard, Elayne Zorn†

Coordinator in Peru: Cecilia Rivera

Funding bodies and supporting institutions: King's College London, The Leverhulme Trust, The British Academy, The University of Liverpool, Pontificia Universidad Católica del Perú, The British Council, Lima, Newcastle University

Other collaborators: Irina Avila, Nick Bugg, Robin Kilpatrick, Marino Luna, Nicholas Ostler, William Rowe, Henry Stobart, Mamerto Torres

Reviewers: Serafín Coronel-Molina, Sabine Dedenbach-Salazar Sáenz, Bruce Mannheim, Zoila Mendoza, Tristan Platt

Introduction

About *Kawsay Vida*

The Package

Kawsay Vida ("life," in Quechua and Spanish, respectively) comprises a course book and interactive multimedia program on DVD, suitable for the teaching and learning of the Quechua language from beginner to advanced levels. The course book is based on contemporary Bolivian Quechua, while the multimedia program contains both a section on Bolivian Quechua (beginner to intermediate levels) and a section on southern Peruvian Quechua (advanced level). The text provides a practical introduction to spoken Quechua through the medium of English, while the multimedia program offers a choice of English or Spanish as the medium of instruction. The DVD is available for both PC and Apple platforms.

The Course Book

The *Kawsay Vida* course book is based around a series of video recordings of speakers using their language in spontaneous speech; clips from many of these recordings are contained in the accompanying multimedia program (see below). *Kawsay Vida* differs from many beginning language courses in this respect. Language in spontaneous utterance and language in the prescriptive form that it takes in many grammars and course books are two different things. Many beginners' manuals proceed from prescription to description; that is, from the rules to their application, or to the pointing out of exceptions, in actual speech. This approach might make life a little easier for the beginner: the samples of language that they encounter at the early stages are carefully crafted in order to present structures and vocabulary according to the author's design. However, they create an artificial environment for the learner, wherein he or she is buffered from the realities of speech variation in its many guises.

Kawsay Vida makes spontaneous spoken language its starting point, leading students straight into the world of the Quechua speaker of Northern Potosí, before moving on to structural explanations and specially designed practical exercises. This approach, we believe, is particularly effective in the case of a language closely bound up with a culture quite different from that of the potential user of the book. The video clips introduce the student to residents of a particular valley in the region, interviewed on location near their homes, giving a sense of immediacy that the printed page and the artificially created text cannot achieve.

The book contains twenty-two units of study. As the student works through these, cross-references take them to relevant sections of the DVD, as a means of reinforcing and expanding the points being studied. The Bolivian and Peruvian Quechua sections of the multimedia program are divided into thematically and grammatically ordered modules, which introduce the user to different aspects of Andean life, while progressing language learning in a structured way. The user engages with the audio, video, and visual material contained in the DVD through a range of interactive exercises, which practice listening and comprehension skills. Once familiarity with the language is acquired, the multimedia program may be used independently from the book.

Kawsay Vida has been piloted over the last ten years with undergraduate and postgraduate students in Latin American Studies programs at the University of Liverpool and Newcastle University. From this experience, we can assert that some seventy-five hours of classroom tuition are needed to cover the twenty-two units. The time required to work through the materials contained in the DVD is harder to calculate, as this will depend on individual learning styles and needs.

The fieldwork and filming on which the book is based were conducted during the summers of 1990, 1991, and 1993, in the cantón of San Pedro de Buenavista, province of Charcas, Northern Potosí, Bolivia.[1] The Quechua spoken in the countryside here is less heavily influenced by Spanish than that spoken in the town, and less mixed with Spanish than the Quechua of Cochabamba. There is some Aymara substratum, and in the countryside Quechua-Aymara bilingualism, or trilingualism with Spanish, persists. Despite local variation, it is easily intelligible across a wide area of the southern Andes, including southern Peru, and can be understood, with some modification in pronunciation, also in Ecuador.

In determining the content of each unit, the production team took the video footage as their starting point. To a large extent, the content of this footage dictated the thematic contents of the book: daily life in the town and surrounding communities of San Pedro de Buenavista. If there seems to be a particular emphasis given to certain activities over others, this is because our visits took place during the dry months in the Andes, including the fiesta season in late June. The fiesta in honor of San Pedro's patrons (Saint Peter and Saint Paul) was a focal point of our attention, as the material reflects.

At the same time, a plan was drawn up as to the grammatical progression the course book should ideally follow, starting from the formation of simple sentences and moving on to more complex constructions. The aim was to spread the study of grammar points, particularly the verb and noun suffixes, evenly and thinly over the total number of units, and to present them in an order that reflected their relative frequency of use in everyday speech. This aim in principle was sometimes constrained in practice by the lack of suitable footage to illustrate a particular point. To resolve this, we devised some units where there is no video, and priority is given instead to the sequencing of grammar points. Overall, we sought a compromise between the wish to present the grammar in the most pedagogically appropriate sequence, and the wish to include the most interesting and technically suitable sequences of video.

The order in which the past tenses are introduced illustrates this compromise. On analyzing the footage, our team found that very few of the speakers interviewed used the direct past tense (indicated by **-rqa-**), which was not necessary for the particular topics of conversation that arose. Moreover, in the most technically satisfactory sequence in which this tense occurs, the speaker also uses constructions that it seemed more appropriate to introduce at a later stage, for example the habitual past tense (constructed with **-q** and **ka-**). On the other hand, the indirect past tense (signaled by **-sqa-**) was found in a sequence where the surrounding language was relatively simple. It was thus preferable to introduce

---

1. Rosaleen Howard conducted filming and fieldwork, with assistance from Rodolfo Malverde in 1990, Mary Jo Dudley in 1991, and Andrew Canessa in 1993. Pedro Plaza is a native speaker of Northern Potosí Quechua and participated in the piloting of the course book at Liverpool.

the use of the **-sqa-** past tense (Unit 11 Chunka jukniyuq) before the use of the **-rqa-** past tense (Unit 12 Chunka iskayniyuq), contrary to what is found in Quechua language course books based on more prescriptive criteria, where usage of **-rqa-** is generally taught first.[2]

The course units were initially written, piloted, and edited during the years 1993 to 1996, a period of much innovation and flux in the field of applied linguistics in Bolivia. Following the introduction of the Programa de Educación Intercultural Bilingüe (PEIB) in 1990, Education Reform Law 1565 (passed in 1994) officialized intercultural bilingual education for speakers of indigenous languages, including Quechua. These reforms involved further revision of the alphabet best suited for the standardized—written—form of the language. In order to show uniformity with language-teaching materials being produced in Bolivia for local educational use, we adopted PEIB orthography for *Kawsay Vida*. In the new (post-2006) political conjuncture language planners have taken further decisions about the standard ("norma") for the written language. These are limited to the spelling of a small number of lexemes and have also been taken into account.

The term "Quechua" refers to a language family within which there are many varieties, some of them closer to each other, and thus more mutually intelligible, than others. Broadly speaking the Quechua languages present dialectological differences that place the varieties of central Peru (departments of Huánuco, Ancash, Cerro de Pasco, Junín, and northern Lima) at one end of a continuum, while the languages (or varieties) spoken in northern Peru, Ecuador, southern Peru, Bolivia, and northwest Argentina are located toward the other end of the scale of difference. Alfredo Torero (1964, 1974) conducted pioneering research on the classification of the Quechua dialects, placing the southern Peruvian and Bolivian varieties of Quechua presented in *Kawsay Vida* within the same dialect grouping.[3]

There are some differences between the Quechua of the "Bolivia" section of the *Kawsay Vida* DVD program, which represents the variety spoken in the valleys of Northern Potosí, and the Quechua of the "Peru" section, which represents the Quechua of Cuzco. For example, the Cuzco speakers regularly use a phrase marker **-mi** when they make affirmations. This marker adds a nuance of "validation" to the statement being made; it is rarely found in the Quechua of Northern Potosí.

There is one notable difference between the current spelling conventions of Bolivian Quechua and those of southern Peruvian Quechua that we observe in our spelling of each variety in the multimedia program. While in Bolivian Quechua the velar fricative /x/ as in English "ham" is written with "j" (**jamuy** 'to come'), in Peru this sound is represented with "h" (**hamuy**). The course book, being based on the Bolivian variety, uses a "j" for this sound; however, in the Peru section of the multimedia program users will encounter the "h." As these materials are prepared as much with Andean as Anglo-American users in mind, we consider it crucial that local norms of spelling—which are the outcome of debates going back to the mid-1980s among language planners in the countries where Quechua is spoken—be adhered to.

The following list summarizes the sounds of Bolivian and southern Peruvian Quechua, giving a phonemic gloss and approximate equivalent pronunciations in English where available.

---

2. It may be that the priority given to *-rqa-* in the order of presentation of the Quechua past tenses in most course books is due to the fact that the function of this tense is somewhat closer to that of past tenses in more familiar, European languages, than is the function of *-sqa-*.

3. See also Gary Parker's classification (1963). Cerrón Palomino 1987 and Mannheim 1991 provide further discussion of the historical development of the Quechua dialects. Grammatical studies of Bolivian Quechua include Lastra 1968, Albó 1974, and Plaza 2009. Course books include Grondín 1971, Bills et al. 1971, Morató Peña 1994, and Plaza 2010. The audiovisual materials on Cochabamba Quechua compiled by the late Roger Anderson and his team are a valuable complement to *Kawsay Vida*, and may be found at http://quechua.ucla.edu/ (Anderson 2005–2011).

a	aqha	open back vowel	
ch	china	plain alveolar affricate	
chh	chhama	aspirated alveolar affricate	"chat"
ch'	ch'arki	ejective alveolar affricate	
j/h	j/hamun	velar fricative	"happy"
i	ichhu	closed mid-vowel	"eat"
k	kachi	velar stop	"cat"
l	lawa	alveolar lateral	"lap"
ll	llama	palatal lateral	
m	mama	bilabial nasal	"man"
n	nina	alveolar nasal	"nice"
ñ	ñaña	palatal nasal	
p	papa	plain bilabial stop	
ph	phuru	aspirated bilabial stop	"pan"
p'	p'ata	ejective bilabial stop	
q	qaqa	plain postvelar stop	
qh	qhura	aspirated postvelar stop	
q'	q'aya	ejective postvelar stop	
r	ruwan	bilabial flap	
s	simi	alveolar sibilant	"sat"
t	tinku	plain alveolar stop	
th	thanta	aspirated alveolar stop	"tap"
t'	t'anta	ejective alveolar stop	
u	ura	closed front vowel	
w	wawa	bilabial glide	"wake"
y	yuraq	palatal glide	"yam"

In addition to the above standards at the level of phonology we have adopted standardized conventions for morpho-phonological representation of the verb suffixes **-chka-** (progressive action; variously pronounced as [**chka ~ sha ~ sa ~ sqa ~ xa**]);[4] **-nchik** (1st-person inclusive; variously pronounced as [**nchis ~ nchix**]); **-p ~ -pa** (genitive; variously pronounced [**x ~ pa ~ pax**]; and **-pti-** (verbal subordinator; pronounced [**xti**]; also commonly written **-qti-**). In the vocabulary given in each unit, and in the vocabulary checklist at the back of the book, where the pronunciation of a word differs from its representation in standardized spelling, the pronounced form is indicated within brackets. For example, the word **lluqalla** 'young boy' is pronounced [lloqalla].

As a result of the social, political, and economic dominance of Spanish since the colonial period, many Quechua speakers became bilingual with the European language in order to be able to communicate across the linguistic divide and in institutional spheres, while Quechua became largely associated with rural, domestic, and intimate settings. The bilingualism that grew from this "diglossic" situation gave rise to language mixture in the speech of many individuals, and words that originated in Spanish eventually became part of Quechua vocabulary, whether or not the speaker was bilingual. The pronunciation of hispanisms in Quechua speech shows different degrees of assimilation to the Quechua sound system, depending on how well established they are in daily use.

4. The letter "x" as in [xa] and elsewhere is a phonetic representation of the aspirated /h/ as pronounced in Spanish *jamón* or English "ham."

One problem posed for writing Quechua, therefore, is whether words of Spanish origin should be written according to their "Quechuaized" pronunciation, or whether they should be written according to Spanish norms. We have used the degree of assimilation into Quechua vocabulary as a guiding precept here. For example, long-established words like "uwija" from Spanish oveja 'sheep' and "waka" from Spanish vaca 'cow' are written according to Quechua spelling rules. But for the most part, due to the varied modes of pronunciation of the Spanish borrowings into Quechua, we have chosen to write these words according to Spanish norms, with an indication in brackets of their most usual Quechua pronunciation, for example "escuela" [iskwila] for "school" and so on.

Another issue that arises in teaching Quechua to second-language learners is whether to teach the hispanisms as part of the Quechua lexicon. For some twenty years now, teaching of Quechua in the formal education system in the Andean countries has become more widespread and is now official policy. This process has given rise to many debates among native-speaking education specialists about the internal development of the language. Should the written materials being produced for educational purposes retain the high level of hispanisms to be found in Quechua speech, or should something be done to regenerate the language's own vocabulary? Those involved in Quechua-language education have often adopted the latter option. An effort is made to replace words of Spanish origin with proper Quechua vocabulary.

Various strategies are used here. For example, new words may be coined, drawing on existing Quechua vocabulary in order to express ideas that originate in the Spanish-speaking society, giving rise to neologisms such as "yachay wasi" (lit. "knowledge house") for "school" in place of "iskwila." Alternatively, attempts are made to revive, sometimes with new meanings, vocabulary that has fallen out of use (archaisms). Here, dictionaries from the colonial period such as the monumental work of the Jesuit scholar Diego González de Holguín (1993 [1608]) are drawn upon, and a word like "qillqay," for example, which originally meant "to draw, carve, or embroider," is put to service as the Quechua word for "to write" using alphabetic script.

You will come across people using many hispanisms in the video clips on the DVD. As our approach is to take the spoken language as a starting point, in the text of the *Kawsay Vida* book we retain these hispanisms to a large extent. However, in the interest of language regeneration by the means described above, we also introduce some of the neologisms and archaisms that Quechua-language education specialists propose, and many of which are now gaining currency in everyday speech.

Each unit of the book opens with a summary of the main grammatical constructions to be featured in that unit. There follows a short section entitled "Kawsay/Andean Life," which provides some cultural context for the material to be covered. The aim is to emphasize the close relationship between language and cultural life, and to motivate the student to use the study of the language as a springboard for further reading on the culture. This is followed by a short piece of text in which these constructions are used, followed in turn by a vocabulary list and grammar notes. There is then a series of exercises in which the structures and vocabulary are put into practice. These include cross-references to the multimedia program. Students are directed to work on specific sections of the DVD, in order to practice and reinforce the language they are studying in any given unit. For example, in Unit 1, exercise "3 Kimsa" directs the student to the DVD in the following way:

> 3 Kimsa ⌘ Qhawana / Video View ▶ DVD
>
> Go to the following section of the *Kawsay Vida* multimedia program:
>
> *Peruvian Quechua > ayllu > qhawana > Casimirawan tupana*
>
> Watch the video clip, and answer the questions below. Do not worry that you do not understand much of the text at this stage. Just listen to the Quechua being spoken. You may click the ENGLISH button to see the translation.
>
> 1. At the start of the clip, Carmen uses three phrases to greet Casimira. Note them down.
> 2. At the end of the clip, how does she say goodbye to her?
> 3. How do people say goodbye in Bolivian Quechua?
> 4. If you were to meet a friend on the road, how would you greet him/her?

In each unit, writing, speaking, and listening skills are variously practiced.

The Multimedia Program

The multimedia program on DVD supports and extends the work carried out by the learner in the classroom that is based on the course book. The material in the Bolivia section of the DVD is based on the same field material as the book, and thus complements the latter. Through still images, sound, movies, and text, the multimedia program provides interactive language drills, aural transcription practice, and electronic grammar and dictionary lookup facilities.

Getting Started with the Multimedia Program
- On PC insert the disc, double click the "Kawsay Vida for PC Set-Up" icon and follow the instructions in the *Installer Wizard*.
- On Apple insert the disc and copy the "Kawsay Vida for Mac" folder to your *Applications Folder*.
- To get started, **double click** on the "Kawsay Vida" icon. This is the only time you should use a double click as you work on the program.
- The title sequence will begin. You may click at any time to bypass this sequence.
- On the Program menu page, click "Preferences" to select your language medium. Click "OK" to return to the Program menu.
- Beginners should start with the Bolivian Quechua section.
- Until you become familiar, you are advised to work down the menus in sequence, or go to the links suggested in the course book units as you progress.
- **Single click** on the menu choices to move around the program. Be patient: the response may be a little slow!
- Be sure to read the **on-screen instructions** as you work through the interactive exercises.

Using the Multimedia Lookup Facility

As you work in the multimedia program, you can use the lookup facility to check the meanings of words and suffixes at any time. You may access the lookup in two ways:

1. Click on the **red question mark** in the top right-hand corner of the screen; when the palette opens, type the item you wish to look up into the search box and click "Find."
2. Alternatively, when you have a piece of Quechua text on-screen, click the ANALYSIS button; then click on any part of the analyzed text (word root or suffix); the palette will open at that item.

Note that when searching for a verb in the dictionary lookup palette, you should enter the verb root only into the search box, not the infinitive form. Thus, for example, to search for the verb "jamuy" (to come) enter "jamu."

When searching for a suffix in the grammar lookup palette, you should enter these into the search box without dashes. Thus, for example, to search for -**yki**- (2nd-person-singular possessive marker) enter "yki."

PART I

1 / Juk

Napaykuna / Greetings

In This Unit...

You learn how to greet someone, inquire after their health, and ask their name and where they are from. You study the verb **kay** 'to be' and the singular forms of personal pronouns. You learn the interrogative pronouns **imayna** 'how?' and **imataq** 'what?' You study the verb suffix **-chka-** used with **kay** to indicate a temporary state; the class-free suffix **-rí** in questions; the class-free suffixes **-pis**, **-lla**, **-taq**, and their combination. You learn basic vocabulary for talking about the family.

KAWSAY / ANDEAN LIFE
The Quechua Language

Quechua language is spoken mainly in rural areas of the Andean region, and in small provincial towns that constitute administrative centers and cantón capitals, such as San Pedro de Buenavista, where the linguistic and ethnographic materials for this course book and DVD were recorded. In Bolivia today the language is taking a stronger hold in the cities as well; Quechua can be widely heard in Cochabamba, where the language demonstrates a greater admixture of Spanish than in rural communities of Northern Potosí such as Sikuya and Coacarí. According to the 2001 census, some 30 percent of the Bolivian population (more than two million people) are speakers of Quechua, while Peru's census of 2007 counted some three and a quarter million speakers, or 13 percent of the total population. In both Cuzco and Cochabamba there exist academies of the Quechua language, whose members are made up mainly of the landed bilingual and urban-dwelling classes, and who promote the language through writing and teaching. Their views on how the language should be written often differ from those of university linguists or government language planners, feeding the ongoing debates about how this formerly unwritten language should be confined to script.

Suggested reading: Mannheim 1991; Adelaar and Muysken 2004; Howard 2011.

– Imaynalla kachkanki?
– Waliqlla kachkani, qamrí?
– Ñuqapis waliqllataq kachkani!

Ñawirina, yachakuna / Read and Learn

Imaynalla kachkanki?	How are you?
Waliqlla kachkani.	I am just fine.
Qamrí?	And you?
Ñuqapis waliqllataq kachkani.	And I am just fine too.
Payrí?	And him/her?
Paypis waliqllataq kachkan.	And s/he is just fine too.

Parlana / Dialogue 1

– Imaynalla kachkanki mamáy (tatáy, ñañáy, wawqíy, turáy)?
– Waliqlla kachkani. Qamrí?
– Ñuqapis waliqllataq kachkani.
– Juanrí?
– Juanpis waliqllataq kachkan. Payrí?
– Paypis waliqllataq kachkan.

Parlana / Dialogue 2

– Imaynalla kachkanki wawqíy (mamáy, tatáy, panáy, turáy, ñañáy)?
– Allinlla kachkani. Qamrí?
– Ñuqapis allinllataq kachkani.
– Mamaykirí (tataykirí, wawqiykirí, panaykirí, turaykirí, ñañaykirí)?
– Mamaypis allinllataq kachkan.

Imataq sutiyki?	What is your name?
Sutiyqa Rosa.	My name is Rosa.
Qampatarí?	And yours?
Sutiyqa Pablo.	My name is Pablo.
Paypatarí, imataq sutin?	And what is his/her name?
Sutinqa María.	Her name is María.

Parlana / Dialogue 3
Imataq sutiyki?
Sutiyqa Rosa.

Parlana / Dialogue 4
Qampatarí, imataq sutiyki?
Sutiyqa Pablo.

Parlana / Dialogue 5
Paypatarí, imataq sutin?
Sutinqa Juan.
Paypatarí?
Sutinqa Luisa.

Maymantataq kanki?	Where are you from?
Boliviamanta kani.	I am from Bolivia.
Qamrí maymantataq kanki?	And you, where are you from?
Inglaterramanta kani.	I'm from England.
Payrí, maymantataq?	And her/him, where is s/he from?
Payqa Texasmanta.	He/she is from Texas.

Parlana / Dialogue 6
– Maymantataq kanki?
– Cochabambamanta kani, qamrí?
– Ñuqaqa Londresmanta kani.
– Juanrí maymantataq?
– Juanqa Madridmanta.

Simi / Vocabulary
Ruway / Verbs
    kay: to be.
    napaykuy: to greet.
    ñawiriy: to read.
    parlay: to speak.
    ruway: to do, to make.
    tinkuy (*Bol.*): to meet.
    tupay (*S. Peru*): to meet.
    watuykuy: to analyze, to inquire; to visit.
    yachakuy: to learn.

Suti / Nouns
    simi: mouth; language; word.
    suti: name; noun.

Ayllu masi / Family Members

allchhi: grandson, granddaughter.
awicha: grandmother.
awichu: grandfather.
ayllu: social group, extended family.
ayllu masi: fellow ayllu member.
cuñada: sister-in-law.
churi: son (*man speaking*).
jatun mama: grandmother.
jatun tata: grandfather.
mama: mother.
mamáy!: "Mother!" (term of address for married woman).
masi: coparticipant in a group or activity.
ñaña: sister of a woman.
pana: sister of a man.
tata: father.
tatáy!: "Father!" "Sir!" (term of address for married man).
tullqa: son-in-law, brother-in-law.
tura: brother of a woman.
ususi: daughter.
wawa: child, son (*woman speaking*).
wawqi: brother of a man.
yawar masi: blood kin.
yuqch'a (*var.* ñuqch'a): daughter-in-law.

Suti ranti / Personal Pronouns

ñuqa [noqa]: I, me.
pay: he; she.
paypata: his/hers.
qam [qan]: you, you.
qampata: yours.

Suti tikrachiq / Adjectives

allin: well, good, fine.
sumaq: well, good, fine, virtuous.
waliq [walex]: fine, well.

Tapuq suti ranti / Interrogative Pronouns

ima: what?
imayna: how?
may: where?
maymanta: where from?

Expressions

Tinkunakama! (Bolivia): "See you later!" "Until the next meeting!"
Tupananchikkama! [Tupananchiskama] (Peru): "See you later!" "Until we meet again!"

Simip k'askaynin / Grammar

Simimanta / Word Structure

Quechua words are agglutinative in structure. A word is made up of a **root** and one or more **suffixes**. Suffixes are attached to the root from left to right. Roots may act as verbs (**verb roots**, e.g., awa- 'weave'), as nouns or adjectives (**noun roots**, e.g., wasi 'house', waliq 'fine'), or as **particles** (freestanding forms with a grammatical function, e.g., mana 'no', arí 'yes'). Suffixes perform a range of grammatical functions. Verbal suffixes attach to roots of the verb class; noun suffixes attach to roots of the noun class; class-free suffixes attach to roots of all grammatical types.

Rimay muyuchina / Verb Conjugation

    kay

        Verb "to be," present tense, singular

(i) The verb **kay** expresses the intrinsic *identity* of a person. The personal pronouns and the verb suffixes combine to mark person in the sentence. In statements of identity the verb **kay** is omitted when the subject is a 3rd-person singular. Statements of identity with the verb **kay** often carry the topic marker -**qa** on the subject of the verb.

1st-person singular	**Ñuqa**-qa María ka-**ni**.	I am María.
2nd-person singular	**Qam**-qa Juan ka-**nki**.	You are Juan.
3rd-person singular	**Pay**-qa Pedro.	He is Pedro.

(ii) The 3rd-person-singular form of **kay** is ka**n**. This form expresses *existence* rather than identity, as in the English "there is/there are" or the Spanish form *hay*. This will be studied in a later unit.

(iii) In the 1st and 2nd persons, the personal pronouns may be omitted without affecting the meaning:

Ñuqa María ka-**ni**.	>>>	María ka-**ni**.	I am María.
Qam Juan ka-**nki**.	>>>	Juan ka-**nki**.	You are Juan.

(iv) In the "Vocabulary" section of each unit, verbs are listed in the infinitive form with a -**y** on the end (e.g., **kay** 'to be'). In order to conjugate the verb, the -**y** is deleted, which leaves the verb **root**. **Suffixes** are added to the verb root to form a word. Thus, the root **ka**- 'be' takes the person suffixes -**ni** (1st-person singular) and -**nki** (2nd-person singular) to form **kani** ("I am") and **kanki** ("you are"), respectively; it takes -**n** (3rd-person singular) to form **kan** ("there is," "there are"). The hyphen (-) will be used in examples throughout the course book for the purpose of grammatical analysis, to show the structure of a word, e.g., **ka-ni** 'be 1st-person singular'.

Ruway k'askaq / Verb Suffixes

    -**chka**-

        Added to **kay** 'to be' to indicate temporary state

When attached to the verb **kay** 'to be', the suffix -**chka**- usually gives the state of "being" a temporary or spatial quality, comparable to the Spanish *estar*:

Waliqlla ka-**chka**-ni.	I'm just fine.
Qamrí imaynalla ka-**chka**-nki?	And how are you?
Juanqa waliqlla ka-**chka**-n.	Juan is just fine.

Note: This suffix has a number of pronunciations, for example: [**chka**], [**shka**], [**sha**], [**sa**]. The written norm is -**chka**-.

Suti k'askaq / Noun Suffixes
Possessive Singular

These suffixes, attached to a noun root, form the possessive adjective in the singular form ("my," "your," "his," "her").

mama-**y**	my mother
mama-**yki**	your mother
mama-**n**	his/her mother

-**y**
　Used in terms of address

The 1st-person-singular possessive suffix -**y** may be added to noun roots to form a term of address. In this case, the last syllable of the word is stressed in speech, and marked with an acute accent in writing:

mamáy!	mother!
datáy!	father!
ñañáy!	sister!

-**manta**
　Originative function; "from"

This noun suffix indicates the point of origin of the action of the verb. In this unit we see its use with the verb **kay** 'to be' to indicate a person's origin:

May-**manta**-taq kanki?	Where are you from?
Bolivia-**manta** kani.	I am from Bolivia.

Wak k'askaq / Class-Free Suffixes
-**qa**
　Topic marker

This suffix marks the topic or subject matter of the sentence, e.g.:

Pay-**qa** waliqlla kachkan.	He is just fine.
Juan-**qa** allinlla kachkan.	Juan is just fine.
Ñuqa-**qa** Londresmanta kani.	I am from London.
Sutin-**qa** Juan.	His name is Juan.

-**lla**
　Limitative function; "just"

This suffix softens or limits the force of the phrase to which it is attached:

waliq	fine	>>>	waliq-**lla**	just fine
ñuqa	I	>>>	ñuqa-**lla**	just me

-taq
Question tag

This suffix translates as "and." When used as a tag on interrogative pronouns it softens the force of the question:

Ima-**taq** sutiyki?	And what is your name?
Ima-**taq** sutin?	And what is his/her name?
Maymanta-**taq** kanki?	And where are you from?
Juan maymanta-**taq**?	And where is Juan from?

-pis
Inclusive function; "also," "even"

This suffix indicates inclusion in a group:

Juanqa waliqlla kachkan.	Juan is just fine.
María-**pis** waliqllataq kachkan.	And María too is just fine.

-pis . . . -lla-taq
"And . . . too"

This combination of suffixes gives the sense of "and that too is the case":

pay-**pis**	waliq-**lla-taq**	
she/he-also	fine-just-and	
and she/he too is just fine		

ñuqa-**pis**	waliq-**lla-taq**	ka-chka-ni
I-also	fine-just-and	be-temporary state-1Psing
and I too am just fine		

-rí
Follow-up question tag; "and/how about . . ."

This suffix is used to ask a follow-up question on the same topic, the speaker having had an answer to a previous question:

Imaynalla kachkanki?	How are you?
Waliqlla kachkani. Qam-**rí**?	I am fine. And you?
Paypata-**rí**?	What about his/hers?

Use of -qa, -pis, and -rí

Notice that the class-free suffixes –**qa**, –**pis**, and –**rí** are mutually exclusive. In any word only one of them will appear at a time; they will never be combined.

Ñuqa-**qa** waliqlla kachkani.	I am just fine.
Pay-**pis** waliqllataq.	S/he is just fine, too.
Qam-**rí** imaynalla kachkanki?	And how are you?

Pronunciation
> Stress Patterns in Quechua

Note that the stress in Quechua falls naturally on the penultimate (next-to-the-last) syllable of the word. Thus, when an additional suffix is added, the stress shifts to the right.

> wáliq   >>>   walíqlla   >>>   waliqllátaq

An exception to this rule is found in the terms of address "mamáy!" and "tatáy!," where stress falls on the final syllable to indicate the special function of the word. Other exceptions to the stress rule will be pointed out as they crop up.

Ruwana / Exercises

1 Juk ⌘ Parlana / Oral Work

Work with a partner to learn and practice dialogues 1–6 above. Vary the vocabulary you use.

2 Iskay ⌘ Qillqana / Written Work

Fill the blanks in the following dialogues:

(a) – _____ kachkanki mamáy/tatáy?
   – Waliqlla _____. Qam____?
   – Ñuqapis waliq____ kachkani.
   – Juana____, imaynalla kachkan?
   – Paypis _____ llataq _____.
   – Payrí?
   – _____ waliqllataq kachkan.
(b) – Imaynalla kachkanki _____ / _____?
   – Allinlla. _____?
   – Ñuqapis _____ kachkani.
   – _____ ykirí?
   – _____ pis waliqllataq kachkan.
(c) Imataq sutiyki? _____ Ana. Qampatarí? _____ Juan.
(d) Maymanta ____ kanki? _____ manta kani. Qamrí? _____ manta kani.

3 Kimsa ⌘ Qhawana / Video View   ▶ DVD

Go to the following section of the *Kawsay Vida* multimedia program:

Peruvian Quechua > Ayllu > Qhawana > Casimirawan tupana

Watch the video clip, and answer the questions below. Do not worry that you do not understand much of the text at this stage. Just listen to the Quechua being spoken. You may click the ENGLISH button to see the translation.

1. At the start of the clip, Carmen uses three phrases to greet Casimira. Note them down:

   (i) _____

   (ii) _____

   (iii) _____

2. At the end of the clip, how does Carmen say goodbye to Casimira?
_____.

3. How do people say goodbye in Bolivian Quechua?
_____.

4. If you were to meet a friend on the road, how would you greet him/her?
_____.

4 Tawa ⌘ Watuykuna / Analysis

Study these Quechua sentences and then answer the questions below:

1. Imaynalla kachkanki mamáy? Ñuqaqa waliqlla kachkani, qamrí?
2. Payqa Carlos. Imaynalla kachkan? Waliqlla kachkan.
3. Ñuqapis waliqllataq kachkani.
4. Payrí, imaynalla kachkan? Paypis allinllataq kachkan.
5. Mamayki, imaynalla kachkan?
6. Qam, maymantataq kanki?
7. Imataq sutiyki?
8. Sutiyqa Juan.
9. Cochabambamanta kani.

(i) How many personal pronouns can you find?
(ii) Identify the verb suffixes and name their functions.
(iii) Identify the noun suffixes and name their functions.
(iv) How many times is a class-free suffix used in the sentences?
(v) How many different ways of asking a question can you identify?

5 Phichqa ⌘ Qillqana / Written Work

Complete the following sentences by adding the missing suffixes or personal pronouns:

1. Ñuqaqa waliqlla kachka____.
2. ____qa allinlla kachkanki.
3. ____qa waliq kachkan.
4. Qamrí, imaynalla ka____nki?
5. ____pis waliqllataq kachkani.
6. Pay____ allinllataq ka____n.
7. Ima____ sutiyki?
8. Paypata____, imataq suti____?
9. May____taq kanki?
10. Ñuqa____ Liverpoolmanta ka____.

6 Suqta ⌘ Parlana / Oral Work

You are walking in the countryside and meet with a person you know from a nearby village. Follow the suggested pattern to have a conversation with her.

Ask her how she is.
She says she is fine.

She asks how you are.
You say you are fine too.
Ask her where she is from; she tells you.
She asks where you are from; you tell her.
Ask her what her name is.
She tells you her name and asks yours.
You tell her your name.
Say goodbye.

2 / Iskay

Runakuna / People

In This Unit...

You learn the terms for identifying different members of social groups. You are taught how to ask and answer questions about them. You study the use of grammatical sentence markers to indicate assertion using suffix **-qa**, interrogation using suffix **-chu**, and confirmation using emphatic suffix **-puni**.

KAWSAY / ANDEAN LIFE
Identities

Cultural identities in the Andes are very diverse, products of the mixed cultural and linguistic heritage of present-day inhabitants. In Spanish, a vocabulary exists for expressing perceptions of racial, ethnic, or class difference when referring to people. In some cases, these terms have been reinforced by their usage in the social sciences; others, such as *indio*, acquired pejorative connotations in everyday language, and alternative usages such as *indígena* have evolved. Throughout the Andes, Quechua speakers use the term "runa" to mean "person" or "human being." In San Pedro de Buenavista, one cultural distinction is expressed through the use of "llaqta runa" to refer to urban-dwelling people, usually Spanish or Spanish-Quechua bilingual (*mestizo* or *cholo* in Spanish); and "campo runa" to refer to the people of the countryside, generally Quechua or Quechua-Aymara bilingual (*indígena* in Spanish).

  Suggested reading: Allen 2002; van Vleet 2008; Howard 2009.

– Pitaq pay?
– Payqa doña Roberta.
– Pay llaqta warmichu?
– Arí, payqa llaqta warmi.

Ñawirina, yachakuna / Read and Learn

Pitaq pay?	Who is she?
Payqa doña Roberta.	She is Doña Roberta.
Robertaqa warmi.	Roberta is a woman.
Payqa llaqta warmi.	She is a town woman.
Pay llaqta warmichu?	Is she a town woman?
Arí, payqa llaqta warmipuni.	Yes, she really is a town woman.

Tapuy / Asking Questions

The grammatical construction of a question in Quechua varies according to whether the question is open (any answer is possible) or closed (only a "yes" or "no" answer is likely). In this unit we study open questions using **pitaq?** ("who is it?") and **imataq sutin?** ("what is his/her name"?). Closed questions are constructed with the -**chu** interrogative suffix.

Open Questions

Pi-**taq** pay?	Who is s/he?
Pi-**taq** Roberta?	Who is Roberta?
Pi-**taq** Juan?	Who is Juan?
Pi-**taq** kanki?	Who are you?
Ima-**taq** sutin?	What is her/his name?

Assertions

Pay-**qa** Roberta.	She is Roberta.
Pay-**qa** Juan.	He is Juan.
Pay-**qa** llaqta warmi.	She is a woman from the town.
Pay-**qa** campo runa.	He/she is a person from the countryside.
Pay-**qa** lluqalla.	He is a young boy.
Pay-**qa** imilla.	She is a young girl.
Pay-**qa** wayna.	He is a young man.
Pay-**qa** sipas.	She is a young woman.
Ñuqa-**qa** Rosa kani.	I am Rosa.
Sutin-**qa** Roberta.	Her name is Roberta.
Roberta-**qa** ñañay.	Roberta is my sister. [woman speaking]
Juan-**qa** wawqiy.	Juan is my brother. [man speaking]

Closed Question

Pay warmi-**chu**?	Is it a woman?
Pay qhari-**chu**?	Is it a man?
Pay lluqalla-**chu**?	Is it a young boy?
Pay imilla-**chu**?	Is it a young girl?
Pay wayna-**chu**?	Is it a young man?
Pay sipas-**chu**?	Is it a young woman?
Pay ayllu runa-**chu**?	Is he an ayllu member?
Pay llaqta runa-**chu**?	Is she a town person?
Qam Rosa-**chu** kanki?	Are you Rosa?
Roberta ñañayki-**chu**?	Is Roberta your sister?
Juan wawqiyki-**chu**?	Is Juan your brother?

Affirmative Responses

Arí, payqa lluqalla.	Yes, he is a young boy.
Arí, payqa wayna.	Yes, he is a young man.
Arí, ñuqaqa Rosa kani.	Yes, I am Rosa.
Arí, payqa ñañay.	Yes, she is my sister.
Arí, payqa wawqiy.	Yes, he is my brother.

Confirming Responses

warmi-**puni**	really a woman
sipas-**puni**	really a young woman
Rosa-**puni** kani.	I am really Rosa.
ñañay-**puni**	really my sister
wawqiy-**puni**	really my brother

Simi / Vocabulary

Suti / Nouns

    campo [kampu]: countryside.
    kawsay: life.
    llaqta: town.

Runa / People
- ayllu runa: member of an ayllu.
- campo runa [kampu]: rural-dwelling person.
- imilla: young girl.
- jawa runa: outsider, foreigner.
- llaqta runa: town-dwelling person.
- lluqalla [lloqalla]: young boy.
- machu runa: old man.
- mozo [musu]: town-dwelling *mestizo*.
- paya: old woman.
- qhari: man; male human being.
- q'ara: outsider.
- runa: person.
- runakuna (*var.* runas): people.
- sipas: young woman.
- warmi: woman; wife; female human being.
- wayna: young man.

Tapuq suti ranti/Interrogative Pronouns
- pi: who?

Expression
- arí: "yes."

Simip k'askaynin / Grammar
Wak k'askaq / Class-Free Suffixes

-chu?

Interrogative marker

This suffix is used to form a closed question, that is, when an answer with "arí" ("yes") or "mana" ("no") is expected. It is placed on the word that is being questioned.

Pay Roberta-**chu**?	Is she Roberta?
Pay lluqalla-**chu**?	Is he a young boy?
Juan wawqiyki-**chu**?	Is Juan your brother?
Qam-**chu** Rosa kanki?	Are you (and not another person) Rosa?
Qam Rosa-**chu** kanki?	Are you Rosa (and not another person)?

-chu . . . -chu?

"Either . . . or?"

The interrogative suffix -**chu** may occur on each of two terms when a relationship between them of "either . . . or?" is being questioned:

Pitaq pay? Juan-**chu** Manuel-**chu**?	Who is that? Is it Juan or Manuel?
Maymantataq kanki?	Where are you from?
La Pazmanta-**chu** Sucremanta-**chu**?	From La Paz or Sucre?

-pis . . . -pis
    "Both . . . and"

The inclusive suffix **-pis** 'also' may occur on each of two terms when a relationship between them of "both . . . and" is being asserted:

| mamay-**pis** taytay-**pis** | both my mother and father |
| warmi-**pis** qhari-**pis** | both women and men |

-puni
    Emphatic function

This suffix is used to reinforce a statement:

| Pay llaqta runachu? | Is s/he a town person? |
| Arí, payqa llaqta runa-**puni**. | Yes, sure, s/he is a town person. |

| Pay wawqiykichu? | Is he your brother? |
| Arí, payqa wawqiy-**puni**. | Yes, sure, he's my brother. |

| Qam Rosachu kanki? | Are you Rosa? |
| Arí, ñuqaqa Rosa-**puni** kani. | Yes, sure, I am Rosa. |

Ruwana / Exercises

1 Juk ⌘ Qillqana / Written Work

Imagine yourself in the marketplace in Bolivia. You are interested in the people you see around you. Match the Quechua sentences on the left to their English equivalents on the right.

1. Pay ayllu runachu?	A. Is he a young boy?
2. Payqa waynapuni.	B. Who is he?
3. Payqa sipas.	C. Is he/she an *ayllu* person?
4. Payqa llaqta runa.	D. He really is a young man.
5. Lluqallachu pay?	E. He is Carlos.
6. Payqa machu runa.	F. What is his/her name?
7. Pitaq pay?	G. Is she a woman from the town?
8. Imataq sutin?	H. She is a town person.
9. Payqa Carlos.	I. Is Juana your sister?
10. Pay llaqta warmichu?	J. He is an old man.
11. Juana ñañaykichu?	K. She is a young woman.

2 Iskay ⌘ Parlana / Oral Work

Look at the photos of different kinds of people in society. Ask and answer questions with your classmates, using the model provided. Use vocabulary from Units 1 and 2.

Pitaq pay?
Pay waynachu?
Payqa waynapuni.
Payqa sipas.
Payqa llaqta warmi.

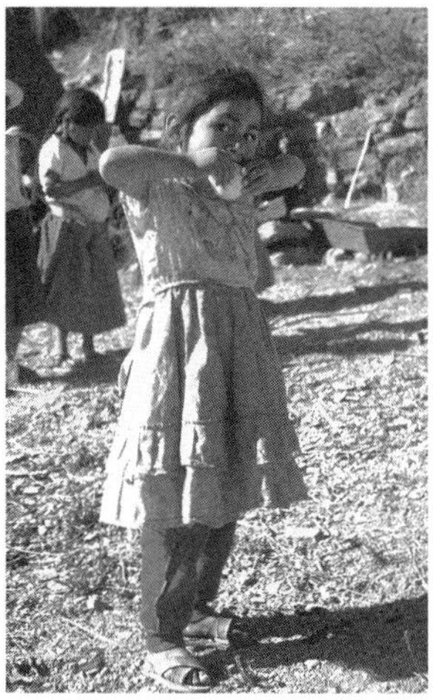

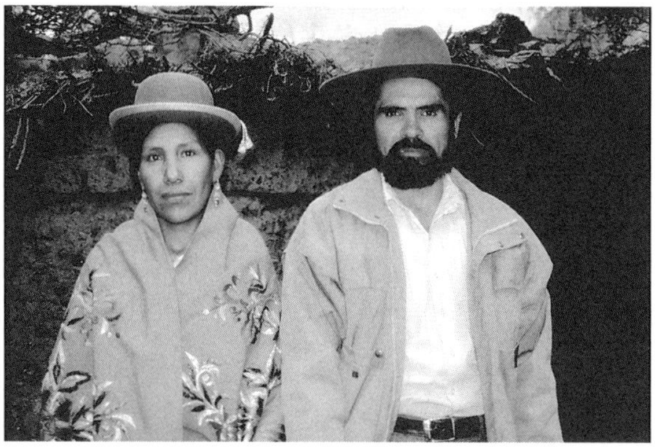

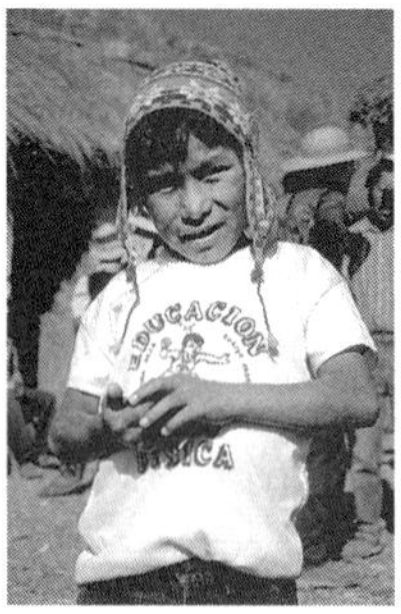

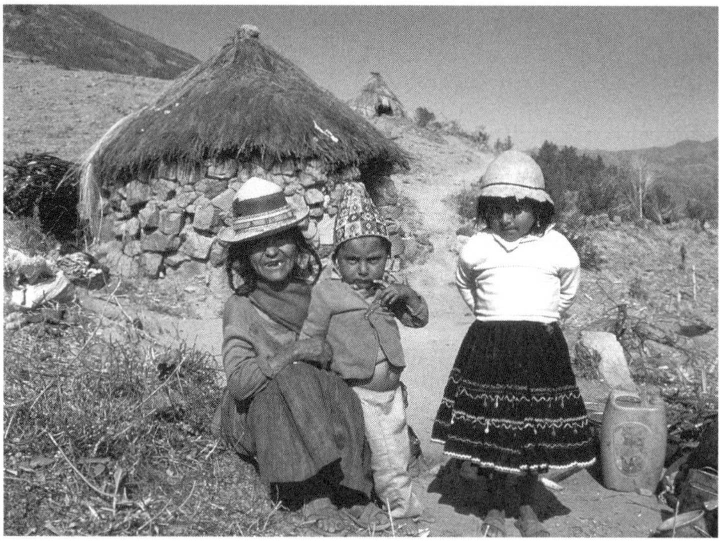

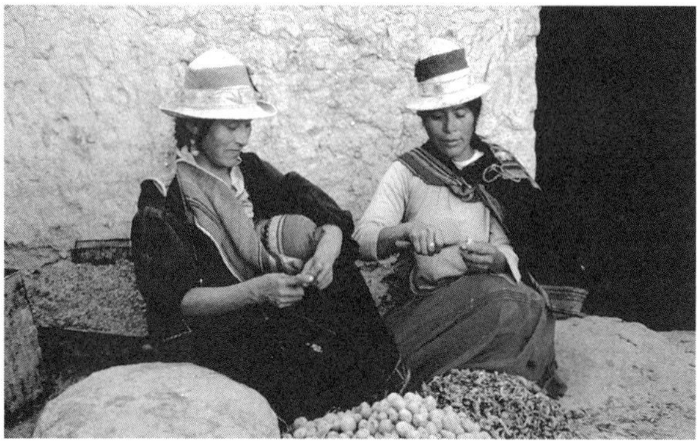

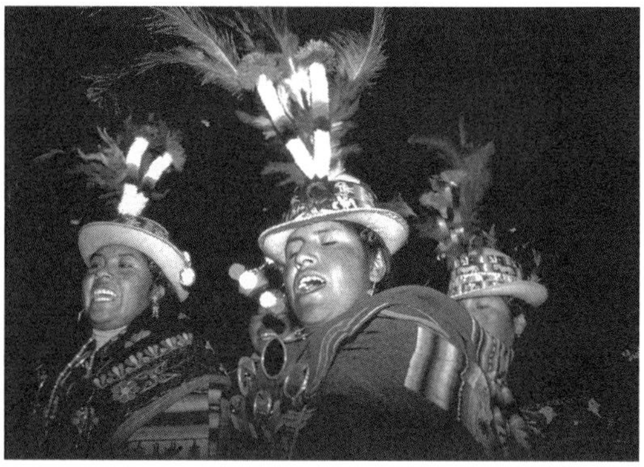

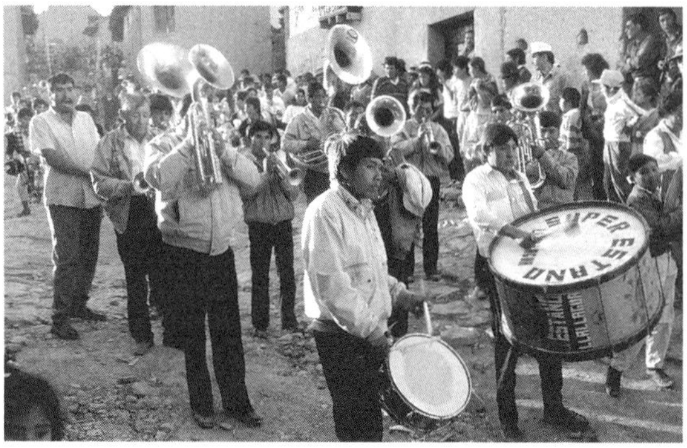

Payrí?
Paypis llaqta warmillataq.
Imataq sutin?
Sutinqa Manuela.
Paypatarí? Imataq sutin?
Sutinqa Luis.

3 Kimsa ⌘ Qillqana / Written Work

Turn the following assertions into the interrogative form. Note the change in the sentence structure that is required. Remember that the verb **kay** 'to be' is not used in 3rd-person-singular assertions and questions regarding identity.

Payqa warmi.   >>>   Pay warmichu?

1. Payqa sipas.   _____?
2. Payqa Juan.   _____?
3. Payqa llaqta runa.   _____?
4 Payqa imilla.   _____?
5. Qamqa waliqlla kachkanki.   _____?
6. Payqa q'ara.   _____?
7. Payqa ayllu warmi.   _____?
8. Payqa Roberta.   _____?
9. Robertaqa panayki.   _____?
10. Juanqa turayki.   _____?

4 Tawa ⌘ Yachana / Practice   ▶ DVD

Go to the following section in the *Kawsay Vida* multimedia program:

Bolivia > Runa > Yachana > Pitaq?

This exercise introduces you to the people of San Pedro de Buenavista who contributed to the making of the "Bolivian Quechua" section of the program. Follow the on-screen instructions, and work through the exercise.

   Copy some of the phrases to your workbook, and practice them.

_____
_____
_____
_____

5 Phichqa ⌘ Qillqana / Written Work

qharichu warmichu?   male or female?
qharipis warmipis   both male and female

List each of the following words in one of the three columns below, according to whether they refer to male or female people or to both indifferently.

2 / ISKAY

warmi	q'ara	mama	ñaña
llaqta warmi	sipas	tata	ususi
machu runa	lluqalla	imilla	churi
paya	qhari	runa	
wayna	mozo	tura	
wawa	llaqta runa	wawqi	
ayllu runa	campo runa	pana	

Warmi	Qhari	Warmipis qharipis

6 Qanchis ⌘ Junt'achina / Gap-Fill Exercise ▶DVD

Go to the following section of the *Kawsay Vida* multimedia program:

Peruvian Quechua > Ayllu > Qhawana > Presentaciónpa ayllun

Read the text and use the translation and lookup facilities in the program to help you with the meaning. Make a list below of all the kin terms that are used in the video. How many of them derive from Spanish and how many are Quechua? Why do you think there is this variation?

_____

_____

_____

_____

7 Qanchis ⌘ Junt'achina / Video Exercise   ▶DVD

Go to the following section of the *Kawsay Vida* multimedia program:

Peruvian Quechua > Ayllu > Hunt'achina > Presentaciónpa ayllun > Audio

On-screen, fill in the gaps in the text. Press return on your computer keyboard to move to the next gap. Use the play bar or the audio button on-screen to stop and start the audio.

When you have completed the gap-fill exercise, identify all the words in the text that refer to members of doña Presentación's family. Check their meanings in the lookup facility, and list them below with their English translations.

_____

_____

_____

_____

8 Pusaq ⌘ Parlana / Oral Work

Imagine you visit a Quechua-speaking friend in his or her home. Ask him/her who the different people in the family are. Use the model below and vary the vocabulary you use.

Pay mamaykichu?	>>>	Arí, payqa mamay.
Chay warmi panaykichu?	>>>	Mana, payqa cuñaday.
Cuñadaykichu?	>>>	Cuñadaypuni.
Pitaq wawqiyki?	>>>	Chay waynaqa wawqiy.
Imataq sutin?	>>>	Sutinqa Jorge.

3 / Kimsa

P'acha / Clothing

In This Unit...

You discover how to ask and answer questions about the items of clothing worn by people in Quechua-speaking regions of the Andes. You encounter the interrogative pronoun **ima** 'what?' and the use of **-taq** in interrogatives. You study the demonstratives **kay**, **chay**, and **jaqay**, and learn how to form negative statements using **mana . . . -chu**.

KAWSAY / ANDEAN LIFE
Clothing

Clothing is one of the most distinctive markers of social, cultural, and regional identity in the Andes. Cloth is traditionally woven from llama and alpaca fiber; since the time of the Spanish Conquest, it has been produced from sheep's wool as well. Textile weaving is a millenarian art in the Andes. Textile designs appearing in clothing and other everyday artifacts are a medium through which weavers signal their ayllu membership, enabling the wearer's place of origin to be recognized when they travel to other regions. The clothing of men and women is differentiated in some respects, although certain items are used by both genders. In Northern Potosí, older women and girls in the more remote communities wear the almilla: a plain black dress of homespun cloth called bayeta. However, the pollera (dirndl skirt) is increasingly replacing the almilla. The most ubiquitous item is the llikita, a decorative woven cloth about one square meter in size, used as a shawl by women and as a cloth for carrying things on the back by men and women alike. The llikita is known as *awayo* in Bolivian Spanish, derived from the Aymara word for the same item. In Northern Potosí too, the aqsu is another type of decorative cloth, worn by women as an overskirt, hanging from the waist and down the back. Andean headgear is typically the felt hat, made in different shapes depending on the region; in the southern Andes, the ch'ullu, a knitted bonnet with earflaps, traditionally made and worn by men, provides extra warmth at high altitudes.

  Suggested reading: Arnold 1997; Zorn 2004; Femenías 2005.

Imataq kay?
Chayqa lliklla.

Ñawirina, yachakuna / Read and Learn

Imataq kay?	What is this?
Kayqa ch'uspa.	This is a coca pouch.
Imataq chay?	What is that?
Chayqa punchu.	That is a poncho.
Imataq jaqay?	What is that over there?
Jaqayqa lliklla.	That over there is a carrying cloth.
Kayqa mana ch'ulluchu.	This is not a knitted hat.

Tapuy / Asking Questions

Open Questions

Imataq **kay**?	What is this?
Imataq **chay**?	What is that?
Imataq **jaqay**?	What is that over there?

Assertions

Kay-qa punchu.	This is a poncho.
Kay-qa lliklla.	This is a carrying cloth/shawl.
Chay-qa ch'uspa.	That is a coca pouch.
Chay-qa ch'ullu.	That is a knitted hat.
Jaqay-qa punchu.	That over there is a poncho.
Jaqay-qa manta.	That over there is a shawl.

Closed Questions

Kay punchuchu?	Is this a poncho?
Chay phulluchu?	Is that a blanket?
Jaqay ch'uspachu?	Is that over there a coca pouch?

Affirmative Responses

| **Arí**, **chay**-qa punchu. | Yes, that's a poncho. |
| **Arí**, **jaqay**-qa phullu. | Yes, that's a blanket over there. |

Negative Responses

| Mana, **mana** ch'ullu-**chu**. | No, it isn't a knitted hat. |
| Mana, **mana** pollera-**chu**. | No, it isn't a peasant skirt. |

Confirming Responses

| Aqsu-**puni**. | It really is a woven overskirt. |
| Chaqueta-**puni**. | It really is a man's jacket. |

Simi / Vocabulary

Suti / Nouns

    p'acha: clothing.

Warmi p'acha / Women's Clothing

    almilla: plain-woven woolen dress.
    aqsu: handwoven overskirt.
    blusa: blouse.
    chharara: stovepipe straw hat (worn by women).
    manta: factory-made shawl.
    pollera [pullira]: dirndl skirt.

Qhari p'acha / Men's Clothing

    bufanda [wuhanta]: sash worn around waist.
    chaqueta [chakita]: embroidered jacket.
    ch'ullu (*var.* lluch'u): knitted cap with earflaps.
    montera [muntira]: cowhide helmet worn in *tinku* fighting.
    pantalon [pantalun]: trousers.
    punchu: poncho.
    unku: short poncho.
    wara: calf-length trousers.

Warmi p'achapis qhari p'achapis / Both Men's and Women's Clothing

    chumpi: woven belt.
    ch'uspa: coca pouch.
    juk'uta: rubber sandal.
    luq'u: floppy felt hat.
    lliklla: handwoven carrying cloth.
    polera: t-shirt.
    sombrero [sumiru]: hat.

Rikuchiq suti ranti / Demonstrative Pronouns

    chay: that.

jaqay: that over there.
kay: this.

Simip k'askaynin / Grammar
Wak k'askaq / Class-Free Suffixes

mana . . . -chu

Negative construction

The *negative* construction is formed by combining the negative particle **mana** and the negative suffix **-chu**. **Mana** is placed immediately before the word or phrase that is to be negated, and **-chu** is placed on the end of the word that is to be negated.[1]

Chayqa **mana** lliklla-**chu**.	That is not a carrying cloth.
Kayqa **mana** warmi p'acha-**chu**.	This is not women's clothing.

-taq

(i) Question tag

Two separate functions of **-taq** 'and' can now be identified. As seen in Unit 1, **-taq** is used on interrogative pronouns to make the question less abrupt:

Imayna-**taq** kachkanki?	And how are you?
Ima-**taq** kay?	And what is this?

(ii) Coordinating suffix

-taq is also used as a coordinating suffix, referring back to something previously stated:

Imillaqa waliqlla kachkan.	The young girl is fine.
Lluqallarí?	And the young boy?
Lluqallapis waliqlla-**taq**.	And the young boy is just fine, too.

Syntax

Noun + Noun Adjectival Construction

One noun may be placed in front of another noun, performing an adjectival function:

llaqta warmi	town woman
warmi wawa	female baby
qhari p'acha	male clothing

Ruwana / Exercises
1 Juk ⌘ Qillqana / Written Work

Study the grammar notes above, look at the pictures, and answer the following questions appropriately:

---

1. The interrogative suffix -**chu** and the negative suffix -**chu** are distinguished from each other by the fact that the negative -**chu** always appears in combination with **mana**.

1. Kay punchuchu?

Chay ch'uspa wawa p'achachu? Mana, _____.

2. Jaqay llikllachu? _____.

Chay chaqueta qhari p'achachu? Arí, _____.

P'ACHA / CLOTHING 35

3. Imataq kay? (bufanda)

_____.

Kayrí imataq? (bufanda)

_____.

Imataq jaqay? (ch'ullu)

_____.

4. Kayrí imataq? (sombrero)

_____.

Chayrí sombrerochu? (ch'ullu)

_____.

2 Iskay ⌘ Qillqana / Written Work

a) Choose an appropriate suffix or pronoun from the list and insert it into the sentences below.

-chka-   -pis
-taq   -lla-
-puni   -rí
-qa   -chu

1. Imaynalla ka_____nki tatáy? Waliq_____ka_____ni.
2. Qam_____? Ñuqa_____waliq_____taq.
3. Pi_____pay? Pay_____lluqalla.
4. Pay sipas_____? Arí, payqa sipas_____.
5. María_____warmi. Juana_____warmi_____taq.
6. Pay wayna_____? Mana, pay_____mana wayna_____. Pay_____lluqalla.
7. Ima_____kay? Chay_____ch'ullu.
8. Jaqay punchu_____? Mana punchu_____, jaqay_____liklla.

b) Translate the sentences into English.

1. _____.
2. _____.
3. _____.
4. _____.
5. _____.
6. _____.
7. _____.
8. _____.

3 Kimsa ⌘ Qillqana / Written Work

List the words for items of clothing in one of the three columns according to whether they refer to male or female items or to both indifferently.

punchu   bufanda
unku   pollera
lliklla   almilla
blusa   chaqueta
ch'ullu   wara
aqsu   luq'u
ch'uspa   chharara
sombrero   montera
manta   pantalón
chumpi

Warmi p'acha	Qhari p'acha	Warmi p'achapis qhari p'achapis

4 Tawa ⌘ Junt'achina / Video Exercise   ▶DVD

Go to the following section in the *Kawsay Vida* multimedia program:

Bolivian Quechua > Kawsay > Junt'achina > Filomena p'achamanta

Watch the video clip and make a list of all the words for items of clothing that doña Filomena uses.
Listen to the audio clip and do the same. Add any new words to the vocabulary list in this unit.

5 Phichqa ⌘ Yuyarina / Review

Give the Quechua translations for the following phrases in the blanks provided.

that little girl	_____
this young boy	_____
boy baby	_____
that young woman over there	_____
woven belt	_____
knitted hat	_____
that man	_____
women's clothing	_____
just fine	_____
yes	_____
this coca pouch	_____
this person	_____
my mother	_____

3 / KIMSA

that country person   _____

overskirt   _____

that town person over there   _____

he is a man   _____

I am Rosa.   _____

Are you Juan?   _____

she is a woman   _____

4 / Tawa

Ruwana / Daily Tasks

In This Unit...

You meet a young woman weaver. You learn to talk about the daily domestic activities that are typical of rural life in Northern Potosí. You study verb conjugation in simple sentences; the use of the progressive suffix -**chka**-; and the use of the direct-object marker -**ta**.

KAWSAY / ANDEAN LIFE
Technologies

Life is changing rapidly in Bolivia: towns are expanding and migration from the countryside to the urban areas is ever increasing. But in the countryside many traditional skills and techniques survive. Production of handwoven textiles for multiple purposes still prevails. Women weave the decorative lliklla, ch'uspa, and punchu on the backstrap loom, while men use the Spanish loom for weaving plain bayeta cloth. Agriculture remains unmechanized in the valleys of Northern Potosí: the land is plowed by means of ox-drawn plowshares driven by a plowman, and the women follow behind, planting seeds in the furrows. People live off the land, and the main staples are potatoes and other species of root vegetable, corn, barley, and quinoa. Sheep and goats are reared in the temperate valleys, while in the colder highland environment llamas and alpacas thrive, providing fleece for textiles and, to a lesser extent, a source of protein. Llamas also serve as pack animals. People build their own houses, using their family networks for labor. Construction materials include local timber for the house frame and roof, and mud and straw for the walls.

Suggested reading: Meyerson 1990; Harris 2000.

– Kay warmi imatataq ruwachkan?
– Payqa awachkan.
– Imatataq awachkan?
– Llikllata awachkan.

Ñawirina, yachakuna / Read and Learn

Imatataq ruwachkanki?	What are you doing?
Llikllata awachkani, qamrí?	I'm weaving an awayo, and you?
Ñuqapis llikllatataq awachkani.	I'm also weaving an awayo.
Payrí, imatataq ruwachkan?	What is s/he doing?
Payqa wallpa uchuta wayk'uchkan.	S/he is cooking chili chicken.

Qallarina / Introduction

Mama Elisaqa awachkan. Imatataq awachkan? Payqa phulluta awachkan. Juanrí, imatataq ruwachkan? Payqa llamk'achkan, papata allachkan. Maríataq lawata wayk'uchkan.

Parlana / Dialogue 1

– Mama Elisa! Imatataq ruwachkanki?
– Awachkani.
– Imatataq awachkanki?
– Phulluta.

Parlana / Dialogue 2

– Tata Juan! Imatataq ruwachkanki?
– Llamk'achkani, papata allachkani.
– Maríarí?
– Payqa lawata wayk'uchkan. Juanapis lawallatataq wayk'uchkan.

Parlana / Dialogue 3

– Qamrí imatataq ruwachkanki?
– _____. (give your own reply)

Simi / Vocabulary

Ruway / Verbs

  Ruwana / Activities

  allay: to dig up, harvest (tubers).
  away: to weave.
  jamk'ay [jank'ay]: to grill, to toast (in frying pan).
  llamk'ay [llank'ay]: to work.
  michiy: to graze animals.
  mikhuy: to eat.
  pallay: to gather; to collect; to pick threads in weaving design.
  pichay: to sweep.
  phuchkay: to spin.
  qarpay: to irrigate.
  t'aqsay: to wash clothes.
  upyay [ukyay]: to drink.
  wayk'uy: to cook.

Suti / Nouns

  chakra: field.
  llamt'a [llant'a]: firewood.
  ruwana: task, activity.
  wasi: house.
  wayñu: Andean song and dance style.

  Away / Weaving

  bayeta: plain-woven cloth.
  kustala: sack.
  millma: wool.
  phullu: blanket.
  wayaqa: woven bag used for carrying food or coca.

  Uywa / Animals

  allpaqa: alpaca.
  allqu: dog.
  karwa (Sp. *cabra*): goat.

kawallu (Sp. *caballo*): horse.
khuchi: pig.
k'anka: rooster.
llama: llama.
misi: cat.
pili: duck.
quwi: guinea pig.
uwija (Sp. *oveja*): sheep.
uywa: animal.
waka (Sp. *vaca*): cow.
wallpa: hen.
wuru (Sp. *burro*): donkey.

Mikhuna / Food

aqha: chicha.
arroz [arus]: rice.
aycha: meat.
cebada [siwara]: barley.
chuqllu: *choclo* (corn on the cob).
ch'arki: sun-dried meat.
ch'uñu: freeze-dried potato.
fideos [firiyus]: pasta.
habas [jawas]: broad beans.
jamk'a [jank'a]: grilled cereal or pulses.
kinwa: quinoa.
lawa: broth (grain-based soup).
mikhuna: food.
mut'i: *mote* (grilled or boiled grains or pulses eaten as side dish or snack).
papa: potato.
papa lisa: *melloco* (Andean tuber).
sara: maize, corn.
sara jamk'a: grilled corn.
trigo [riwu]: wheat.
t'anta: bread.
uchu: chili pepper; chili-based dish eaten on festive occasions.
uqa: *oca* (Andean root vegetable).
yaku: water.

Simip k'askaynin / Grammar

Rimay muyuchina / Verb Conjugation

    Present Tense—Singular

All verbs are regular in Quechua. In the basic conjugation, person suffixes are added to the verb root. This form of the verb expresses a general truth, simple present tense, and in some contexts a recent past.

away 'to weave'

1st-person singular	**ñuqa** awa-**ni**	I weave
2nd-person singular	**qam** awa-**nki**	you weave
3rd-person singular	**pay** awa-**n**	s/he weaves

Note: The use of the personal pronoun is not obligatory. Thus **awani** alone also means "I weave."

Ruway k'askaq / Verb Suffixes

Use of Verb Suffixes

Suffixes are added to the verb root to mark person, tense, and other meanings:

Present tense	awa-**ni**	I weave
Present progressive aspect	awa-**chka**-**nki**	you are weaving

-chka-
    Indicates progressive aspect

This suffix shows action in progress:

ruwa-ni I do   >>>   ruwa-**chka**-ni   I am doing

Order of Verb Suffixes

Person suffixes are the verb suffixes that appear farthest to the right on the verb form. They may be followed by other, class-free, suffixes. Other verb suffixes are placed to the left of the person suffix and follow a particular order:

awa	–	chka	–	ni	–	puni
weave	–	progressive aspect	–	1st-person singular	–	really

I really am weaving.

Suti k'askaq / Noun Suffixes

Use of Noun Suffixes

Suffixes are added to the noun root to mark the relationship between entities, for example that between subject and object; and temporal, spatial, and possessive relationships:

wasi	–	lla	–	y	–	manta	–	puni
house	–	just	–	my	–	from	–	really

just from my house, really

-ta
    Direct-object marker

This suffix is added to the noun form that is the object of the action of the verb. The object normally precedes the verb in the Quechua sentence.

Phullu-**ta** awa chka ni.   I am weaving a blanket.

-ta also appears on the interrogative pronoun **ima**, when **ima** is acting as the object of the verb, for example:

Ima-**ta**-taq ruwa chka nki?   What are you doing?

Sentence Structure

Standard word order in a Quechua sentence is **SUBJECT** > **OBJECT** > **VERB**.

SUBJECT	OBJECT	VERB
ñuqaqa	punchuta	awachkani
I	A PONCHO	AM WEAVING

I am weaving a poncho.

However, this standard order may not always be adhered to in everyday speech.

Noun Suffix Order

On the noun root, noun suffixes generally precede class-free suffixes. However, the limitative suffix -lla- presents an exception. Notice where it is placed in the following conjunctive construction in which three class-free suffixes combine:

-pis -lla- . . . -taq
   Conjunctive function; "and just also . . ."

-lla- and **–taq** are separated and wrapped around any noun or verb person suffix appearing at the end of the word.

Ñuqa-**pis** punchu-**lla-ta-taq** awachkani.   I also am just weaving a poncho.
Pay-**pis** t'antata mikhu-**lla-n-taq**.   S/he is also eating bread.

Ruwana / Exercises

1 Juk ⌘ Qillqana / Written Work

Fill in the gaps in the texts below:

1. - Mama Elisa! Ima_____taq ruwa_____nki?
- Awachka_____.
- Imatataq awachka_____?
- Phullu_____.

2. Tata Juan imata_____ruwachka_____? Papa_____allachkan.
Maríarí? Maríapis papa_____allachka_____n_____.

3. Qam, ima_____taq ruwachka_____? Ñuqaqa_____. (supply your own answer)

2 Iskay ⌘ Parlana / Oral Work

Work with a partner to create some dialogues in which you talk about what other people are doing. Use the structures and vocabulary introduced above.

3 Kimsa ⌘ Yachana / Practice

Answer the question according to the model, using the cues provided. Note that the object marker **-ta** appears in both the question and the answer.

Imataraq ruwachkanki? (llikIla away)   >>>   Llikllata awachkani.

Imatataq ruwachkanki?
1. (phullu away) _____.
2. (chumpi away) _____.
3. (kustala away) _____.
4. (aqsu away) _____.
5. (llikIla away) _____.
6. (ch'uspa away) _____.

4 Tawa ⌘ Yachana / Practice

Answer the questions according to the model, using the cues provided.

Imatataq ruwachkanki? (uwija michiy)   >>>   Uwijata michichkani.
Maríarí imatataq ruwachkan? (chakra qarpay)   >>>   Payqa chakrata qarpachkan.

Imatataq ruwachkanki?
1. (uwija michiy) _____.
2. (llamt'a pallay) _____.
3. (millma phuchkay) _____.

Maríarí imatataq ruwachkan?
4. (wasi pichay) _____.
5. (papa allay) _____.
6. (kinwa wayk'uy) _____.

Juanrí imatataq ruwachkan?
7. (uqa mikhuy) _____.
8. (yaku upyay) _____.

5 Phichqa ⌘ Qillqana / Written Work

Answer the question according to the model, using the cues provided.

Imatataq ruwachkanki? (punchu away)   >>>   Punchuta awachkani.
Qamrí?   >>>   Ñuqapis punchullatataq awachkani.

Imatataq ruwachkanki?
1. (ch'uspa away) _____.
Qamrí? _____.
2. (aqha upyay) _____.
Qamrí? _____.
3. (t'anta ruway) _____.
Qamrí? _____.
4. (uqa allay) _____.
Qamrí? _____.
5. (p'acha t'aqsay) _____.
Qamrí? _____.

6. (ch'uñu mikhuy) _____.
Qamrí? _____.

6 Suqta ⌘ Yachana / Practice

Complete the following question/answer sequences, using the cues provided.

Imatataq ruwachkanki? (Sara jamk'ay) >>> Sarata jamk'achkani.
Maríarí, imatataq ruwachkan? (llamt'a pallay) >>> Llamt'ata pallachkan.

1. Imatataq ruwachkanki? (mikhuna wayk'uy)
_____.

Maríarí, imatataq ruwachkan? (llamt'a pallay)
_____.

2. Carmen imatataq ruwachkan? (millma phuchkay)
_____.

Juanrí, _____? (wasi pichay)
_____.

3. Chay wayna _____? (lliklla away)
_____.

Payrí, _____? (uwija michiy)
_____.

4. Chay sipas _____? (lawa mikhuy)
_____.

Chay runarí, _____? (chakra qarpay)
_____.

5. Imatataq mikhuchkanki? (ch'arki)
_____.

Payrí, imatataq mikhuchkan? (ch'uñu)
_____.

6. _____? (t'anta)
_____.

Chay warmirí, _____? (aycha)
_____.

7 Qanchis ⌘ Qhawana / Video View   ▶DVD

Go to the following section in the *Kawsay Vida* multimedia program:

Bolivian Quechua > Kawsay > Qhawana > Imigdia awaymanta

Watch the video clip and answer the following question:

Mama Imigdia imatataq awachkan? _____.

Write out the answer to the question three times, using a different word in each instance, to describe other items that she might weave. Use the vocabulary from Unit 3.

1. _____.
2. _____.
3. _____.

8 Pusaq ⌘ Rikuna / Browse   ▶DVD

Go to the following section in the *Kawsay Vida* multimedia program:

Peruvian Quechua > Mikhuy > Rikuna > Mikhuy wayk'unapaq

Browse through the exercise, and note below the vocabulary it contains for referring to types of food and dishes eaten in southern Peru.

_____

_____

_____

_____

5 / Phichqa

Maymantataq jamunki? / Where Do You Come From?

In This Unit...

You are introduced to a fiesta sponsor from the ayllu Coacarí, which is located in the cantón of the same name, not far from Chiru Q'asa. The fiesta sponsor and his group have walked for several days to attend the fiesta in San Pedro. You learn to ask where people are from, and how long it takes to get to places. You study the plural forms of the present tense; uses of the noun suffixes **-manta** and **-pi**; questions using **machkha** 'how many'/'how much'? You also learn further use of **-pis**; contrastive use of **-taq**; and numerals up to ten.

KAWSAY / ANDEAN LIFE
The Fiesta Cycle

Fiestas in the Andes are religious occasions held in honor of the particular religious patron—Catholic saint, manifestation of Christ, or the Virgin Mary—attributed to each village or urban neighborhood. The festival calendar is bound up with the agricultural cycle. The planting season begins around September, before the rains come in November, allowing seeds to germinate and crops to grow. There is some early harvesting around Carnival time in February, but the main harvest season falls in April and May. From June to September, the ground lies relatively fallow and the climate is dry and hot. This is the height of the festive season, with each little town and village in the countryside celebrating its patron; long pilgrimages take place, such as the one to the shrine of Santiago in Macha, Northern Potosí, on July 24. Travel in the dry season is easier, and urban migrants return in great numbers to their provincial towns of origin to pay their respects to the saint and to catch up with family and friends. Festivals are celebrated with religious ceremonies in the churches and in people's houseyards, and with music, dance, food, and drink. San Pedro de Buenavista celebrates its patronal fiesta for Saint Peter and Saint Paul on June 28 and 29 each year.

Suggested reading: Sallnow 1987; Rasnake 1988.

Maymantataq kanki?
Ayllu Coacarímanta kani.

Ñawirina, yachakuna / Read and Learn

Maymantataq jamunkichik?	Where do you (*pl.*) come from?
Ñuqayku Coacarímanta jamuyku.	We (*excl.*) come from Coacarí.
Ñuqanchik Coacarímanta jamunchik.	We (*incl.*) come from Coacarí.
Maymantataq kankichik?	Where are you (*pl.*) from?
Ñuqayku Coacarímanta kayku.	We (*excl.*) are from Coacarí.
Ñuqanchik Coacarímanta kanchik.	We (*incl.*) are from Coacarí.
Machkha díapi chayamunkichik?	How many days did it take you (*pl.*) to get here?
Kimsa díapi chayamuyku.	It took us (*excl.*) three days to get here.
Imapitaq jamunkichik?	How did you (*pl.*) get here? [*lit.* "In what did you come?"]
Chakillapi jamuyku.	We (*excl.*) just came on foot.
Machkhataq jamunkichik?	How many of you have come?
Iskaylla jamuyku.	Just two of us (*excl.*) have come.

Qallarina / Introduction

Tata Máximoqa parlachkan. «Ñuqayku Coacarí ayllumanta kayku» ñin. Paykunaqa kimsa díapi San Pedro llaqtaman chayamunku. «Chay ayllu Coacaríqa karupi kachkan» ñin. Tata Máximoqa akullichkan.

Parlana / Dialogue

Mama Rosa (R): – Maymantataq jamunkichik?
Tata Máximo (M): – Ñuqaykuqa Coacarímanta jamuyku.
R: – Chay llaqtarí karupichu?

M: – Karupi.
R: – Machkha díapi chayamunkichik?
M: – Kimsa díapi chayamuyku.
R: – Imapitaq jamunkichik?
M: – Chakillapi jamuyku.
R: – Machkhataq jamunkichik?
M: – Suqtalla jamuyku.

Simi / Vocabulary

Ruway / Verbs

    akulliy: to chew coca leaves.
    chayay: to arrive.
    chayamuy: to arrive (in the direction of the speaker).
    jamuy: to come
    puriy: to walk, to move, to work (machinery).
    yupay: to count.

Ruway tikrachiq / Adverbs

    kunan: now.

Suti / Nouns

    auto [awtu]: car.
    avión: plane.
    carro [karu]: bus.
    chaki: foot.
    día [diya]: day.
    mayu: river.
    p'unchaw [p'unchay]: day, daylight.
    yupay: number.

    Chunkakama yupaykuna/ Numbers up to Ten

    juk: one.
    iskay: two.
    kimsa: three.
    tawa: four.
    phichqa: five.
    suqta: six.
    qanchis: seven.
    pusaq: eight.
    jisq'un: nine.
    chunka: ten.

Suti tikrachiq / Adjectives

    karu: far.

Suti ranti / Personal Pronouns
    ñuqanchik: we (*inclusive*).
    ñuqayku: we (*exclusive*).
    paykuna: they.
    qamkuna: you (*plural*).

Tapuq suti ranti / Interrogative Pronouns
    imapi: how/by what means of transport? (*lit.* "in what?")
    machkha: how much, how many?
    maymanta: where from?

Expressions
    ñin: "s/he says."

Simip k'askaynin / Grammar
Rimay muyuchina / Verb Conjugation
    Simple Present Tense, Singular and Plural

chayay 'to arrive'

ñuqa chaya-**ni**	I arrive	ñuqanchik chaya-**nchik**	we (incl.) arrive
		ñuqayku chaya-**yku**	we (excl.) arrive
qam chaya-**nki**	you (sing.) arrive	qamkuna chaya-**nkichik**	you (pl.) arrive
pay chaya-**n**	he, she arrives	paykuna chaya-**nku**	they arrive

These endings are used on all verbs. The use of the personal pronoun is not obligatory. Tense is understood as present or recent past according to context. See how the verb is used in the following examples:

Ñuqa Coacarímanta chayamu**ni**.	I arrive here from Coacarí.
Pay Coacarímantachu chayamu**n**?	Does s/he arrive here from Coacarí?
Karumantachu chayamu**nkichik**?	Do you (pl.) arrive here from far away?

    kay 'to be'
        Simple present tense, singular and plural

ñuqa ka-**ni**	I am	ñuqanchik ka-**nchik**	we (incl.) are
		ñuqayku ka-**yku**	we (excl.) are
qam ka-**nki**	you (sing.) are	qamkuna ka-**nkichik**	you (pl.) are
pay (ka-**n**)	he, she is	paykuna ka-**nku**	they are

  kan
    "There is/there are"

When **kan** is used, the meaning is "there is/there are":

Machkha lliklla **kan**?	How many carrying cloths are there?
Kimsalla **kan**.	There are just three.

ñuqayku/ñuqanchik
   Exclusive "we"/inclusive "we"

In Quechua there are two forms for the 1st-person plural, "we":

ñuqayku   excludes the addressee ("we but not you")
ñuqanchik   includes the addressee ("we all")

The verb endings agree with the pronoun endings:

ñuqa**yku** chaya-**yku**   we but not you arrive
ñuqa**nchik** chaya-**nchik**   we all arrive

Suti k'askaq / Noun Suffixes

-manta
   "From"; "after"

This suffix indicates movement in space or time from the point of origin:

Llaqta-**manta** jamuchkanku.   They are coming from town.
Sipas-**manta** kaypi tiyakuni. I have lived here since [I was] a girl.
Chay-**manta** chayanku.   Then they arrived.

It also indicates place of origin in statements of identity:

San Pedro-**manta** kanku.   They are from San Pedro.

   -**pi**
      "In"; (i) periods of time; (ii) means of transport; (iii) mode of speaking

The basic sense of this suffix is "in." In this unit it is used to indicate a period of time within which an action occurred; or a means of transport by which a journey was made. -**pi** also marks a language in which someone is speaking.

(i)   Kimsa día-**pi** chayamuyku.   We (excl.) arrive here in three days.
(ii)   Auto-**pi**-chu jamunkichik?   Did you (pl.) come by car?
(iii) Aymara-**pi** parlanku.   They talk in Aymara.

   -s/-**kuna**
      Noun plural marker

The pluralization of nouns is not an inherent category of Quechua grammar, so "papa" may refer to "a potato" or to "potato**es**" as a group; "siku" may refer to "a panpiper" or to a group of "panpiper**s**." The generalized presence of noun plural marking in Quechua is one example of the influence of Spanish syntax upon the language.

Plural agreement between nouns and verbs is therefore not a strict requirement in Quechua, although it often occurs in practice. Thus the following sentences are grammatically correct:

Warmi**s**qa jamun.   The women have come. (noun in plural, verb in singular)
Runa**kuna**qa chayamun.   The people have arrived here. (noun in plural, verb in singular)
Machkha wawataq kan?   How many children are there? ("how many?" implies plural, noun in singular)

In Bolivian Quechua the Spanish plural suffix -**s** has taken a strong hold in the spoken language, and you will hear it in the speech of the people of San Pedro de Buenavista in the Kawsay Vida video clips. Where pluralization occurs, -**s** is used to pluralize nouns ending in a vowel, while -**kuna** pluralizes nouns ending in a consonant:

mayu	river	>>>	mayu-**s**	rivers
awaq	weaver	>>>	awaq-**kuna**	weavers

We reproduce this usage in many of the exercises both in the course book and in the multimedia program.

In Bolivia in recent years, an effort has been made to promote –**kuna** as the standard plural marker in the written form and to discourage use of the Spanish -**s**. However, it is worth noting that this does not remove the influence of Spanish norms in this aspect of Quechua grammar.

In Peruvian Quechua, the Spanish -**s** is not used; –**kuna** is the pluralizing suffix, as the "Peruvian Quechua" section of the Kawsay Vida program illustrates.

Wak k'askaq / Class-Free Suffixes

-**pis** 'also' and -**taq** 'and'
    Coordinating suffixes

Note how the functions of -**pis** 'also' and -**taq** 'and' differ in the following sentences:

(i) Payqa San Pedromanta   S/he is from San Pedro,
    ñuqa-**pis** San Pedro-**lla**-manta-**taq** kani.   and I am from San Pedro, too.
(ii) Payqa La Pazmanta   S/he is from La Paz,
    ñuqa-**taq** San Pedromanta.   and I am from San Pedro.

-**pis** creates an effect of inclusion in relation to what was previously stated (the same is the case), whereas -**taq** creates an effect of contrast (something different is the case).

-**ri**
    Insistent coordinative

The coordinative suffix -**ri** without an accent (unstressed -**ri**) may be found in both interrogative and affirmative sentences. Used in questions, it makes the question more insistent, and sometimes challenging:

Imataq sutiyki-**ri**?   Now what is your name?
Chay llaqta-**ri** karuchu?   Is that town far at all?

In affirmatives it is used with the demonstrative pronoun **chay**, for example, to construct a causal phrase:

chayri   in that case

Tapuq suti ranti / Interrogative Pronoun
    machkha
        "How much? How many?"

Machkha may stand alone:

Machkha-taq kankichik? How many are you?

Or **machkha** may qualify a following noun; in this case, note how the question suffix **-taq** is placed on the end of the qualified noun:

Machkha wasi-**taq** kan?   How many houses are there?

Note the construction in the following type of reply:

Machkha-taq jamunkichik?   How many of you have come?
Kimsalla jamuyku   Just three of us have come.

Ruwana / Exercises
1 Juk ⌘ Qillqana / Written Work
Practice the following dialogue according to the model, using the cues provided.

Maymantataq jamunkichik? (Coacarí)	>>>	Ñuqaykuqa Coacarímanta jamuyku.
Machkha díapitaq chayamunkichik? (3)	>>>	Kimsa díapi chayamuyku.
Imapitaq jamunkichik? (avión)	>>>	Aviónpi jamuyku.

1. Maymantataq jamunkichik? (Chiru Q'asa)
_____.

Machkha díapitaq chayamunkichik? (2)
_____.

Imapitaq jamunkichik? (chaki)
_____.

2. Maymantataq jamunki? (Macha)
_____.

Machkha díapitaq chayamunki? (4)
_____.

Imapitaq jamunki? (kawallu)
_____.

3. Maymantataq paykuna jamunku? (Cochabamba)
_____.

Machkha p'unchawpitaq chayamunku? (1)
_____.

Imapitaq chayamunku? (auto)
_____.

4. Maymantataq jamunkichik? (Francia)
_____.

Machkha díapitaq chayamunki? (3)
_____.

Imapitaq jamunki? (avión)

_____.

5. Maymantataq jamunkichik? (Chile)

_____.

Machkha díapitaq chayamunkichik? (4)

_____.

Imapitaq jamunkichik? (carro)

_____.

2 Iskay ⌘ Parlana / Oral Work

Study the model then ask and answer the questions, using your own ideas.

Maymantataq kanki?	>>>	Londresmanta kani.
Payrí, maymantataq?	>>>	Paypis Londresllamantataq. *or* Paytaq Nueva Yorkmanta.
Machkhataq jamunkichik?	>>>	Chunkalla jamuyku.

1. Maymantataq kanki?
2. Tata/mama/masi/ykirí, maymantataq?
3. Qamkunarí maymantataq kankichik?
4. Machkhataq jamunkichik?
5. Paykuna maymantataq chayamunku?
6. Machkhataq jamunku?
7. Paykuna Brasilmantachu jamunku?
8. Qamkuna Españamantachu chayamunkichik?

3 Kimsa ⌘ Qhawana / Video View   ▶DVD

Go to the following section in the *Kawsay Vida* multimedia program:

Bolivian Quechua > Runakuna > Qhawana

1) Watch the following video clips: (i) **Coacarímanta jamuy**; (ii) **fiestaman riy**.
2) Note down the sentences in each clip which refer to where people come from and contain the suffix –**manta**. Look up and note down the English translation.

_____
_____
_____

4 Tawa ⌘ Yachana / Practice   ▶DVD

Go to the following section in the *Kawsay Vida* multimedia program:

Bolivian Quechua > Runakuna > Yachana > Akllanapaq (1)

Do the multiple-choice exercise, following the on-screen instructions. This exercise helps you review material you have studied in previous units. Use the lookup facility to check any meanings you are not sure of. Note down any new vocabulary or structures you find.

5 Phichqa ✣ Watuykuna, Inglés Simiman Tikrana / Analyze and Translate into English

Study the model and answer the following questions concerning each Quechua sentence below.

(i) Analyze the following sentences into their grammatical parts.
(ii) Explain the function of the suffixes.
(iii) Translate into English.

Machkhataq kankichik? >>> Machkha-taq ka-nkichik
how many-question suffix be-you plural >>> how many are you?

1. Ima llaqtamantataq kankichik?

2. Llikllatachu awachkanki?

3. Maymantataq jamunkichik?

4. Chay lluqalla ch'uñuta mikhuchkanchu?

5. Chay runa mana papatachu allan.

6. Suqta p'unchawmanta chayamuyku.

7. Qanchis wasichu kan?

8. Chay imillas, machkha ovejatataq michichkanku?

9. Chakrata qarpankichikchu?

_____

_____

10. Chay llaqta warmi imatataq ruwachkan?

_____

_____

6 Suqta ⌘ Qillqana / Written Work

You meet a Bolivian Quechua friend along the road. Write a short conversation with them in Quechua. Include questions about how they and their family are; ask them where they are coming from and what they are doing. Ask what other people are doing also.

6 / Suqta

Maymantaq richkanki? / Where Are You Going?

In This Unit...

You meet some more members of the Coacarí fiesta sponsors' party. You learn how to ask where people are going, and what they are going there for. You study the verb suffix **-mu-**, which indicates the direction of an action; and a verbal construction expressing purpose with verbs of movement. You study the noun suffix **-pi**, which denotes location in space.

KAWSAY / ANDEAN LIFE
Geography and Travel

The peoples of the Andes have always been mobile, taking advantage of the variety of natural environments that their mountainous geography provides—from the high tundra (puna) at over 10,000 feet, to the temperate valleys (qhichwa) above 6,000 feet, to the subtropical foothills (yunka) above 3,000 feet—and the different crops that can be grown at each altitude. The festival season provides an ideal opportunity for people from rural communities such as Sikuya, Qayarani, and Coacarí (featured in the multimedia program) to journey to their local town—here the cantón capital of San Pedro de Buenavista—to celebrate with music, song, and ritual, and to visit the markets that accompany the fiestas. Road networks in Northern Potosí have been improving since the 1990s, but there are still many communities whose inhabitants make journeys of several days on foot to reach the urban centers.

Suggested reading: Brush 1977; Gade 1999.

Fiesta ruwaq jamuchkayku.

Ñawirina, yachakuna / Read and Learn

Maymantaq richkanki?	Where are you going?
Potosíman richkani.	I am going to Potosí.
Maymantaq richkankichik?	Where are you (*pl.*) going?
Llaqtaman richkayku.	We are (*excl.*) going to town.
Imamantaq richkankichik?	What are you (*pl.*) going for?
Fiesta ruwaq richkayku.	We are going (*excl.*) to sponsor the fiesta.
Pitataq pusamuchkankichik?	Who are you (*pl.*) bringing?
Sikuta pusamuchkayku.	We are bringing (*excl.*) the panpipe players.
Maypitaq tiyakunki?	Where do you live?
La Pazpi tiyakuni.	I live in La Paz.

Qallarina / Introduction

Paykunaqa Coacarímanta kanku. Chaypi tiyakunku. Kunan San Pedro llaqtaman richkanku. Kimsa díapi chayamuchkanku. Paykuna San Pedroman fiesta ruwaq jamuchkanku.

Qhawana / Video View ▶DVD

Go to the following section in the *Kawsay Vida* multimedia program:

Bolivian Quechua > Runakuna > Qhawana > Coacarímanta jamuy

Watch the video clip. Use the translation and lookup facilities to check any meanings you are not sure of.

Simi / Vocabulary

Ruway / Verbs

    apamuy: to bring.
    apay: to carry.
    ayqiy: to escape.
    chimpay: to approach; to cross over (river, street).
    ñiy: to say.
    pukllay: to play.
    pusay: to bring, lead, guide (a person).
    phaway: to fly, run.
    q'ipimuy: to bring on one's back.
    q'ipiy: to load onto one's back.
    rantiy: to buy, to barter.
    riy: to go.
    takiy: to sing.
    tarpuy: to sow (seeds and tubers).
    tiyakuy: to live, to reside.
    tusuy: to dance.

Suti / Nouns

    Chhiqakuna / Places

    aqha wasi: bar where chicha is sold.
    aya wasi: cemetery.
    chhiqa: place.
    escuela [iskwila]: school.
    feria: market.
    jampiy wasi: hospital.
    jatun yachay wasi: university.
    kancha: corral; houseyard; sports ground; football pitch.
    larqha (*var.* rarqha, larq'a): irrigation canal.
    molino [mulinu]: mill.
    monte [munti]: bush; hilly woodland.
    muju: seed.
    ñan: road, path.
    pukyu: spring (of water).
    puna: high moorland.
    qhuya: mine.
    tusuy wasi: nightclub, discotheque.
    urqu: hill, mountain.
    valle [walli]: warm valley region.
    yachay wasi: school.
    yunka: Andean foothills.

    Fiesta/Raymi / Religious Festivals

    alférez [alhiris]: fiesta sponsor (ritual role).

chinki: fiesta sponsor's sister (ritual role); small drum played by fiesta sponsor's sister in ritual.

estandarte [istantarti]: pennant (religious icon).

fiesta [hista]: religious festival.

fiesta ruwaq: fiesta sponsor.

iglesia [inlisya]: church.

iñiy wasi: church.

raymi: religious festival.

siku: panpipe player; panpipe.

tullqa: fiesta sponsor's brother-in-law (ritual role).

Wak simi / Other Words

ñisqa: so-called.

Simip k'askaynin / Grammar

Ruway k'askaq / Verb Suffixes

-**mu**-

(**i**) On verbs of movement: movement toward speaker

When used on verbs of movement, -**mu**- indicates an action in the direction of the speaker, for example:

Llaqtaman chaya-**mu**-n.   S/he arrives at the town (where the speaker is).

but

Llaqtaman chayan.   She/he arrives at the town (in another place).

(**ii**) On verbs of activity

The suffix -**mu**- indicates that the subject moves to another place to perform an activity:

Papata alla-**mu**-n.   S/he has gone to dig up potatoes.
Fiestapi tusu-**mu**-ni.   I go to dance in the fiesta.

but

Papata allan.   S/he digs up potatoes.
Fiestapi tusuni.   I dance in the fiesta.

-**mu**- + -**chka**-

Suffix order

Note that the directional suffix -**mu**- precedes -**chka**- in the verb:

Wasiman chimpa-**mu**-**chka**-n.   S/he is approaching the house.

-**q**

Nominalizing suffix: (**i**) agentive

This suffix is attached to the verb root, producing a nominalized form that indicates the "doer" of an action. In this nominalized form, all suffixes that attach to the new form will be of the noun class.

ruway	to make	>>>	ruwa-**q**	maker
parlay	to speak	>>>	parla-**q**	speaker
llamk'ay	to work	>>>	llamk'a-**q**	worker
tusuy	to dance	>>>	tusu-**q**	dancer

Nominalizing suffix: (**ii**) purposive

When followed by a verb of movement, -**q** indicates the purpose of the action, for example:

Fiesta ruwa-**q** chayamun. S/he arrives to sponsor the fiesta.
Papa alla-**q** richkan. S/he is going to dig up potatoes.

The person is marked on the verb of movement in question, as follows:

tusu-**q ri**-ni	I go to dance	tusu-**q ri**-nchik	we (incl.) go to dance
		tusu-**q ri**-yku	we (excl.) go to dance
tusu-**q ri**-nki	you (sing.) go to dance	tusu-**q ri**-nkichik	you (pl.) go to dance
tusu-**q ri**-n	s/he goes to dance	tusu-**q ri**-nku	they go to dance

Suti k'askaq / Noun Suffixes

-**man**

"to," "at," "to get"

This suffix indicates movement toward a place, and arrival at a place:

May-**man**-taq richkan?	Where is s/he going?
Chakra-**man** richkan.	S/he is going to the field.
May-**man**-taq purichkanku?	Where are they walking to?
Qhuya-**man** llamk'aq rinku.	They go to work in the mine.
Ima-**man**-taq richkan?	What is s/he going for/to get?
T'anta-**man** richkan.	S/he is going for/to get bread.

-**pi**

Indicates location in space; "in," "on"

The most frequent use of -**pi** is to indicate the place where the action of the verb takes place, or the location of a person or object in space: in or on a place. Whereas -**man** expresses movement to a place, and -**manta** expresses movement from, -**pi** indicates stationary action or activity.

Mayu-**pi** t'aqsachkan.	S/he is washing clothes in the river.
May-**pi**-taq tiyakunki?	Where do you live?
Jaqay wasi-**pi** tiyakuni.	I live in that house.
Llaqta-**pi** takichkan.	S/he is singing in the town.
La Paz-**pi** aymarata parlanku.	They speak Aymara in La Paz.

Ruwana / Exercises

1 Juk ⌘ Junt'achina / Video Exercise ▶DVD

Go to the following section in the *Kawsay Vida* multimedia program:

Bolivian Quechua > Runakuna > Junt'achina > Coacarímanta jamuy

Working on-screen, do both the video and audio gap-fill exercises. Click on the video and audio buttons to get started, and follow the on-screen instructions. There are three levels of difficulty here; you can work through each text three times with different gaps to fill each time.

2 Iskay ⌘ Qillqana / Written Work

Ask and answer according to the model, using the cues provided:

Maymantaq richkankichik? (llaqta) >>> Llaqtaman richkayku.
Imamantaq richkanki? (t'anta) >>> T'antaman richkani.

1. Maymantaq richkankichik? (rarqha)
_____.

2. Imamantaq chay larqhaman richkankichik? (yaku)
_____.

3. Maymantaq richkanki? (llaqta)
_____.

4. Imamantaq llaqtaman richkanki? (fiesta)
_____.

5. Maymantaq paykuna richkanku? (aqha wasi)
_____.

6. Qharikuna imamantaq chakraman jamunku? (papa)
_____.

7. Chay lluqallarí maymantaq phawachkan? (urqu)
_____.

8. Awaq warmi imamantaq punaman rin? (allpaqa millma)
_____.

9. Maymantaq qamkuna purichkankichik? (Oruro)
_____.

10. Maymantaq tullqa chimpachkan? (iglesia)
_____.

3 Kimsa ⌘ Qillqana / Written Work

Practice using the suffix **-q** as an agentive ("doer"). Change the following sentences as shown in the model. Note how the direct-object marker **-ta** is no longer needed when the verb is in the agentive form. Note how the translation differs.

Payqa fiestata ruwachkan. >>> S/he sponsors a fiesta.
Payqa fiesta ruwaq. >>> S/he is a fiesta sponsor.

1. Sipasqa uwijata michichkan.
   _____.

2. Chay waynaqa llamt'ata pallachkan.
   _____.

3. Chay qhariqa bayetata awachkan.
   _____.

4. Mama Elisaqa phulluta awachkan.
   _____.

5. Gabrielqa librota qillqachkan.
   _____.

6. Ronaldoqa futbolta pukllachkan.
   _____.

7. Shakiraqa televisionpi takichkan.
   _____.

4 Tawa ⌘ Qillqana / Written Work

Practice using the suffix **-q** in the purposive construction, with verbs of movement. Ask and answer according to the model, using the cues provided:

Imamantaq richkankichik? (fiesta ruway)   >>>   Fiesta ruwaq richkayku.

1. Imamantaq chay sipas jamuchkan? (tusuy)
   _____.

2. Waynas imamantaq fiestaman rinku? (charanku tocay)
   _____.

3. Imamantaq chimpachkankichik? (mikhuy)
   _____.

4. Tullqa chinki ñisqa imamantaq llaqtaman jamunku? (fiesta ruway)
   _____.

5. Chay warmirí imamantaq jamun? (takiy)
   _____.

6. Qamrí imamantaq jamuchkanki? (futbol pukllay)
   _____.

7. Chay runas imamantaq chakraman richkanku? (llamk'ay)
   _____.

5 Phichqa ⌘ Parlana / Oral Work

Work in groups of more than two and practice the following dialogue. Make the conversation relate to your own lives.

– Maymantataq qamkuna jamuchkankichik?
– _____manta jamuchkayku.
– Maymantaq richkankichik?
– _____man richkayku.
– Imamantaq jaqayman richkankichik?
– _____q richkayku.
– _____imatataq ruwachkanku?
– Paykunaqa _____nku.

6 Suqta ⌘ Yachana / Practice ▶DVD

Go to the following section in the *Kawsay Vida* multimedia program:

Bolivian Quechua > Runakuna > Yachana > Akllana (2)

Work through the exercise. Note how the "-**q** + verb of movement" structure works. Use the lookup facility to check meanings you are not sure of. Note any new vocabulary below:

_____

_____

7 Qanchis ⌘ Qillqana / Written Work

Insert the suffix -**mu**- into the following sentences. Translate both versions, noting how the addition of this suffix changes the meaning.

Wasiman chimpachkan.	>>>	Wasiman chimpa-**mu**-chkan.
S/he is approaching the house.	>>>	S/he is approaching this house (where I am).
Chakrapi mujuta tarpuyku.	>>>	Chakrapi mujuta tarpu**mu**yku.
We plant seeds in the field.	>>>	We go to plant seeds in the field (over there).

1. Sarata chakramanta apani.
_____.
_____.

2. Tullqa alférezman parlaq chimpachkan.
_____.
_____.

3. Montepi llamt'ata pallachkanku.
_____.
_____.

4. Qhuyapi llamk'achkan.
_____.
_____.

5. Paypis conciertopi tocallantaq.
_____.
_____.

6. Qamkuna yachay wasiman phawankichik.
_____.
_____.

8 Pusaq ⌘ Parlana / Oral Work

Talk about where actions and events take place.

Maypitaq tiyakunki?	>>>	Cochabambapi tiyakuni.
Tatayki mamayki maypitaq tiyakunku?	>>>	San Pedropi tiyakunku.
Londrespichu tiyakunki?	>>>	Mana, Bristolpi tiyakuni.
Maypitaq llamk'ankichik?	>>>	Chicagopi llamk'ayku.

1. Maypitaq tiyakunki?
_____.

2. Qamrí, maypitaq tiyakunki?
_____.

3. Maypitaq (ñañayki/wawqiyki/mamayki/tatayki) tiyakun?
_____.

4. (Londres/Birmingham/Boston/Oruro)pichu tiyakunki?
_____.

5. Maypitaq paykuna futbolta pukllanku?
_____.

6. Ronaldorí maypitaq pukllan? _____.

7. Qam, maypitaq p'achaykita rantinki? (*name a store of your choice*) pichu?
_____.

9 Jisq'un ⌘ Yachana / Practice ▶DVD

Go to the following section in the *Kawsay Vida* multimedia program:

Bolivian Quechua > Runakuna > Yachana > Maymantataq

Do the exercise, following the on-screen instructions.

10 Chunka ⌘ Yachana / Practice   ▶DVD

Go to the following section in the *Kawsay Vida* multimedia program:

Bolivian Quechua > Runakuna > Yachana > Maypitaq

Do the exercise, following the on-screen instructions.

11 Chunka jukniyuq ⌘ Qhichwaman tikrana / Translate into Quechua

Translate the following sentences into Quechua. Use the suffix -**mu**- where appropriate.

1. They are buying potatoes at the market.
_____.

2. He is bringing the firewood in a bundle on his back.
_____.

3. Carmen has gone to church to hear Mass.
_____.

4. The panpipe players have arrived.
_____.

5. Is she bringing the children to the fiesta?
_____?

6. They haven't brought any food.
_____.

7. Has the fiesta sponsor arrived?
_____?

8. Who is the fiesta sponsor bringing?
_____?

9. That young woman has come to sell t-shirts.
_____.

10. We are studying languages at the university.
_____.

7 / Qanchis

Yuyarina / Review

A Look Back

Ima k'askaqkunataq kaykama yachakusqa kanku? What suffixes have been studied so far?

Verb Conjugation Suffixes

-n	3rd-person singular (Unit 1)
-nchik	1st-person plural, inclusive (Unit 5)
-ni	1st-person singular (Unit 1)
-nki	2nd-person singular (Unit 1)
-nkichik	2nd-person plural (Unit 5)
-nku	3rd-person plural (Unit 5)
-yku	1st-person plural, exclusive (Unit 5)

Verb Suffixes

-chka-	state of being temporal/spatial (Unit 1); progressive (Unit 4)
-mu-	directional (Unit 6)
-q	agentive; purpose (Unit 6)

Noun Suffixes

-kuna/-s	plurals (Unit 5)
-manta	"from," "after" (Unit 5)
-man	"to" (Unit 6)
-n	3rd-person-singular possessive (Unit 1)
-pi	"in" (Unit 5)
-s/-kuna	plurals (Unit 5)
-ta (i)	direct-object marker (Unit 4)
-y	1st-person-singular possessive (Unit 1)
-yki	2nd-person-singular possessive (Unit 1)

Class-Free Suffixes

-chu	interrogative (Unit 2); negative (Unit 3)
-lla	limitative (Units 1, 4)
-pis	"also"; includer (Units 1, 2, 4, 5)
-puni	emphatic (Unit 2)
-qa	topic marker (Unit 1)
-ri	insistent coordinative tag (Unit 5)
-rí	follow-up question tag (Unit 1)
-taq	question tag (Unit 1); coordinating suffix (Unit 3, 4, 5)

Ñawirina, kutichina / Read and Answer the Questions

Tata Siskoqa San Pedroman richkan. Payqa tullqa kachkan. Mama Elisapis San Pedrollamantaq richkan. Payqa chinki kachkan. Tullqawan chinkiwan fiesta ruwaq richkanku. Paykunaqa alférezta pusachkanku. Charawaytuman chayanku. Chaypi Mama Filomena paykunata suyachkan. Chaypi parlanku.

– Imaynalla Mama Filomena, waliqllachu?
– Waliqlla waliqlla, qamkunarí?
– Ñuqaykupis waliqlla kachkayku.
– Maymantataq chayamuchkankichik?
– Toracarímanta.
– Fiestamanchu richkankichik?
– Arí, chayman richkayku. Jaku khuska!

Chaymanta fiestaman rinku. Mama Filomenatapis pusallankutaq.

1 Juk ⌘ Inglespi kutichiy! / Answer in English

1. What place-names are mentioned in the text?
_____

2. What verbs in the text indicate movement?
_____

3. What ways of asking a question can you find in the text?
_____

4. What words are used to refer to people in the text?
_____

5. How many people are going to the fiesta?
_____

2 Iskay ⌘ Qhichwapi kutichiy! / Answer in Quechua

1. Pitaq chinki?
_____

2. Tullqa, chinki La Pazmanchu richkanku?
_____

3. Imamantaq San Pedroman richkanku?
_____

4. Imatataq mama Filomena Charawaytupi ruwachkan?
_____

5. Imatataq paykuna chaypi ruwanku?
_____

6. Imaynataq Mama Filomena kachkan?
_____

7. Maymantataq Mama Elisa, Tata Sisko kanku?
_____

8. Mama Filomena fiestamanchu richkan?
_____

Simi / Vocabulary

    kutichiy (v): to respond, to answer.
    khuska (adv): together.
    jaku!: let's go!
    suyay (v): to wait for.

Ruwana / Exercises

1 Juk ⌘ Junt'achina / Gap-Fill Exercise

Fill the gaps in the sentences with the most appropriate suffixes, choosing from the ones provided in brackets.

1. Paykunaqa Toracarí_____jamuchkanku.   [pi | manta | chu]
2. Paykunaqa San Pedro_____richkanku.   [man | chu | manta]
3. Ñuqayku chakraman richka_____.   [yku | nkichik | nchik]
4. Chakra qarpa_____richkani.   [ta | kuna | q]
5. Paykunaqa qhuya llamk'aq_____kanku.   [nku | pis | kuna]
6. Chaymantataq sara_____apamuni.   [pis | ta | man]
7. Ima_____taq jamuchkankichik?   [manta | ri | man]
8. Ñuqaqa qillqani, qillqa_____kani.   [chka | q | y]

2 Iskay ⌘ Simi tikrana / Sentence Transformation

In each sentence, substitute another word of your choosing for the **boldface** words. Make a new sentence while keeping the same grammatical structure. Check any meanings you are not sure of.

1. **Ch'uspa**ta awachkan.
_____

2. **Mama**yqa aychata wayk'uchkan.
_____

3. Tata Francisco **ch'uñu**ta q'ipimun.
_____

4. **Sikus**tachu suyachkanki?
_____

5. Tatayqa **fiesta ruwa**q.
_____

6. **Llaqta**pi llamk'ayku.
_____

7. **Jatun yachay wasi**man yachakuq rinku.
_____

8. **Chaki**pi urqumanta jamunku.
_____

9. **Mayu**manta chimpamuchkan.
_____

10. Wawakunaqa **yaku**man rin.
_____

3 Kimsa ⌘ Yachana / Practice   ▶DVD

Go to the following section of the *Kawsay Vida* multimedia program:

Peruvian Quechua > Ayllu > Yachana

Choose *yachanapaq (1)* and *yachanapaq (2)*. Do these exercises for general review of points studied so far. Use the space below to note any differences between Peruvian and Bolivian Quechua that you come across.

_____

_____

_____

PART II

8 / Pusaq

Allin kay / Health

In This Unit . . .

You acquire the vocabulary to talk about your health, including words for the parts of the body. You learn the interrogative phrase **imayki** 'what of yours?'. You practice the possessive form in the singular. You are introduced to the basics of person/object-marking in verbs.

KAWSAY / ANDEAN LIFE

Health and Sickness

Causes of illness and forms of treatment are perceived variously in Andean societies. In rural areas, certain illnesses are attributed to an imbalance in the sick person's relationship with the natural world, perhaps arising from neglect of ritual observances that must be performed at certain times of the year: offerings to the pachamama in the month of August, for example. The services of shamans (yatiri) are called upon to correct the imbalance, and they do this by means of ritual gestures, using incense, sprinkling alcohol, and prayers in Aymara and Quechua. Even in urban settings, people call on the yatiri to tend to their health problems, often turning to hospitals and Western-style doctors only as a last resort.

Suggested reading: Crandon-Malamud 1993.

Jampiq jamun.

Ñawirina, yachakuna / Read and Learn

> Imaykitaq nanasunki? — Where does it hurt you? [*lit.* "What of you hurts you?"]
> Wiksay nanawan. — My stomach hurts me.

Qallarina / Introduction

Mama María unqusqa kachkan. Uman nanan. Juanpis unqusqallataq. Wiksan nanachkan. Jampiq jamun. Payqa tapun:

Parlana / Dialogue

Jampiq (J): – Imaynalla mama María?
María (M): – Mana allinchu. Unqusqa kachkani.
J: – Imaykitaq nanasunki?
M: – Umay nanawan.
J: – Umaykichu nanasunki?
M: – Arí, umaypuni.
J: – Rinriyki nanasunkichu?
M: – Mana, mana rinriychu nanawan.
J: – Tata Juanrí?
M: – Paypis unqusqallataq
J: – Payta imantaq nanan?
M: – Wiksan nanan.
J: – Wiksallanchu nanan?
M: – Arí, wiksallanpuni nanan.

Simi / Vocabulary

Ruway / Verbs

    chiriy: to be cold.
    ch'akiy: to be thirsty.
    jampiy: to cure, heal.
    k'ajay: to have a temperature.
    mayllay: to wash (one's face, hands, body; food).
    nanay: to hurt.
    puñuy: to sleep.
    q'uñiy: to be hot, to be on heat (animals).
    ruphay: to burn; to be sunny.
    tapuy: to ask.
    unquy: to be ill.
    yariqay (*var.* yarqhay): to be hungry.

Suti / Nouns

    chiri: cold.
    jampiq: doctor.
    pachamama: female earth deity; mother earth.
    puñuna: bed.

    Kurku / Body (Exterior)

    chanka: leg.
    chukcha: hair.
    kiru: teeth.
    kunka: neck.
    kurku: body.
    maki: hand.
    ñawi: eye.
    ñuñu: breast.
    qallu: tongue.
    qara: skin.
    qunqur: knee.
    rikra (*var.* likra): arm.
    rinri (*var.* ninri): ear.
    sillu: fingernail.
    sinqa: nose.
    tullu: bone.
    uma: head.
    uya: face.
    wasa: back.

    Ukhu / Body (Insides)

    k'iwicha: liver.
    phusa: lungs.
    rurun: kidney.

sunqu: heart.
ukhu: insides; interior space.
wiksa [wisa]: stomach.
yawar: blood.

Suti tikrachiq / Adjectives

kusisqa: happy.
llakisqa: sad.
unqusqa: ill, sick.

Expressions

Jukta tapurisqayki: "I'll ask you a question."

Simip k'askaynin / Grammar

Ruway k'askaq / Verb Suffixes

-**wan**- and -**sunki**

Person object–marker in the verb, singular

The suffix -**wan** marks the verb when there is a 1st-person-singular object (me) and a 3rd-person-singular subject (he/she/it).

Nana-**wa**-n.	It hurts me.
Chiri-**wa**-n.	I'm cold. [*lit.* "It is cold to me."]
Yariqa chka-**wa**-n	I'm hungry (right now).

-**sunki** marks the verb when there is a 2nd-person-singular object (you) and a 3rd-person-singular subject.

Nana-**sunki**.	It hurts you.
Nana-**sunki**-chu?	Does it hurt you?
Yariqa-**sunki**-chu?	Are you hungry?

While it is possible to analyze -**wan** as "-**wa**- + -**n**" (i.e., 1st-person-singular object + 3rd-person-singular subject), -**sunki** is not analyzable in this way and is best learnt as a synthetic suffix (i.e., 2nd-person-singular object + 3rd-person-singular subject).

The 3rd-person personal object has no explicit marker in the verb. For clarity, the object can be expressed by the personal pronoun with direct object marker -**ta**, but this is not obligatory:

Chiri-n.	S/he is cold. [*lit.* "It colds him/her."]
Pay-**ta** chiri-n.	S/he is cold.
Chakin nana-n.	His/her foot hurts.

-**ni**-

Connective suffix

This suffix is used to facilitate pronunciation where a noun ends in a consonant and the possessive suffixes are added. It has no meaning in itself.

qunqur knee   >>>   qunqur-**ni**-y   my knee

kawsay	life	>>>	kawsay-**ni**-yki	your life
yawar	blood	>>>	yawar-**ni**-n	his blood

Ruwana / Exercises

1 Juk ⌘ Parlana / Oral Work

Ask and answer questions to find out the words for parts of the body in Quechua. Follow the model, then add ideas of your own. Point to parts of your body, or use a picture.

Jukta tapurisqayki, mamáy/tatáy.
Kay, imataq qhichwapi? (nose)   >>>   Qhichwapiqa sinqa.
Kayrí? (hand)   >>>   Chaytaq qhichwapiqa maki.

1. (eye)
2. (knee)
3. (mouth)
4. (tooth)
5. (nose)
6. (foot)
7. (back)
8. (hair)
9. (arm)
10. (face)

2 Iskay ⌘ Parlana / Oral Work

Working in pairs, practice the dialogue below. Substitute the **boldface** words for other vocabulary referring to different parts of the body.

– Imaynalla, mamáy/tatáy?
– Mana allinchu. Unqusqa kachkani.
– Imaykitaq nanasunki?
– **Umay** nanawan.
– **Umay**kichu?
– Arí, **umay**puni.
– **Rinri**ykichu nanasunki?
– Mana, mana **rinri**ychu nanawan.
– Juanrí?
– Paypis unqusqallataq.
– Imantaq nanan?
– **Wiksa**n nanan.
– **Wiksa**llanchu?
– Arí, **wiksa**llanpuni.

3 Kimsa ⌘ Qillqana / Written Work

Practice the use of impersonal verbs combined with the suffixes -**wan** and -**sunki** where appropriate. Follow the model and vary the vocabulary by substituting the italicized impersonal verbs for the ones listed below.

Chiriy >>> *Chiri*sunkichu? >>> Arí, *chiri*chkawan/mana, mana *chiri*chkawanchu.
Juantarí, *chiri*nchu? >>> Arí, paytapis *chiri*chkallantaq/mana, mana payta *chiri*chkanchu.

1. yariqay (qam; wawa)
___

2. ruphay (qam; paykuna)
___

3. nanay (qam; Manuel)
___

4. ch'akiy (qam; Paulina)
___

4 Tawa ⌘ Parlana / Oral Work

Compose a conversation with a Quechua speaker. Follow the prompts, and elaborate with your own ideas.

Greet the person; ask how they are.
They say they are hot.
Ask them if they are thirsty.
They say they are very thirsty.
Offer them some water to drink ("upyariy!" "drink"!).
Ask them if they are hungry.
They say they are not hungry.
They ask you if you are hungry.
You say yes, you are hungry.
They offer you some *mote* to eat ("mikhuriy!" "eat!").

5 Phichqa ⌘ Simi yachana / Vocabulary Practice

Find or make a drawing of the human body and label it, using the vocabulary you know.

6 Suqta ⌘ Rikuna / Browse ▶DVD

Go to the following section in the *Kawsay Vida* multimedia program:

Peruvian Quechua > Hampikuy > Rikuna > Hampikuy

Browse through the images on-screen, and study their accompanying text. Use the translation and analysis facilities to identify the vocabulary for: (i) words for parts of the body; (ii) words for symptoms of illness; (iii) names of medicinal plants; (iv) words to describe healing techniques. Note the words under their headings in the box below.

Parts of the Body	Symptoms	Names of Plants	Curing Techniques

7 Qanchis ⌘ Yachana / Practice ▶DVD

Go to the following section in the *Kawsay Vida* multimedia program:

Peruvian Quechua > Hampikuy > Yachana > K'askarachinapaq

Use this exercise to reinforce your knowledge of the vocabulary identified in exercise 6. Advanced grammar structures can be disregarded until a later stage in the program.

9 / Jisq'un

Chhiqa / Places

In This Unit...

You meet a Chayantaka charango player, who describes learning songs from the spirits of the waterfalls. You talk about the landscape and the places people go. You study the reflexive suffix -**ku**- and its combination with the suffix -**mu**-. You meet the causative suffix -**chi**-, which marks delegated action. You practice the interrogative marker -**chu**- and learn another use of -**ta**.

KAWSAY / ANDEAN LIFE
Music

Quechua-speaking peoples in the Andes participate in a rich musical culture. Music—and in particular song—helps in many ways to sustain the very use of the language in social life. Musical traditions are diverse, and a range of wind, string, and percussion instruments has evolved in part from pre-Columbian times and in part under European influence. In San Pedro de Buenavista a vibrant musical culture is evident in both the town and the countryside, with different instrument types and song versification characterizing each. The ubiquitous Andean song and dance form is the wayñu, which is performed especially by young people in the fiestas. In the indigenous communities, it is typical for the men to play the wayñu tunes on the charango while the women sing in a characteristic high-pitched register and dance in a circle.

Suggested reading: Stobart 2006.

Charankuta tocachkani.
Phaqchasman takiyta uyarikamuni.

Ñawirina, yachakuna / Read and Learn

Takiyta uyarikuni.	I listen to the song.
Versota apakamun.	He brings back the tune for himself.
Imillasta tusuchin.	He makes the girls dance.

Qallarina / Introduction

Kay runaqa Chayantakamanta, charankuta tocan. Charanku tocaqqa ch'in lomasman, wayq'usman, phaqchasman ima rin, ñin. Chay phaqchaspi sirinus ñisqata uyarikun; jaqaymanta versosta apakamun, ñin. Chaymantataq imillasman versosta uyarichin, yachachin, ñin. Charanku tocaqqa fiestapi wayñusta tocan; runakunataq kusikun. Wakin charanku tocaqkunaqa sirinusman charankuta tutantinta saqimunku, ñin. Sut'iyaytataq mask'amunku, ñin.

Simi / Vocabulary

Ruway / Verbs

    apakamuy: to bring for oneself.
    atiy: to be able.
    jurqhuy [orqhoy]: to extract; to take something out of an inner space.
    kawsay: to live (be alive).
    kusiy: to be happy.
    kutimuy: to come back.
    kutiy: to return, to go back.
    llakiy: to be sad.

lluqsiy: to go out.
mask'ay: to look for something.
mast'ay: to spread out on a surface.
munakuy: to love.
munay: to want, to like.
phukuy: to blow.
qhatiy: to herd animals, to follow.
qhawakuy: to watch.
qhaway: to look at.
rikuy: to see.
saqiy: to leave something.
sayay: to stand.
sut'iyay: to dawn, to get light.
tocay [tukay]: to play (a musical instrument).
uyarikuy: to listen attentively; to obey.
uyariy: to hear; to listen.
yachachiy: to teach.
yachay: to know.
yaykuy: to enter, to go in.

Ruway tikrachiq / Adverbs

tutantin: all night.

Suti / Nouns

charanku: charango.
jallp'a (*var.* allpa): earth, land.
qhichwa: Quechua language; warm valley region.
sirinu (Sp. *sireno*): female water spirit.
sut'iyay: dawn.
takiy: song.
tinku: ritual battle between two halves of a community.
tuta: night.
t'iyu: sand.
urpi: dove.
verso [wirsu]: tune.

Chhiqa / Places

lomas: hills.
machay: cave, rock overhang.
punku: door, doorway.
qallpa: uncultivated plot of land.
qaqa: rock, boulder.
qucha: lake.
wayq'u: small river, gully.

Suti tikrachiq / Adjectives
    ch'in: silent.

Positional Particles
    chawpi: center, middle.
    jawa: outside.
    pata: above.
    ukhu: inside.
    ura: below.
    wasa: behind.

Partitive Adjective
    wakin: some.

Conjunctions
    chaymanta: then; after that; from there.
    ima: and (*closes a list*).

Simip k'askaynin / Grammar
Ruway k'askaq / Verb Suffixes
    -**ku**-

  (**i**) Action for the benefit of the subject of the verb

This suffix indicates the action of the verb is performed for the personal benefit of the subject of the verb:

uyarini	I listen	>>>	uyari-**ku**-ni	I listen attentively
apan	s/he carries	>>>	apa-**ku**-n	s/he carries for him/herself

  (**ii**) Reflexive/semi-passive aspects

With transitive verbs -**ku**- usually indicates reflexivity:

Llaqtapi tukuy imata qhawani.	In the city, I look at everything.
Llaqtapi sumaqta qhawa-**ku**-ni.	In the city, I look out for myself.
Juanqa llaki-**ku**-n.	Juan feels sad.
Ñuqanchik kusi-**ku**-nchik.	We feel happy.

-**ku**- can also be interpreted as a "middle voice," as in:

Kanchapi qhichwa simiqa uyari-**ku**-n.   The Quechua language is heard in the marketplace.

    -**ku**- + -**mu**- >>> -**kamu**-
        "Go (and do) for oneself"

When combined with -**mu**-, -**ku**- precedes -**mu**- and -**ku**- changes to -**ka**- for reasons of vowel harmony:

Taki-**ku**-ni.	I sing to myself.	>>>	Taki-**ka**-**mu**-ni.	I go to have a sing.
Uyari-**ku**-ni.	I listen.	>>>	Uyari-**ka**-**mu**-ni.	I listen.

-chi-
   Indicates delegated action; causative function

When the suffix **-chi** is used, the subject of the verb does not execute the action of the verb but rather causes another person to do so. For example:

Qhichwata yachani.	I know Quechua.
Qhichwata paykunata yacha-**chi**-ni.	I teach them Quechua [lit. "cause them to know"].
Charanku tocaqqa imillasman versosta yacha-**chi**-n.	The charango player teaches the tunes to the girls.
Quchata rikunku.	They see the lake.
Turistasman quchata riku-**chi**-nku.	They show the tourists the lake [lit. "cause them to see"].

Suti k'askaq / Noun suffixes

-ta
   Adverb marker

-ta serves to form adverbial phrases of space and time:

lunes-**ta**	on Monday
tutantin-**ta**	all night
sut'iyay-**ta**	at dawn
ñan-**ta**	along the road

Syntax

Expressing Location and Orientation in Space

(i) By use of demonstrative pronouns **kay, chay, jaqay**

The demonstrative pronouns **kay** 'this', **chay** 'that', and **jaqay** 'that over there' take noun suffixes to express spatial orientation and location. Compare the following:

kay-pi	here
chay-pi	there
jaqay-pi	over there
kay-man	to here
chay-man	to there
jaqay-man	to over there
kay-manta	from here
kay-manta	from there
jaqay-manta	from over there

(ii) By use of positional particles

chawpi 'middle'	jawa 'outside'
pata 'above'	ukhu 'inside'
ura 'below'	

These words can be used in a number of ways to describe position in space.
   (i) They can combine with noun suffixes to describe location as follows:

pata-pi	on top
pata-manta	from up there
pata-man	to up there

(ii) They can act as postpositional phrases as follows:

ñan **chawpi**	the middle of the road
urqu **pata**	the mountain top
wasi **ukhu**	the interior of the house
llaqta **ura**	the place below the town

(iii) They can act as adjectival phrases positioned in front of a noun to qualify it in spatial terms:

chawpi p'unchaw	midday
jawa runa	outsider, foreigner
ura mayu	down river
pata wasi	the house at the top

(iv) In all cases, they may take noun suffixes as follows:

kancha **chawpi**-pi	in the middle of the yard
wasi **ukhu**-pi	inside the house
urqu **pata**-man	to the top of the mountain
jawa runa-ta rikun	he/she sees the outsider
ura mayu-manta	from down river

(v) Words that describe particular spaces, such as **punku** 'door, doorway' and **kancha** 'yard', may be used in compound phrases to describe location:

wasi punku	house doorway
Inti Punku	Sun Door (location at Machu Picchu)
wasi kancha	houseyard

Ruwana / Exercises

1 Juk ⌘ Watuykuna / Analysis

(i) Following the examples, decide how the presence or absence of -**ku**-, -**mu**-, and -**kamu**- contributes to the meaning of the sentences below:

jallp'ata llamk'an	s/he works the land
jallp'ata llamk'akun	s/he works the land for him/herself
jallp'ata llamk'amun	s/he goes to work the land
jallp'ata llamk'akamun	s/he goes to work the land for him/herself

1. Versota uyarini.
2. Versota uyarimuni.
3. Versota uyarikuni.
4. Versota uyarikamuni.
5. Tinkuta qhawakun.

6. Tinkuta qhawan.
7. Tinkuta qhawakamun.
8. Tinkuta qhawamun.
9. Ch'uñuta apamunchik.
10. Ch'uñuta apakunchik.
11. Ch'uñuta apanchik.
12. Ch'uñuta apakamunchik.

(ii) Use the suffixes **-ku-**, **-mu-**, **-kamu-** in whole sentences, to express different meanings. Make three sentences for each of the following verbs, using vocabulary of your choice, as in the model:

parlay	>>>	Inglaterrapi inglésta parlani.
	>>>	Jatun yachay wasipi qhichwata parlakuni.
	>>>	Franciaman francésta parlamuni.
	>>>	Boliviaman qhichwata parlakamuni.

1. mikhuy

_____.
_____.
_____.

2. llamk'ay

_____.
_____.
_____.

3. rantiy

_____.
_____.
_____.

2 Iskay ⌘ Qillqana / Written Work

Rewrite the following sentences by changing the subject of the verb and using the suffix **-chi-**. Make all necessary changes, as shown in the model:

Wawaqa mikhun. (mama)   >>>   Mamaqa wawata mikhuchin.

1. Waynaqa unqun. (chiri)
_____.

2. Marinaqa wayk'un. (doña Elisa)
_____.

3. Lluqallaqa qhichwata yachan. (yachachiq)
_____.

4. Sipasqa fiestapi tusun. (charanku tocaq)
_____.

5. Imillasqa wayñusta takin. (fiesta ruwaq)
_____.

6. Payqa versosta uyarin. (sirenos)
_____.

3 Kimsa ⌘ Qillqana / Written Work

(i) Complete the following sentences appropriately with either -**man**, -**manta**, or -**pi**.

1. Llaqta ura_____uwijasta qhatiq rinku.
2. Ñuqayku mayu pata_____t'aqsayku.
3. Chay warmiqa wasi ukhu_____lluqsimun.
4. Allquqa wasi jawa_____puñuchkan.
5. Autoqa ura ñan_____sayan.
6. Yachakuqkunaqa escuela_____yaykun.
7. Kunturqa urqu pata_____kawrasta qhawamun.
8. Payakunaqa wasi punku _____parlanku.

(ii) Translate the following pairs of sentences into English, showing the differences in meaning:

1. Mama Filomena pata chakraman papata apan.
   Mama Filomena chakra patapi ch'uñuta mast'an.
   _____.
   _____.

2. Tata Vitalioqa wasi ukhupi puñuchkan.
   Tata Vitalioqa ukhu wasita pichamun.
   _____.
   _____.

3. Ura mayuman sarata tarpuq rinku.
   Mayu uramanta t'iyuta jurqhunku.
   _____.
   _____.

4 Tawa ⌘ Parlana / Oral Work

Ask and answer the questions about people's movements using the relevant noun suffix, as shown in the model.

Sisku urqu**man**chu richkan? (yachay wasi)   >>>   Mana, mana urqu**man**chu richkan; yachay wasi**man** richkan.

1. Luisa yunkamanchu phawachkan? (monte)
2. Mariyanu yachay wasimantachu ayqichkan? (iñiy wasi)
3. Pedro wayq'umantachu kutimunchu? (chakra)
4. Qamkuna tusuqkunatachu qhawakamunkichik? (futbol pukllaq)
5. Waynas mayutachu purichkanku? (ñan)

5 Phichqa ⌘ Parlana / Oral Work

Use the structures suggested in the box to conduct interviews with different kinds of Quechua-speaking people.

Charanku tocaqta parlanki:	
Sirenos	– Chay sirenosman rinkichu?
	– Sirenosman rini.
	– Imamantaq rinki?
Verso uyarikuq riy	– Versota uyarikuq rini
	– Chaymantarí imatataq ruwanki?
Apakamuy	– Versosta apakamuni
	– Chaymantarí?
imillasman yachachiy	– Chaymantataq imillasman versota yachachini

1. Chakra llamk'aqta parlanki:
   chakras
   papa tarpukuq
   papata allakamuy
   wasiyman apamuy

2. Siku tocaqta parlanki:
   fiestas
   siku phukukamuq riy
   tusukamuy
   aqhata upyaykuy

6 Suqta ⌘ Rikuna / Browse   ▶DVD

Go to the following section in the *Kawsay Vida* multimedia program:

Bolivian Quechua > Fiesta > Rikuna > Fiesta kaqkuna

Browse through the exercise to learn what the different participants do in the fiesta. Note below any sentences that contain **-ku-**, **-mu-**, **-kamu-**, **-chi-**.

_____
_____
_____
_____

7 Qanchis ⌘ Qhawana / Video View   ▶DVD

Go to the following section in the *Kawsay Vida* multimedia program:

Bolivian Quechua > Fiesta > Qhawana > Primitiva fiestamanta

Watch the video and note below the phrases in the text that contain the suffixes **-ku-** and **-chi-**. Translate them into English.

_____

_____

_____

_____

8 Pusaq ⌘ Junt'achina / Video Exercise   ▶DVD

Use the same section in the *Kawsay Vida* multimedia program:

Bolivian Quechua > Fiesta > Junt'achina > Primitiva fiestamanta

Follow the on-screen instructions, and do (i) the audio and (ii) the video gap-fill exercises. You can work through each text three times, gradually increasing the level of difficulty.

9 Jisq'un ⌘ Takirisun! Tusurisun! / Let's Sing and Dance!

Here is a wayñu sung by Luzmila Carpio. See how much of the text you can understand. Listen to the recording and sing and dance!

ACACIOMANTA

Urpillay kutimuy ari
Mayllapitaq purichkanki   (x 2)
Manachus atinki chayri
Imapaqñataq kawsani   (x 2)
Munasqatay
Imapaqñataq kawsani   (x 2)
Imayna mamap wawanpis
Wasillanpi llaqtallanpi   (x 2)
Nuqap wawa munakusqay
Ni wasinpi ni llaqtanpi   (x 2)
Munasqatay
Ni wasinpi ni llaqtanpi   (x 2)

(Sung by Luzmila Carpio; see video available online)

10 / Chunka

Away / Weaving

In This Unit . . .

You meet a craftsperson from the community who explains the art of weaving. You learn how to ask questions about specialized activities. You study possessive constructions; the use of the noun suffix -**wan**; and more about the noun suffix -**manta**.

KAWSAY / ANDEAN LIFE
Weaving

Weaving is one of the most ancient crafts in Andean societies, having evolved in pre-Columbian times and still flourishing today. Both men and women weave. In the case of Bolivia it is generally the women who weave the intricately patterned carrying cloths (lliklla), ponchos (punchu), belts (chumpi), and coca pouches (ch'uspa); they use a backstrap or horizontal loom. The Bolivian men produce plain-woven cloth for making tailored dresses (almilla) and trousers (pantalon); they work on an upright frame loom, the design of which is of Spanish origin. Woven textile production yields clothing (p'acha) as well as functional items such as sacks (kustala), horse blankets (karuna), and blankets for bedding (phullu). Textiles were used as trade and ritual items in precolonial times, and still retain much of their function as a source of real and symbolic wealth today, especially in the tourist market.

Suggested reading: Arnold 1997; Zorn 2004.

Imataq kaypa sutin?
Kaypa sutinqa awana.

Ñawirina, yachakuna / Read and Learn

Imataq kaypa sutin?	What is this [*object's*] name?
Kaypa sutinqa lliklla.	This object's name is "lliklla."
Imawantaq rantikunki?	What do you buy it with?
Qullqiwan rantikuyku.	We buy it with money.
Chay wich'uñari imamantataq?	What is that weaving pick made from?
Chay wich'uñaqa llama tullumanta.	That weaving pick is made from llama bone.

Qallarina / Introduction

Boliviapipis Perupipis runaqa warmipis qharipis ayllukunapi awanku. Awanapi llikllata, aqsuta, chumpita, ch'uspata, phulluta, wakkunatapis oveja millmamanta, llama millmamanta, allpaqa millmamanta ima awanku.

    Kaypi mama Imigdia Cruz awachkan. Awaymanta parlachkan. Payqa llikllata awachkan. Wich'uñawan wich'un. Chay wich'uña tullumanta, llama tullumanta. Chay llama tulluta punaman mask'amunku ñin, sarawan rantikunku ñin.

Qhawana / Video View   ▶DVD

Go to the following section in the *Kawsay Vida* multimedia program:

Bolivian Quechua > Kawsay > Qhawana > Imigdia awaymanta

Watch the video and listen to doña Imigdia describe the art of weaving. Study the language of the text, using the lookup facilities on-screen.

Simi / Vocabulary

Ruway / Verbs

    aqhay: to make chicha (corn beer).
    karuna: horse blanket.
    k'antiy: to twist, ply yarn.
    tiyay: to be (located in space).
    wich'uy: to beat threads down with the weaving pick.

Suti / Nouns

    awana: loom.
    chuwa: wooden dish.
    k'anti: spindle for twisting yarn.
    k'aspi: stick.
    k'uychi: rainbow.
    llimp'i: color.
    manka: clay cooking pot.
    mathi: gourd (used as recipient for liquids).
    phuchka: spindle for spinning.
    qullqi: silver; money.
    q'aytu: thread, yarn.
    rantina: merchandise.
    t'uru: clay.
    wich'uña: weaving pick.
    wiphala: rainbow flag of the indigenous organizations.
    wislla: spoon.

Suti tikrachiq / Adjectives

    jatun: big.
    juch'uy: small.

    Llimp'i / Colors

    anqas: blue.
    ch'iqchi: pale gray.
    ch'umpi: brown.
    kulli: purple.
    mullu: pink (shell-colored).
    panti: dark red.
    puka: red.
    q'illu: yellow.
    q'umir: green.
    rosado [rusadu]: pink.
    uqi: lead gray.
    yana: black.
    yuraq: white.

Tapuq suti ranti / Interrogative Pronouns
>   imawan: what with?
>   pipta: whose?

Simip k'askaynin / Grammar

Suti k'askaq / Noun Suffixes

> *Vowel* + **-p**/*consonant* + **-pa**
>> Genitive marker

The genitive suffix is the basis for forming possessive adjectives. The genitive suffix has two forms in Bolivian Quechua: **-p**, pronounced [**x**] ('**j**'), after words ending in a vowel, and **-pa**, pronounced [**pa**] or [**pax**], after words ending in a consonant.

ñuqa	I	>>>	ñuqa-**p** [noqax]	my
qam	you	>>>	qam-**pa** [qampax]	your
pay	s/he	>>>	pay-**pa** [paypax]	his/her
María	Mary	>>>	María-**p** [Mariyax]	Mary's
Juan	John	>>>	Juan-**pa** [xuwanpax]	John's

> Possessive Phrases

The possessive phrase using the possessive adjectives is formed by adding the genitive suffix to the word indicating the *possessor*, and the appropriate possessive suffix to the word indicating the item *possessed*:

Maria-**p** wasi-**n**	Mary's house
Juan-**pa** allqu-**n**	John's dog
ñuqa-**p** llaqta-**y**	my town

The rule can be summarized as follows:

> Singular forms

ñuqa-**p** [noqax] wasi-**y**	my house [lit. "of me my house"]
qam-**pa** [qanpax] wasi-**yki**	your house [lit. "of you your house"]
pay-**pa** [paypax] wasi-**n**	his/her/its house [lit. "of him his house"]

> Plural forms

ñuqayku-**p** [noqaykux] wasi-**yku**	our house (excl.) [lit. "of us our house"]
ñuqanchik-**pa** [noqanchexpax] wasi-**nchik**	our house (incl.) [lit. "of us our house"]
qamkuna-**p** [qankunax] wasi-**ykichik**	your house [lit. "of you your house"]
paykuna-**p** [paykunax] wasi-**nku**	their house [lit. "of them their house"]

Note that the possessive adjective is not obligatory for the phrase to make sense:

| wasi-**y** | my house |
| chakra-**yku** | our (excl.) field |

Possessive Pronouns

    Vowel + **-pta** /consonant + **-pata**

There is much regional variation in the formation of the Quechua possessive pronouns. Here we present one Bolivian variation, common among speakers in San Pedro de Buenavista. The genitive suffixes take the forms **-pta** (pronounced 'jta' [xta]) and **-pata**, respectively. When a word ends in a vowel, **-pta** is added; when a word ends in a consonant, **-pata** is added, as in the following examples:

ñuqa-p sutiy	my name	>>>	ñuqa-**pta**	mine
qam-pa sutiyki	your name	>>>	qam-**pata**	yours
pay-pa sutin	his/her name	>>>	pay-**pata**	his, hers
Juan-pa wasin	John's house	>>>	Juan-**pata**	John's
María-p wawan	Mary's baby	>>>	María-**pta**	Mary's

Summary:

    Singular forms

ñuqa-pta [noqaxta]	mine
qam-pata [qanpata]	yours
pay-pata [paypata]	his/hers

    Plural forms

ñuqayku-pta [noqaykoxta]	ours (*excl.*)
ñuqanchik-pata [noqanchexpata]	ours (*incl.*)
qamkuna-pta [qankunaxta]	yours
paykuna-pta [paykunaxta]	theirs

The genitive marker in Bolivia has other variant forms, such as: ñuqa-qpata [noqaxpata], ñuqa-ypata [noqaypata], etc.

    -wan

        (**i**) Instrumental; "with"

In this function **-wan** indicates the instrument with which an action is performed:

Makilla-**wan** ruwanku.   They just make it with their hands.

        (**ii**) Accompaniment; "with"

In this function **-wan** indicates the person or object which accompanies a noun:

María-**wan** jamuni.   I came with María.

        (**iii**) Coordinative function; "both . . . and"

The suffix **–wan** is repeated on the two elements in the sentence which go together, producing the sense of "both . . . and" in English translation.

Mama Imigdia puka q'aytu-**wan** yana q'aytu-**wan** awachkan.   Doña Imigida weaves with both red yarn and black yarn.

-manta

(i) "From, out of"

-**manta** is used to indicate what a thing is made of:

Kay lliklla llama millma-**manta**.	This cloth is made out of llama wool.
Aqhata sara-**manta** ruwanchik.	We make chicha from corn.

(ii) "About"

-**manta** may also indicate the topic one is talking about:

Simi-**manta** parlachkan.	He is talking about languages.
Away-**manta** parlachkan.	She is talking about weaving.

Syntax

Adjectives

Adjectives precede the noun in Quechua. Thus:

puka t'ika	red flower
yana qucha	black lake
jatun wasi	big house
juch'uy punchu	small poncho

Noun + Noun Adjectival Construction

When two nouns come together, the first noun describes or qualifies the second, performing the function of an adjective. Thus word order can alter meaning, as is seen by comparing the following two expressions:

llama tullu	llama bone
tullu llama	skinny llama

Coordinating Ideas in a Sentence

There are a number of ways of coordinating ideas in a Quechua sentence. These commonly give rise to translation as "and" in English. Various suffixes may be used depending on the type of coordination in question. Here we review those seen so far.

(i) Juxtaposition

The idea of "and" may be expressed merely by juxtaposing a series of statements. It is only formally present in the translation.

Lomasman rin wayq'usman rin phaqchasman rin.   He goes to the hills, the ravines, and the waterfalls.

In this case the possibility is left open that other elements may be added.

(ii) **ima**

The particle **ima** may be added at the end of a list of elements; in this case **ima** closes off the list; it gives rise to "and" in the translation:

Lomasman wayq'usman phaqchasman **ima** rin.   He goes to the hills, the ravines, and the waterfalls.

(iii) -pis . . . -pis

The repetition of **-pis** 'also' on two or more elements in a sentence conveys the idea of items belonging in a set, but thought of as separate items:

Llaqtapi t'antata-**pis** misk'ita-**pis** rantikuni.   I buy bread and sugar in town.

(iv) -wan . . . -wan

The repetition of **-wan** 'with' on two or more elements in a sentence conveys the idea of two items belonging together; this structure can be translated as "both . . . and":

Luis-**wan** Pedro-**wan** chakrapi llamk'anku. Luis and Pedro work in the fields.

(v) -tawan (-ta + -wan)

This compound suffix is used to add one more item to a list. In the usage here it is the direct object of a verb:

Almillata llikllata chumpi-**tawan** churakun.   She wears a dress, a shawl, and a belt.

In questions **-tawan** can be translated as "and what else?":

Ima-**tawan** churakunki?   And what else do you wear?
Pantalón-**tawan**.   And trousers as well.

(vi) -taq

This suffix is used to mean "and" when contrasting a statement with a previous one:

Ñuqa phuchkani pay-**taq** awan.   I spin and he weaves.

(vii) -taq . . . -taq

The repetition of **-taq** 'and' on two or more elements in a sentence conveys the idea of two elements both being the case, although not necessarily both at the same time:

Mama Imigdia phuchkan-**taq** k'antin-**taq**.   Doña Imigdia both spins and twists yarn.

(viii) -rí

The stressed **-rí** is used to repeat a question that has been previously posed, while directing it toward another subject; it can be translated as "and":

Tatayki-**rí** maypitaq llamk'achkan?   And where does your father work?

(ix) -ri:

The unstressed **-ri** is used on questions to make them insistent or challenging:

yachankichu-**ri**?   and do you know? (I don't think you do)

(x) **-taqri** (**-taq** + **-ri**):

This suffix compound translates as "and" in describing a sequence of actions. It is stylistically more forceful than **-taq** alone:

phuchkaspa-**taqri** k'antina   and then after spinning one has to twist (the yarn)

Ruwana / Exercises

1 Juk ⌘ Junt'achina / Video Exercise   ▶DVD

Go to the following section in the *Kawsay Vida* multimedia program:

Bolivian Quechua > Kawsay > Junt'achina > Imigdia awaymanta

Follow the on-screen instructions, and do (i) the audio and (ii) the video gap-fill exercises. You can work through each text three times, gradually increasing the level of difficulty.

2 Iskay ⌘ Qillqana / Written Work

Answer these questions about the introductory text:

1. Pitaq awachkan? _____
2. Imatataq awachkan? _____
3. Imawantaq wich'uchkan? _____
4. Imamantataq chay wich'uña? _____
5. Chay wich'uña k'aspichu? _____
6. Chay llama tulluta maymantataq mask'akamunku? _____
7. Qullqiwanchu llama tulluta rantikunku? _____

3 Kimsa ⌘ Yachana / Practice   ▶DVD

Go to the following section in the *Kawsay Vida* multimedia program:

Bolivian Quechua > Fiesta > Yachana > Fiesta kaqkuna practice (2)

Do the multiple-choice exercise, following the on-screen instructions.

4 Tawa ⌘ Qillqana / Written Work

Answer the questions below, following the model provided:

Piptataq chay awana? (Juana)   >>>   Juanapta.
Piptataq chay chuwa? (Manuel)   >>>   Manuelpata.

1. Piptataq chay wich'uña? (mama Imigdia) _____
2. Piptataq kay manka? (mamay) _____
3. Piptataq chay llikla? (ñuqa) _____
4. Piptataq kay charanku? (jaqay wayna) _____
5. Piptataq chay chakra? (aylluyku) _____
6. Piptataq kay k'aspi? (Juanpa allqun) _____

5 Phichqa ⌘ Parlana / Oral Work

Ask questions to find out the names of your classmates, using the full possessive construction, as in the model provided:

Imataq qampa sutiyki?	>>>	Ñuqap sutiyqa María.
Qampatarí?	>>>	Ñuqaptaqa Andrés.
Paypatarí?	>>>	Paypa sutinqa Filomena.
Chay warmiptarí?	>>>	Chay warmip sutinqa Elisa.
Chay sipaspatarí?	>>>	Chay sipaspa sutinqa Paula.
Chay waynaptarí?	>>>	Chay waynap sutinqa Edmundo.

6 Suqta ⌘ Qillqana / Written Work

(i) Answer the question according to the model:

Imamantataq chay punchu? (llama millma)   >>>   Chay punchuqa llama millmamanta.

1. Imamantataq chay wich'uña? (llama tullu)
   _____

2. Imamantataq chay chuwa? (t'uru)
   _____

3. Imamantataq kay lliklla? (allpaqa millma)
   _____

4. Imamantataq kay awana? (k'aspi)
   _____

(ii) Answer the question according to the model:

Imawantaq awachkanki? (wich'uña)   >>>   Wich'uñawan awachkani.

5. Imawantaq wayk'uchkanki? (llamt'a)
   _____

6. Imawantaq mikhunku? (wislla)
   _____

7. Imawantaq chakrata qarpanku? (yaku)
   _____

8. Imawantaq aqhachkanki? (sara, yaku)
   _____

9. Imawantaq wich'unki? (wich'uña)
   _____

10. Imawantaq k'antin? (k'anti)
    _____

7 Qanchis ⌘ Qillqana / Written Exercise

Fill the gaps in the following sentences with the suffixes -**pis**, -**taq**, -**wan**, or -**tawan**, as appropriate. Follow the model.

Tata Julio papata_____ uqata_____ tarpun.   >>>   Tata Julio papatapis uqatapis tarpun.

1. María_____ Martina_____ fiestapi takinku tusunku ima.
2. Justinaqa puka q'aytu_____ q'illu q'aytu_____ chumpita awachkan.
3. Daniel punchuta ch'ullu_____ churakun.
4. Carlosqa yunkapi_____ punapi_____ tarpun.
5. Ñuqaqa qhichwata_____ inglésta_____ parlani.

8 Pusaq ⌘ Yachana / Practice   ▶DVD

Go to the following section in the *Kawsay Vida* multimedia program:

Bolivian Quechua > Fiesta > Yachana > Akllana (4)

Do the multiple-choice exercise, following the on-screen instructions.

9 Jisq'un ⌘ Llimp'imanta Parlana / Talk about Colors

Answer the questions about the colors of different items. Use the particle **ima** to close off your list, as in the model.

Chay k'uychipi ima llimp'itaq tiyan?   >>>   Q'illu, puka, kulli, q'umir, anqas **ima** tiyan.

1. Chay wiphalapi ima llimp'itaq tiyan? (red, yellow, green, blue, purple)
_____

2. Ima llimp'itaq kay llikllapi tiyan? (yellow, brown, red, green)
_____

3. Ima llimp'itaq kay saras kanku? (white, black, red)
_____

4. Ima llimp'itaq p'achayki? (answer according to what you are wearing)
_____

10 Chunka ⌘ Parlana / Oral Work

Interview a Quechua weaver, using the questions suggested and adding ideas of your own.

– Imatataq ruwachkanki, mamáy?
– Awachkani.
– Imatataq awachkanki?
– _____

– Imawantaq awachkanki?
– _____

– Kay wich'uña imamantataq?
– _____

– Chay wich'uña uwija tullumantachu?
– _____

– Chay wich'uñata rantikunkichu?
– _____

– Imawantaq wich'uñata rantikunki?
– _____

– Ima llimp'itaq kay q'aytuykiri?
– _____

11 Chunka iskayniyuq ⌘ Tikrana / Translation

Translate into Quechua:

1. My head hurts. _____
2. Is this your loom? _____
3. Where is their house? _____
4. Whose are those llamas? _____
5. Her child is ill. _____
6. Our (incl.) town is far. _____
7. Does your stomach hurt? _____
8. What is she talking about? _____
9. They have gone to the mine to work. _____
10. He has gone to live in the Chapare. _____

11 / Chunka jukniyuq

Simikuna / Languages

In This Unit...

You meet don Vitalio Mareño, from the community of Sikuya, who talks about the languages that people speak in the region of San Pedro de Buenavista. You practice asking questions about languages. You study the indirect past tense as indicated by -**sqa**-; additional uses of -**manta** and -**ta**; the class-free suffixes -**ña** 'already' and -**raq** 'still'; and the attributive suffix -**yuq**.

KAWSAY / ANDEAN LIFE
Languages

Quechua is only one of the many indigenous American languages spoken in Bolivia. It first spread here in the decades prior to Spanish arrival in the Andes, as the Incas expanded their territorial control southward from Cuzco into the high plateau region around Lake Titicaca and eastward to the warm fertile valleys of Cochabamba. In the Bolivian highlands, Quechua coexists with the two languages that were here before that expansion: Aymara, widely spoken around La Paz and Oruro, and Chipaya, still spoken by some two thousand people in the altiplano southwest of Oruro. According to the 2001 census, an estimated thirty-six languages are spoken in Bolivia, many of these by Amazonian peoples in the departments of Beni, Trinidad, and Santa Cruz. Around San Pedro de Buenavista people mainly speak Quechua and Spanish, with some Aymara used in the communities on the west bank of the river.

Suggested reading: Howard 2007; Crevels and Muysken 2009.

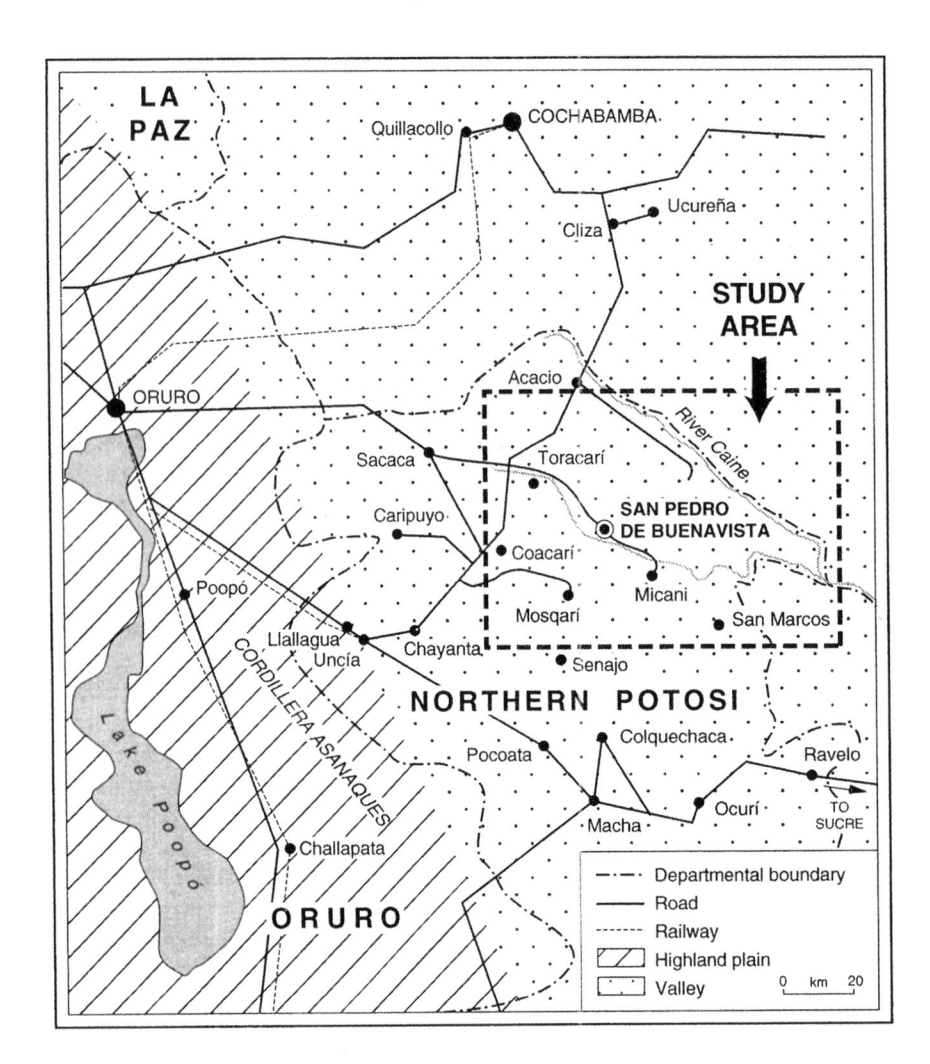

Kay suyupiqa qhichwapis aymarapis parlakunku.

Ñawirina, yachakuna / Read and Learn

Maypitaq aymarata parlanku?	Where do they speak Aymara?
Punapi aymarata parlanku.	They speak Aymara in the puna.
Kay llaqtapi mana aymarata parlankuñachu.	They don't speak Aymara in this town anymore.
Ñawpaqtaqa aymarata parlaqkuna kasqanku.	In the old days it is said they were Aymara speakers.
Chay parlaqkunaqa wañupunkuña.	The ones that spoke [it] have already died out.

Qallarina / Introduction

Bolivia suyupiqa imaymana runakuna tiyan, kimsa chunka suqtayuq "pueblos indígenas" ñisqa tiyan, ñin. Paykunaqa punapi, vallepi, yunkapi, amazonía ñisqapi ima tiyakunku. Chantapis Boliviapiqa kimsa chunka suqtayuq simi parlakun ñin. Wakin simiqa manaña anchatachu parlakun, chinkapuchkanku, wañupuchkanku. Wakin runaqa siminkuta qunqapuchkanku, p'inqakunku, ñin, manaña wawasninmanpis mama siminkuta yachachichkankuchu, castilla simillata astawan munanku. Jinapis, qhichwa simiwan aymara simiwan astawan parlakun ayllukunapiqa, wawapis waynapis sipaspis sumaqta parlankuraq.

Tata Vitalio Mareño Sikuyapi tiyakun. Payqa simimanta parlan. Sikuyapi aymarata manaña parlankuchu. Ñawpaqtaqa parlasqanku, ñin. Kay qhipa pachapi aymara parlaqkuna wañupunkuña. Kunan qhichwallataña parlanku, ñin.

Qhawana / Video View ▸ DVD

Go to the following section in the *Kawsay Vida* multimedia program:

Bolivian Quechua > Runakuna > Qhawana > Vitalio simimanta

Watch the video and listen to what don Vitalio says about language use in Sikuya. Study the language of the text, using the lookup facilities on-screen.

Simi / Vocabulary

Ruway / Verbs

    chinkachiy: to lose.
    chinkakuy: to get lost.
    chinkapuy: to disappear completely.
    chinkay: to be lost; to disappear.
    p'inqay: to be ashamed.
    qunqapuy: to forget completely.
    qunqay: to forget.
    rikhuriy: to appear.
    wañupuy: to die out.
    wañuy: to die.

Ruway tikrachiq / Adverbs

    ancha: very.
    anchata: a lot, very much.
    astawan: more.
    manaña: no more, not any more.
    ña: already.
    ñawpaqta (*var.* ñampaqta): before, firstly (*time*); in front (*space*).
    pisita: a little.
    qhipa: later, recent.
    qhipata: afterward, later (*time*); behind (*space*).
    sumaqta: well, good-heartedly.

Suti / Nouns

    ayllu: rural community; extended family network.
    chipaya: Chipaya language.
    guaraní: Guaraní language.
    imaymana: all sorts of things.
    kastilla simi: Spanish language.
    kichwa: Quechua language (*Ecuador*).

mama simi: mother tongue.
mapudungun: Mapuche language.
pacha: period of time, world, space.
qhichwa: Quechua language (*central Peru, Bolivia*).
runa simi: Quechua language (*southern Peru*).
suyu: territory, region.

Suti tikrachiq / Adjectives

achkha: many.
pisi: little (in quantity).

Conjunction

chantá: then.

Tapuq suti ranti / Interrogative Pronouns

imaynata: how, in what way?
maypi: where?

Simip k'askaynin / Grammar

Rimay muyuchina / Verb Conjugation

-**sqa**-

Indirect past tense marker

This tense is used to indicate: (**i**) events not personally witnessed; (**ii**) information suddenly realized or discovered. To form the tense, the suffix -**sqa**- is inserted into the verb to the left of the person marker:

Ñuqa qunqa-**sqa**-ni	I forgot, had forgotten	Ñuqayku qunqa-**sqa**-yku	we (excl.) forgot, had forgotten
		Ñuqanchik qunqa-**sqa**-nchik	we (incl.) forgot, had forgotten
Qam qunqa-**sqa**-nki	you (sing.) forgot, had forgotten	Qamkuna qunqa-**sqa**-nkichik	you (pl.) forgot, had forgotten
Pay qunqa-**sqa**	he, she, forgot, had forgotten	Paykuna qunqa-**sqa**-nku	they forgot, had forgotten

The 3rd-person-singular marker -**n** is deleted in Bolivian Quechua when the tense suffix -**sqa**- is used.

In traditional stories and accounts of history -**sqa**- is the typical tense marker:

Inka pachapi tukuypis ayllupi kawsa-**sqa**-nku.   In Inca times everybody lived in ayllus.

The *indirect* past tense suffix -**sqa**- contrasts with the direct past tense suffix -**rqa**-, to be studied in Unit 12.

Suti k'askaq / Noun Suffixes

-ta
> Adverb marker

The suffix **-ta** is added to adjectival roots to form adverbs, in a way similar to the **-ly** of English (wonderful > wonderful-**ly**) and **-mente** of Spanish (pleno > plena-**mente**).

sumaq	beautiful, fine	>>>	sumaq-**ta**	beautifully, well
ñawpaq	first	>>>	ñawpaq-**ta**	in the old days, formerly; in front, ahead
qhipa	later	>>>	qhipa-**ta**	later on; behind
lunes	Monday	>>>	lunes-**ta**	on Monday

The interrogative root **imayna-** takes **-ta** in questions that ask about the manner of an action:

Imayna-**ta**-taq parlanku?	How do they speak (it)?
Allin-**ta** parlanku.	They speak (it) well.
Sumaq-**ta** yachanku.	They know (it) finely.

-yuq
> Attributive marker; "with"; use with numerals above 10

Quechua has a decimal numeral system. The component numerals are as follows:

chunka	ten
pachak	a hundred
waranqa	a thousand
junu	a million

The suffix **-yuq** ("with" in the sense of having an attribute) is used to form compound numerals. The connective suffix **-ni-** is needed when **-yuq** is added to a number word ending in a consonant. In long numerals, the suffix **-yuq** appears at the end of the string, as follows:

11	chunka juk-**ni**-**yuq** [lit. "ten with one"]
12	chunka iskay-**ni**-**yuq** [lit. "ten with two" and so on]
13	chunka kimsa-**yuq**
14	chunka tawa-**yuq** . . .
20	iskay chunka [lit. "two tens"]
21	iskay chunka juk-**ni**-**yuq** [lit. "two tens with one" and so on]
200	iskay pachak
201	iskay pachak juk-**ni**-**yuq** . . .
2000	iskay waranqa
2010	iskay waranqa chunka-**yuq**

Use this grid to practice forming long numbers:

junu	waranqa	pachak	chunka	(units)
2	5	3	7	6
iskay junu	phichqa waranqa	kimsa pachak	qanchis chunka	suqta-**yuq**
10	9	8	3	2

Wak k'askaq / Class-Free Suffixes

-ña and -raq

As "class-free" suffixes, -ña 'already' and -raq 'still; yet' may be attached to words of all grammatical categories: noun and verb forms, and particles such as **mana**. In the case of verb forms, they are positioned after the person marker.

-ña

Perfective aspect; "already"

This suffix indicates completion of the action or state of affairs indicated by the word to which it is attached:

parlanku	they speak	>>>	parlanku-ña	they already speak
sumaq	beautiful	>>>	sumaq-ña	already beautiful
sipas	young woman	>>>	sipas-ña	already a young woman
mana	no, not	>>>	mana-ña	no more, not anymore

Mana-**ña** munanchu.   S/he does not want (it) anymore.

This suffix may also act as an adverbial root:

Ña-chu rinki?   Are you going already?

-raq

We identify three principle uses of the suffix -raq. (i) -raq may indicate that an action which began in the past is "still" continuing into the present; (ii) combined with the negative particle **mana**, -raq indicates that an action has "not yet" occurred; (iii) -raq may indicate that an action or state of affairs is "prior to" another action or state of affairs. In this unit we look at uses (i) and (ii). Use (iii) will be studied in Unit 14.

(i) Imperfective aspect; "still"

-**raq** may show that an action or state of affairs is not yet completed; that it is still the case:

| Puñuchkan-**raq**. | S/he is still sleeping. |
| Tatasniykirí kawsanku-**raq**-chu? | Are your parents still alive? |

In this usage, -**raq** contrasts with the perfective -**ña** meaning 'already'. Compare the following examples:

| Fiestata ruwachkanku-**ña**. | They are already celebrating the fiesta. |
| Fiestata ruwachkanku-**raq**. | They are still celebrating the fiesta. |

mana-raq/mana . . . raq

(ii) Imperfective aspect; "not yet"

The suffix -**raq** may be combined with the negative particle **mana** to convey the idea of action not yet carried out. Note that the position of -**raq** in the negative statement carries variation in emphasis. Compare the following examples:

mana-raq yachanichu   I do **not** know **yet** (where the emphasis is on "not yet")

or

mana yachani-**raq**-chu   I do **not know** yet (where the emphasis is on "not know")

The contrast between "perfective" -**ña** and "imperfective" -**raq** can be better appreciated in the negative forms. Compare the following examples:

| Aymarata mana-**ña** parlankuchu. | They do **not** speak Aymara **any longer**. |
| Aymarata mana-**raq** parlankuchu. | They do **not** speak Aymara **yet**. |

Suffix Order

Class-free suffixes are always placed to the right of all noun-class suffixes, in the case of nouns, and to the right of all verb-class suffixes, in the case of verbs. This is with the exception of -**lla**-, as noted in Unit 4. Thus, class-free suffixes always appear near the end of a word; more than one class-free suffix may appear on any one word, and so their order has to be learned. In these examples the class-free suffixes are in bold:

Noun roots

wasi-**lla**-manta-**chu**?	just from the house?
wasi-**lla**-pi-**raq**-**puni**	really still just in the house
chay-**lla**-manta-**puni**	really just from there

Verb roots

Kawsa-ku-chka-nku-**raq**-**chu**?	Are they still alive?
Kawsa-ku-chka-lla-nku-**raq**.	They are still alive.
Yacha-ku-chka-ni-**ña**.	I am learning already.

Ruwana / Exercises

1 Juk ⌘ Junt'achina / Video Exercise   ▶ DVD

Go to the following section in the *Kawsay Vida* multimedia program:

Bolivian Quechua > Runakuna > Junt'achina > Vitalio simimanta

Working on-screen, do both the video and audio gap-fill exercises in this section. There are three levels of difficulty here; you can work through each text three times with different gaps to fill each time.

2 Iskay ⌘ Qillqana / Written Work

Answer the following questions on the **Vitalio simimanta** video studied in exercise 1:

1. Don Vitalio maypitaq tiyakun?
_____

2. Chay Sikuyapi aymarata parlankuraqchu?
_____

3. Ñawpaqtaqa ima simitataq Sikuyapi parlasqanku?
_____

4. Chay aymara parlaqkuna kawsakuchkankuraqchu?
_____

5. Kay qhipa runakuna ima simillataña parlanku?
_____

Answer the following questions about yourself:

6. Qam maypitaq tiyakunki?
_____

7. Wasiykipirí, ima simikunatataq parlankichik?
_____

3 Kimsa ⌘ Qillqana / Written Work

Ask and answer questions about where different languages are spoken, how well they are spoken, and how many speakers there are, using the prompts provided. Use the suffixes **-pi** and **-ta** in your answers as appropriate.

Maypitaq aymarata parlanku? (Coacarí)	>>>	Coacarípi aymarata parlanku.
Imaynatataq parlanku? (sumaq)	>>>	Sumaqta parlanku.
Machkha chipaya parlaqkuna kan? (2,000)	>>>	Iskay waranqa chipaya parlaqkuna kan.

1. Maypitaq qhichwata parlanku? (Bolivia, Peru, Ecuador, Argentina, Colombia)
_____

Machkha qhichwa parlaqkuna kan? (8 million)
_____

Imaynatataq parlanku? (wakin allin, wakin pisi)
_____

2. Maypitaq aymarata parlanku? (Peru, Bolivia, Chile)

Machkha aymara parlaqkuna kan? (2.5 million)

Imaynatataq parlanku? (waliq)

3. Oruropi ima simitataq parlanku? (castilla simi, qhichwa, aymara)

Imaynatataq parlanku? (sumaq)

4. Ecuador suyupi ima simistataq parlanku? (kastilla simi, kichwa)

Machkha runataq kichwata parlanku? (1.6 million)

5. Brasil suyupi guaraníta parlankuchu? (pisi)

Maypitaq astawan guaraníta parlanku? (Paraguay)

6. Españapi qhichwatachu parlanku?

Ima simikunatataq Españapi parlanku? (kastilla simi, catalán, euskara)

7. Ñawpaqta maypitaq qhichwata parlasqanku? (Perúlla)

Ñawpaqta ima simitataq Boliviap punanpi astawan parlasqanku? (aymara, pukina)

8. Bolivia suyupi machkha simitaraq parlanku?

9. Qampa llaqtaykipi machkha runataq kanku?

10. Qamrí, ima simikunatataq parlanki?

4 Tawa ⌘ Qillqana / Written Work

Answer the following questions according to the model:

Qhichwata yachankiñachu? >>> Arí, yachaniña. *or* Manaraq yachanichu.
Bolivia suyupi pukinata parlankuraqchu? >>> Bolivia suyupi manaña pukinata parlankuchu.

1. Qhichwata yachankiñachu?
_____

2. Kastilla simita yachankichikñachu?
_____

3. Peru suyupi aymarata parlankuraqchu?
_____

4. Sikuyapi aymarata qunqapunkuñachu?
_____

5. Chay aymara parlaqkuna wañupunkuñachu?
_____

5 Phichqa ⌘ Parlana / Oral Work

Interview a Bolivian person in Quechua about the languages of their country. You may use the questions provided below or others of your choice. The answers are up to you!

- Kay Boliviapi ima simitataq parlanku?
- Ñawpaqtarí, ima simitataq parlasqanku?
- Maypitaq chipayata parlankuraq?
- Qam ima simitataq yachanki?
- Warmiykirí/Qusaykirí/Ayllu masiykirí ima simitataq parlan?
- Wawasniykichikwan ima simipitaq parlankichik?
- Yachay wasipi ima simipitaq yachachinku?

6 Suqta ⌘ Yuyarina / Review

Translate the following sentences into Quechua:

1. That house is built from stone.   _____
2. They make chicha with water.   _____
3. She's drinking from a gourd.   _____
4. She's weaving the belt from llama wool.   _____
5. They trade the potatoes for corn.   _____
6. His llama is escaping from the corral.   _____
7. Is your mother ill?   _____
8. Does she have a stomach ache?   _____
9. They don't speak Guaraní in Chile.   _____
10. Doña Imigdia is talking about her loom.   _____

12 / Chunka iskayniyuq

P'achamanta / Clothing Styles

In This Unit...

You meet doña Filomena, who discusses clothing. You practice describing styles of dress. You learn to contrast present customs with those of the past, by using the direct past and past habitual tenses. You produce complex sentences containing a main verb and a subordinate verb.

KAWSAY / ANDEAN LIFE
Social Change

The lives of Quechua-speaking peoples in the rural communities of Northern Potosí, as everywhere in the Andes, have been changing at an increasingly rapid pace since the 1990s. This change comes as a result of many factors. Road networks have improved, bringing rural areas into closer contact with urban centers. This in turn has entailed both increased access to formal schooling and more frequent contact with urban lifestyles; these changes have influenced cultural norms in matters of language use, eating habits, and clothing styles, and have created a desire for consumer goods. Equally, NGO- and government-funded development projects have driven changes in agricultural and construction techniques. The impact of such institutional interventions in rural life in the last twenty years cannot be overestimated; much of the conversation of the people you meet in *Kawsay Vida* focuses on the difference between life in the past and the way things are now.
  Suggested reading: Healy 2001.

Imayuqtaq kachkanku?

Almillayuq kachkan.

Pollerayuq kachkanku.

Vestidoyuq kachkanku.

Ñawirina, yachakuna / Read and Learn

sipas kaspa...	as a young woman...
Imatataq churakuq kanki?	What did you put on?
Imatawantaq churakuq kanki?	What else did you put on?
Qaynaqa pullirata churakurqani	Yesterday I put on a skirt
chay jawa chumpitawan.	and then a belt.
Imayuqtaq kachkanki?	What are you wearing?
Punchuyuq kachkani.	I am wearing a poncho.

Qallarina / Introduction

Mama Filomena p'achakunamanta parlan. Sipas kaspa, pay almillata, chumpita, aqsuta ima churakuq. Umanpi achkha chukchayuq kaq, tullmayuq kaq. Kunanqa sumaq pullirayuq kachkan. Paypa blusan q'illu llimp'iyuq kachkan.

Qhawana / Video View   ▶ DVD

Go to the following section in the *Kawsay Vida* multimedia program:

Bolivian Quechua > Kawsay > Qhawana > Filomena p'achamanta

Watch the video; listen to what doña Filomena says about the clothes she used to wear when she was young, and what she is wearing now. Study the language of the text, using the lookup facilities on-screen.

Simi / Vocabulary

Ruway / Verbs

    churay: to put, to place.
    churakuy: to put on (clothes).
    simp'ay: to braid, to plait.
    yanapay: to help.

Ruway tikrachiq / Adverbs

    jina: thus, in that way.
    kunan p'unchaw: today.
    kunitan: right now.
    qayna: yesterday.

Suti / Nouns

    chumpa: pullover.
    kachi: salt.
    kalsuna: man's trousers of homespun cloth.
    qhariwarmi: male and female couple, married couple.
    simp'ay: plait, braid.
    tinkuq: participant in ritual battle.

tullma: hair tie (for braided hair).
vara [wara]: staff of authority.

Suti tikrachiq / Adjectives
musuq: new.
thanta: old (*referring to clothes*).

Tapuq suti ranti / Interrogative Pronouns
imatawan: what else?
imayuq: with what attributes?

Conjunctions
chay jawa: then, after that, on top of that.

Simip k'askaynin / Grammar
Ruway k'askaq / Verb Suffixes
-spa

Subordinate verb marker in complex sentences

The suffix **-spa** enables the construction of complex sentences containing more than one verb, such as in the English: "When they arrived they cooked the meal," in which "they cooked the meal" is the main verb phrase and "when they arrived" is the subordinate verb phrase.

-spa marks the subordinate verb, and indicates that the action of the subordinate verb is carried out either:

(i) Simultaneously with the main verb:

Sipas ka-**spa** fiestapi tusun.	Being a young girl, she dances in the fiesta.
Ñanta puklla-**spa** jamuchkanku.	They come along the road playing.
Taki-**spa** kusikunchik.	We feel happy as we sing.

or

(ii) Prior to the main verb:

Mikhu-**spa** wasimanta lluqsirqanku.	After they had eaten they left the house.
Charanku tocaqqa serenosta uyariku-**spa** versosta apakamun	After listening to the water spirits, the charango player brings back the tunes.

Where -**spa** is followed by -**qa** a conditional relationship between the two actions is indicated:

Uyari-**spa**-**qa** lluqsinqa.   If s/he hears, s/he will go out.

-**spa** is only used when the action of the main verb and the action of the subordinate verb are performed by the same person. The person of the subordinate verb is not formally marked; rather, person is marked on the main verb.

Rimay muyuchina / Verb Conjugation

-rqa-

Direct past tense marker

This tense is used to indicate information gained through firsthand witness; often referred to as the 'direct knowledge' past tense. To form this tense, the suffix -**rqa**- is inserted into the verb to the left of the person marker: puñu-ni >>> puñu-**rqa**-ni. Here is the full conjugation:

ñuqa puñu-**rqa**-ni	I slept	ñuqayku puñu-**rqa**-yku	we (excl.) slept
		ñuqanchik puñu-**rqa**-nchik	we (incl.) slept
qam puñu-**rqa**-nki	you (sing.) slept	qamkuna puñu-**rqa**-nkichik	you (pl.) slept
pay puñu-**rqa**	he, she slept	paykuna puñu-**rqa**-nku	they slept

The direct past suffix -**rqa**- contrasts with the indirect past suffix -**sqa**- (see Unit 11). Compare the following examples:

llaqtaman ri-**rqa**	he went to town (I saw him)
llaqtaman ri-**sqa**	he went to town (so I was told)

Notice that in both tenses the 3rd-person-singular marker -**n** is deleted.

-q + ka-

Habitual past tense marker

This tense indicates an action performed habitually in the past, usually translated as "used to" in English, or *solía* in Spanish. To conjugate the tense, the verb root takes the agentive suffix -**q**. This is followed by the verb **kay** used as an auxiliary verb. The auxiliary is marked by the relevant person suffix:

puri-ni   I walk   >>>   puri-**q kani**   I used to walk

Here is the full conjugation:

ñuqa puri-**q ka**-ni	I used to walk	ñuqayku puri-**q ka**-yku	we (excl.) used to walk
		ñuqanchik puri-**q ka**-nchik	we (incl.) used to walk
qam puri-**q ka**-nki	you (sing.) used to walk	qamkuna puri-**q ka**-nkichik	you (pl.) used to walk
pay puri-**q**	he, she used to walk	paykuna puri-**q ka**-nku	they used to walk

Note how the auxiliary verb form **ka-n** is omitted in the 3rd-person singular.

Suti k'askaq / Noun Suffixes

-yuq

Attributive

This suffix is added to the noun root to indicate some attribute of the person or thing referred to by the noun. Expressions with -**yuq** often serve to define social status:

warmi-**yuq**	married (man speaking)
qusa-**yuq**	married (woman speaking)
mana mama-**yuq**	orphaned

qullqi-**yuq**	wealthy
vara-**yuq**	community authority [lit. "staff holder"]
mana qullqi-**yuq**	poor
wasi-**yuq**	householder
mana jallp'a-**yuq**	landless
mana kachi-**yuq**	saltless (of food)

Typical examples of use of -**yuq**:

Machkha wata-**yuq**-taq kanki?	How old are you?
Iskay chunka tawa-**yuq** wata-**yuq** kani.	I am twenty-four years old.
Pay machkha wawa-**yuq**-taq?	How many children does she have?
Payqa kimsa wawa-**yuq**.	She has three children.

The use of the negative **mana** with the suffix -**yuq** produces the meaning 'without' or '-less'. In this case, the negation expressed by **mana** does not require the suffix -**chu**.

Compare:

mana wasi-**yuq** runa	a homeless person

with:

Payqa mana wasi-**yuq**-chu.	He does not own a house.

-**tawan**
    Coordinative; "and . . . as well"; "else"

This is a compound suffix (-**ta** + -**wan**) used to mark one more item in a list, when the item is the object of the verb:

Imatataq churakuchkanki?	What are you wearing?
Almillata.	A homespun dress.
Ima-**tawan**-taq?	What else?
Chumpi-**tawan**	Also a belt.

Ruwana / Exercises

1 Juk ⌘ Junt'achina / Video Exercise   ▶ DVD

Go to the following section in the *Kawsay Vida* multimedia program:

Bolivian Quechua > Kawsay > Junt'achina > Filomena p'achamanta

Do both the video and audio gap-fill exercises in this section. There are three levels of difficulty here; you can work through each text three times with different gaps to fill each time.

2 Iskay ⌘ Qillqana / Written Work

Answer these questions on the **Filomena p'achamanta** video studied in exercise 1:

1. Mama Filomena imamantataq parlan?

_____

2. Sipas kaspa imatataq churakuq?

3. Ñawpaqta umanpiqa imayuqtaq kaq?

4. Kunanrí imayuqtaq kachkan?

5. Aqsuyuqchu kachkan?

6. Blusanri ima llimp'iyuqtaq?

3 Kimsa ⌘ Parlana qillqana / Oral and Written Work

Ask and answer according to the model:

qam; churakuy; aqsu, chumpi >>> Imatataq churakurqanki?
>>> Aqsuta churakurqani
>>> Imatawantaq churakurqanki?
>>> Chumpitawan churakurqani

1. qam; apamuy; ch'ullu, bufanda

2. pay; rantikuy; chumpi, ch'uspa

3. tata Pablo; chinkachiy; manta, punchu

4. mama Luisa; apakamuy; aqsu, pollera

5. qamkuna; rikuy; tinku, tusuqkuna

4 Tawa ⌘ Rikuna / Browse ▶ DVD

Go to the following section in the *Kawsay Vida* multimedia program:

Bolivian Quechua > Kawsay > Rikuna > Qayna

Work through the exercise, using the lookup and translation facilities. Choose three sentences from the exercise that contain the direct past tense and note them below.

5 Phichqa ⌘ Yachana / Practice ▶ DVD

Go to the following section in the *Kawsay Vida* multimedia program:

Bolivian Quechua > Kawsay > Yachana > Qayna imatataq ruwarqanku

Follow the on-screen instructions, and work through the exercise.

6 Suqta ⌘ Parlana Qillqana / Oral and Written Work

Ask and answer the questions, using the cues provided; in some cases you are free to supply your own ideas in the answer.

1. Jallp'ayuqchu kanki? (arí/mana)

2. Chay tinkuq umanpiqa imayuqtaq kachkan? (montera)

3. Chay qhariwarmi wasiyuqñachu kanku? (arí/mana)

4. Llikllayki ima llimp'iyuqtaq mamáy? (puka, yana, q'umir, q'illu)

5. Ñañayki wawayuqñachu? (arí/mana)

6. Warmiyuqñachu/Qusayuqñachu kanki? (arí/mana)

7. Aylluykichik yachaywasiyuqñachu? (arí/mana)

8. Kunan p'unchaw, ima p'achayuqtaq kachkanki?

7 Qanchis ⌘ Yachana / Practice ▶ DVD

Go to the following section in the *Kawsay Vida* multimedia program:

Bolivian Quechua > Fiesta > Yachana > Fiesta kaqkuna practice (3)

Follow the on-screen instructions, and work through the exercise. Make a note below of three sentences from the exercise containing the suffix **-yuq**.

8 Pusaq ⌘ Watuykuna / Analysis

Identify the verb forms in the following sentences. In each case, which is the main verb, and which is the subordinate verb? What tenses do you identify here?

1. Tatayqa Oruropi tiyakuspa qhuyapi llamk'aq.
2. Mama Elisaqa unqusqa kaspa anchata puñuchkan.
3. Ayllu runasqa chakraman tarpuq rispa mayuta chimpachkarqanku.
4. Ñawpaqtaqa takispa tususpa fiestata ruwaq kayku.
5. Qaynaqa Genoveva kachita rantikuspa llaqtamanta chayamusqa.
6. Mama Imigdiaqa llikllata wich'uñawan wich'uspa awachkan.
7. Mama Filomenaqa sipas kaspa achkha chukchayuq kaq, simp'aynin achkha kaq.
8. Chay runas monterata churakuspa tinkuman risqanku.

9 Jisq'un ⌘ Qhawana / Video View   ▶ DVD

Go to the following section in the *Kawsay Vida* multimedia program:

Bolivian Quechua > Fiesta > Qhawana > Roberta negociomanta

Watch the video and listen to doña Roberta talk about how she used to go to the fiestas as a market trader. Make a note below of the verb forms in the past habitual tense that she uses.

_____

_____

_____

10 Chunka ⌘ Qillqana / Written Work

Make a complex sentence from the elements provided, following the model:

juch'uy karqa; awaq karqa   >>>   Juch'uy kaspa awaq karqa.

1. Sipas karqa; aymarata parlaq karqa
_____

2. La Pazpi tiyakurqa; universidadpi yachachiq karqa
_____

3. Wasi jawapi karqani; punchuta churakurqani
_____

4. Perupi tiyarqayku; qhichwata yacharqayku
_____

5. Charanku tocaq phaqchaman rirqa; versota apamurqa
_____

6. Phaqchamanta versota apamurqa; imillasman yachachirqa
___

7. Tatamamaywan tiyakurqani; paykunata yanapaq kani
___

11 Chunka jukniyuq ⌘ Parlana / Oral Work

Interview a young man and/or woman who went to a fiesta and make a dialogue about the clothes they wore. You may use the questions provided and others of your choosing.

– Qayna fiestaman rirqankichu?
– Ima p'achayuqtaq rirqanki?
– Imatawan churakurqanki?
– Chay jawarí, imatataq churakurqanki?
– Ima llimp'iyuqtaq p'achayki?
– Yachakuq masiykirí, ima p'achayuqtaq rirqa?

13 / Chunka kimsayuq

Yuyarina / Review

A Look Back

Ima k'askaqkunataq kaykama yachakusqa kanku? What further suffixes have been studied so far?

Verb Conjugation Suffixes

-q + ka-	habitual past tense construction (Unit 12)
-rqa-	direct past tense marker (Unit 12)
-sqa-	indirect past tense marker (Unit 11)

Verb Suffixes

-chi-	causative indicator (Unit 9)
-ku-	reflexive functions (Unit 9)
-spa	verb subordinator; same subject (Unit 9)
-su-	2nd-person object marker (Unit 8)
-wa-	1st-person object marker (Unit 8)

Noun Suffixes

-manta	"from"; "out of"; "about" (Units 5, 10, 11)
-nchik	1st-person-plural possessive, inclusive (Unit 10)
-nku	2nd-person-plural possessive (Unit 10)
-p/-pa	genitive; "of" (Unit 10)
-pi	"in"; locative (Units 5, 8)
-pta/-pata	possessive pronoun markers (Unit 10)
-ta	adverb marker (Units 9, 11)
-taqri	"and"; sequencer (Unit 10)
-tawan	"and"; "and what else?" (Units 10, 12)
-wan	"with" (Unit 10)
-ykichik	1st-person-plural possessive, exclusive (Unit 10)
-yku	3rd-person-plural possessive (Unit 10)
-yuq	attributive marker (Units 11, 12)

Class-Free Suffixes

-ña	"now; already" (Unit 11)
-ni-	connective (Unit 8)
-raq	"still"; "not yet" (Unit 11)

Ruwana / Exercises

1 Juk ⌘ Qillqana / Written Work

Answer the following questions, choosing a word from the ones suggested in brackets to form your answer. Make any grammatical additions or changes to the chosen word as necessary.

María ima ruwaqtaq llaqtaman rirqa? (arroz rantiy; waturikuy; misa uyariy) >>> Misa uyariq rirqa.

1. Qam ima ruwaqtaq chakraman rirqanki? (puñuy; papa allay; wasi pichay)
   _____

2. Imataq sutiyki? (Jorge, Cristina, Fernando)
   _____

3. Vitalio imamantaq punaman risqa? (kachi; ch'uñu; llama millma)
   _____

4. Imataq kay? (ch'uspa; wayaqa; kustala)
   _____

5. Imatataq chay warmi churakuchkan? (aqsu; almilla; chumpi)
   _____

6. Sipaskuna imatataq urqupi ruwachkanku? (phuchkay; takiy; michiy)
   _____

7. Imatataq wawaykiman qararqanki? (papa; ch'arki; t'anta)
   _____

8. Imatawantaq wawaykiman qararqanki? (ch'uñu; aycha; papa)
   _____

9. Imawantaq mamayki wayk'un? (sara; papa; ch'uñu)
   _____

10. Imaynataq Juanpa tatan kachkan? (allinlla; mana allinchu; waliqlla)
    _____

11. Maymantaq qayna turayki/wawqiyki rirqa? (qhuya; mayu; puna)
    _____

12. Maymantataq jamuchkanki? (pata; ura; Oruro)
    _____

13. Tata Juan maymantataq llamt'ata pallamusqa? (monte; mayu; wayq'u)
    _____

14. Pitaq chay runa? (fiesta ruway; qhuya llamk'ay; yachachiy)

_____

13. Qam imilla/lluqalla kaspa piwantaq pukllaq kanki? (ñaña; wawqi; masi)

_____

14. Qam imilla/lluqalla kaspa maypitaq tiyakuq kanki?

_____

15. Machkha watayuqtaq kanki?

_____

16. Machkha yachakuqkunataq claseykipi kan?

_____

2 Iskay ⌘ Parlana, qillqana / Oral and Written Work

Working with a partner, create a conversation with a rural Quechua speaker in which you talk about the clothing worn in his/her community, today and in the past. Use appropriate adverbs of time and tenses.

3 Kimsa ⌘ Yachana / Practice   ▶ DVD

Go to the following section in the *Kawsay Vida* multimedia program:

Bolivian Quechua > Runakuna > Yachana > Akllana (1) and (2)

Do the multiple-choice exercises as review exercises. Follow the on-screen instructions. Note below any structures or vocabulary that are new to you:

_____

_____

_____

4 Tawa ⌘ Junt'achina / Video Exercise   ▶ DVD

Go to the following section in the *Kawsay Vida* multimedia program:

Peruvian Quechua > Ayllu > Hunt'achina > Martap ayllun

Follow the on-screen instructions, and do (i) the audio and (ii) the video gap-fill exercises. You can work through each text three times, gradually increasing the level of difficulty. Note any structures or vocabulary that are new to you:

_____

_____

_____

PART III

14 / Chunka tawayuq

Awayta yachay / Learning to Weave

In This Unit

You hear doña Filomena describe how she learned to weave. You practice talking about different skills. You study the nominalizing suffix -**y** and the "infinitive as object" construction; the noun suffix -**paq**; interrogative **jayk'aq** 'when?'; further use of -**pis**; emphatic -**pacha**; diminutive -**itu**; and ways of describing a sequence of actions using -**spataq**.

KAWSAY / ANDEAN LIFE
Learning Skills for Life

Despite the encroachments of the modern world, rural Andean life has remained largely subsistence based into the twenty-first century. Many skills are needed in order to clothe, feed, and house a family. Manual forms of technology are used, and skills are acquired informally as part of socialization into the community, rather than being learned formally in school and college. Weaving, presented in unit 10, is one such skill. In this unit doña Filomena describes how girls learn increasingly complex forms of weaving as they move from one stage of life to the next. Weaving, as all forms of community-based technology, is learned by watching and doing, rather than by applying abstract cognitive rules. And yet, as studies by anthropologists have shown, the patterns and techniques used in Andean textile production are the result of highly complex intellectual processes.

Suggested reading: Stobart and Howard 2002.

Kay warmi awayta yachan.

Ñawirina, yachakuna / Read and Learn

Jayk'aqmantataq awayta yachanki?	How long have you known how to weave?
Juch'uymantapacha.	Ever since [I was] small.
Ñawpaqta phuchkaniraq.	First of all I spin.
Chumpi away yachaspataqri...	And once I know how to weave a belt...
chay jawa llikllapaq phuchkani	after that I spin for a carrying cloth.

Qallarina / Introduction

Boliviapipis Perupipis runakunaqa sumaqta awayta yachanku. Awanapaqqa ñawpaqta millmataraq phuchkanku. Phullupaqqa rakhullata phuchkanku, chumpipaq astawan ñañullata phuchkanku. Llikllapaq, inkuñapaq, ch'uspapaqqa astawan ñañuta saltaspaq phuchkayta yachanku. Chantapis pisimanta pisi awayta yachakunku. Wawallaraq kaspa ñawpaqta juch'uy chumpita awanku. Chaymantaraq sipas kaspaqa llikllata saltasniyuqta imaymana llimp'iyuqta awayta yachakunku. Wakin ayllupi waynakunapis ch'ulluta t'ipayta yachanku.

Mama Filomena awayta yachan. Juch'uymantapacha awayta yachan, ñin. Juch'uy kachkaspaqa chumpitaraq awayta yachakusqa. Chumpita awayta yachaspataqri phulluta awasqa. Chay jawa llikllata awasqa. Mama Filomenaqa sumaqta awayta yachan.

Simi / Vocabulary

Ruway / Verbs

    astay: to fetch and carry.
    lat'ay: to crawl.
    qallariy: to begin.

qillqay: to write.
riqsiy: to know (a place, person); to recognize.
samariy: to rest.
tukuy: to finish; to pretend (to be).
t'ipay: to knit.
uyway: to nurture (children, animals).
watay: to tie up.
wiñay: to grow, to grow up (children, animals).

Ruway tikrachiq / Adverbs

ajina: so; like this; thus.
jina: like.
pachan: unchanged; remains the same.
pisimanta pisi: little by little.
qayna p'unchaw: yesterday.
qayna wata: last year.

Suti / Nouns

inkuña: small cloth for carrying coca leaves.
killa: month; moon.
uña: newborn offspring.
wallpa uchu: spicy chicken.
wata: year.

Suti tikrachiq / Adjectives

ñañu: thin (*referring to yarn*).
rakhu: thick (*referring to solid objects*).

Tapuq suti ranti / Interrogative Pronouns

imapaq: what for?
jayk'aq: when?
jayk'aqmanta: since when?
pipaq: who for?

Simip k'askaynin / Grammar

Ruway k'askaq / Verb Suffixes

-y

Infinitive marker

The suffix -y turns a verb root into an infinitive, which acts as a noun form:

qillqa-	write	>>>	qillqa-**y**	to write; writing
awa-	weave	>>>	awa-**y**	to weave; weaving
taki-	sing	>>>	taki-**y**	to sing; singing
tusu-	dance	>>>	tusu-**y**	to dance; dancing

Infinitive as object

As a noun (or nominalized) form, the infinitive may take noun-class suffixes. For example, the infinitive may be the object of verbs such as: **yachay** 'to know', **atiy** 'to be able', **munay** 'to want', **tukuy** 'to finish', **qallariy** 'to begin'. In this case, the infinitive form takes the direct object marker **-ta**:

ñuqa	llamk'**ay-ta**	yachani	I know how to work
qam	llamk'**ay-ta**	yachanki	you know how to work
pay	llamk'**ay-ta**	yachan	s/he knows how to work
ñuqayku	llamk'**ay-ta**	yachayku	we (excl.) know how to work
ñuqanchik	llamk'**ay-ta**	yachanchik	we (incl.) know how to work
qamkuna	llamk'**ay-ta**	yachankichik	you all know how to work
paykuna	llamk'**ay-ta**	yachanku	they know how to work

The tense of the main verb may vary, for example:

paykuna llamk'**ay-ta** yacha-ku-**rqa-nku**	they learned how to work
paykuna llamk'**ay-ta** yacha-ku-**chka-nku**	they are learning to work
paykuna llamk'**ay-ta** yacha-**q kanku**	they used to know how to work

Suti k'askaq / Noun Suffixes

-paq

Benefactive; "for"

The suffix **-paq** marks the beneficiary of an action:

Pi-**paq**-taq millmata apamun?	Who does he/she bring the wool for?
Maman-**paq** apamun.	S/he brings (it) for his/her mother.
Pi-**paq**-taq chay pizarrón?	Who is that blackboard for?
Yachay wasi-**paq**.	It's for the school.
Ima-**paq**-taq phuchkanki?	What (item) are you spinning for?
Phullu-**paq** phuchkani.	I am spinning for (to weave) a blanket.

-itu; -ita; -situ

Diminutives

These suffixes are derived from the Spanish diminutive, as in *chiquito* "little" or *ahorita* "just now." They indicate smallness, and also affectivity. The suffix may appear at the end of a noun root; it may be followed by a possessive suffix; or it may appear as an infix, as in "kunitan" "just now," composed of **kunan** + **-ita**. Thus, these diminutive forms have blended into the grammatical structure of Bolivian Quechua.

In southern Peruvian Quechua, Spanish influence in this area of the grammar is not evident; the diminutive suffix **-cha** is common; e.g., urpi**cha**y 'my little dove.' Examples of **-cha** can be found in the "Peruvian Quechua" section of the *Kawsay Vida* multimedia program. The following are Bolivian Quechua examples of diminutive usage:

misi	cat	>>>	misi-**situ**	little cat
k'aspi	stick	>>>	k'aspi-**situ**	little stick

juch'uy	little	>>>	juch'uy-**situ**	very little
wawa	child	>>>	waw-**ita**	little child
ajina	like this	>>>	ajin-**ita**-n	a little like this
kunan	now	>>>	kun-**ita**-n	just now

Wak k'askaq / Class-Free Suffixes

-**pacha**

Temporal emphatic

-**pacha** may operate (**i**) as an adverbial root meaning 'unchanged'; (**ii**) as a suffix whereby the meaning of the word to which it is attached is emphasized. There is usually a temporal dimension to the meaning:

(**i**)	**pacha**llan kachkanki	you have not changed
(**ii**)	juch'uymanta-**pacha**	right since (being) small
(**ii**)	kunan-**pacha**	right now
(**ii**)	chayan-**pacha**	she/he arrives right now
(**ii**)	awani-**pacha**	I weave right now

-**spataqri** (-spa + -taq + -ri)

Conjunctive function; "and after (doing)"

This compound suffix, made up of the verbal subordinator -**spa** + -**taq** + -**ri**, has a conjunctive function and is used to express a sequence of actions. The verb form ending in -**spataqri** describes the first stage of a sequence and the following verb describes the second stage:

Phuchka-**spataqri**, k'antina.   And after spinning, one braids.
Tuku-**spataqri**, samarina.   And after finishing, one rests.

Note that -**taqri** translates as "and" and provides a stylistically more forceful effect than -**taq** alone.

-**raq**

(**iii**) Imperfective aspect; "first of all"

In some contexts, -**raq** can be interpreted as expressing priority in a sequence:

Kayta-**raq** ruwani.   First I do this.
Wawaypaq-**raq** wayk'uni.   I cook for my child first.

Ruway / Exercises

1 Juk ⌘ Qillqana / Written Work

Read the introductory text again and answer the following questions:

1. Awanapaq ñawpaqta imataraq ruwanku?

_____

2. Imaynatataq phullupaq phuchkanku?

_____

3. Wawa kaspa imataraq awanku?

_____

4. Waynakunarí awaytachu yachanku?

5. Jayk'aqmantataq mama Filomena awayta yachan?

6. Juch'uy kachkaspa, imatataq ñawpaqta awasqa?

7. Chumpita awayta yachaspataqri imatataq awarqa?

8. Phullu jawa imatataq awasqa?

9. Qam awayta yachankichu?

10. Qam imakunatataq ruwayta yachanki?

2 Iskay ⌘ Ñawirina, waturikuna / Reading and Analysis

(i) Read the following text and underline the phrases in it which contain the "infinitive as object" construction; list the phrases below and translate them into English.

Ayllupi mamakunaqa wawankuta ñuñuwanpuni uywayta munanku. Wawasninkuta wasanpi q'ipispa paykunawan khuska apanku, ajinata parlayta yachachinku. Wiñaspataq wawakunaqa lat'aytaraq atinku, chaymanta sayarispa puriyta qallarinku. Jatun wawakunaqa qharipis warmipis mamankuta yanapayta qallarinku. Uña wawata munakuspa q'ipiyta atinku, pukllachinku, qhawanku ima. Ayllupipis yanapayta qallarinkuña. Yakuta mayumanta astamunku, uwijata michiyta atinku, awaytapis yachakunkuña.

e.g., Wawankuta ñuñuwanpuni *uywayta munanku.* >>> They want to breastfeed their children [*lit.* "raise at the breast"].

(ii) Translate the following sentences into Quechua, using the verbs provided in brackets.

1. I want to learn Quechua. (munay)

2. We (*incl.*) want to go to Bolivia. (munay)

3. Do you know how to cook spicy chicken? (yachay)

_____

4. The baby can walk now. (atiy)

_____

5. The young people have started to sing already. (qallariy)

_____

6. The young men have finished working. (tukuy)

_____

3 Kimsa ⌘ Rikuna / Browse ▶ DVD

Go to the following section in the *Kawsay Vida* multimedia program:

Peruvian Quechua > Wawa uyway > Rikuna

Browse through the exercise and note the phrases in which the "infinitive as object" construction is used. Write them down below:

_____

_____

_____

_____

4 Tawa ⌘ Qillqana / Written Work

Ask and answer questions according to the model:

Jayk'aqtaq llikllata awarqanki? (qayna wata)   >>>   Qayna wata awarqani.

1. Jayk'aqtaq sarata tarpurqanku? (qayna p'unchaw)

_____

2. Jayk'aqtaq tata Simón alférez kasqa? (qayna wata)

_____

3. Jayk'aqtaq aqharqankichik? (Carnavalpi)

_____

4. Jayk'aqtaq chay wakata rantikurqankichik? (iskay killaña)

_____

5. Jayk'aqtaq wasiykita ruwarqanki? (kimsa wataña)

_____

5 Phichqa ⌘ Qillqana / Written Work

Ask and answer questions according to the model:

Jayk'aqmantataq phuchkayta yachanki? (juch'uy)   >>>   Juch'uymantapacha phuchkayta yachani.

1. Jayk'aqmantataq k'antiyta yachanki? (juch'uysitu)

2. Jayk'aqmantataq qillqayta yachankichik? (qayna wata)

3. Jayk'aqmantataq wawayki awayta yachan? (imillita)

4. Jayk'aqmantataq llaqtaman riyta yachanki? (wawita)

5. Jayk'aqmantataq llama qhatiyta yachanku? (juch'uy)

6. Jayk'aqmantataq tarpuyta yachanki? (wayna)

7. Jayk'aqmantataq aqsuta manaña churakunkuchu? (chunka wata)

8. Jayk'aqmantataq wawayki parlayta yachan? (watan)

9. Jayk'aqmantataq chakraykichikpi sarata tarpunkichik? (Todos Santos)

10. Jayk'aqmantataq samarichkankichik? (qayna p'unchaw)

6 Suqta ⌘ Qillqana / Written Work

Answer the questions according to the model:

Millmata phuchkasparí, imatataq ruwanki? (q'aytu k'antiy)   >>>   Millmata phuchkaspataq, q'aytuta k'antini.

1. Q'aytuta k'antisparí, imatataq ruwanki? (lliklla away)

2. Llikllata awasparí, imatawan awanki? (inkuña away)

3. Punchuta churakusparí, maymantaq rinki? (llaqta)

4. Almillata churakuspari, imatawan churakunki? (chumpi, aqsu)
___

5. Qam feriaman rispari, imatataq rantikunki?
___

7 Qanchis ⌘ Qillqana / Written Work

Practice the suffix -**paq**. Answer the questions according to the model:

Imapaqtaq chay inkuña? (kuka)	>>>	Kukapaq.
Pipaqtaq chay sara? (mamay)	>>>	Mamaypaq.

1. Imapaqtaq chay q'aytu? (phullu) ___
2. Pipaqtaq chay aqha? (alférez) ___
3. Pipaqtaq chay t'anta? (wawa) ___
4. Imapaqtaq chay millma? (lliklla) ___
5. Pipaqtaq chay aycha? (ñuqayku) ___
6. Imapaqtaq chay iPod ñisqa? (uyarina) ___
7. Imapaqtaq chay laptop ñisqa? (qillqana) ___

8 Pusaq ⌘ Yachana / Practice   ▶ DVD

Go to the following section in the *Kawsay Vida* multimedia program:

Peruvian Quechua > Mikhuna > Yachana > Mikhuy wayk'uy (4)

(i) Work through the exercise, noting how the suffix -**paq** is used.
(ii) Note down the words for different kinds of food.

___
___
___
___
___

9 Jisq'un ⌘ Qillqana / Written Work

Revise the suffixes -**ña** and -**raq**. Answer the questions according to the model:

Llaqtaman riyta yachankiñachu?	>>>	Manaraq yachanichu.
or	>>>	Mana yachaniraqchu.
or	>>>	Arí, yachaniña.

1. Aqha upyayta yachankiñachu? _____
2. San Pedrota riqsinkiñachu? _____
3. Qhichwa parlayta atinkiñachu? _____
4. Wawayki ñawiriyta yachanñachu? _____
5. Tatayki llaqtamanta kutimunñachu? _____

10 Chunka ⌘ Parlana, qillqana / Oral and Written Work

Practice the "infinitive as object" construction, by asking and answering the following questions.

1. Qamrí? Ima ruwaytataq yachanki? _____
2. Awaytachu yachanki? _____
3. Phuchkaytachu yachanki? _____
4. Uwija michiy . . . _____
5. Llama qhatiy . . . _____
6. Papa tarpuy . . . _____
7. Aqhay . . . _____
8. Salsa tusuy . . . _____
9. Wayñu takiy . . . _____

11 Chunka jukniyuq ⌘ Yuyarina / Review

Translate into Quechua:

1. I can sing. _____
2. I want to learn Aymara. _____
3. Do you speak Quechua yet? _____
4. Does she know how to spin? _____
5. Do you know how to chew coca? _____
6. The baby started to talk. _____
7. She is learning to write. _____
8. They want to go to school. _____

15 / Chunka phichqayuq

Fiesta ruwana tiyan / Having to Sponsor a Fiesta

In This Unit...

You meet doña Primitiva, who describes the preparations involved in sponsoring a fiesta. You learn how to talk about obligations and getting things done. You study the nominalizing suffix **-na** and additional uses of the causative suffix **-chi-**.

KAWSAY / ANDEAN LIFE
Fiesta Sponsorship

In addition to their religious function, fiestas generate a great deal of social, cultural, and economic activity, and the system of fiesta sponsorship (or system of ritual "cargos"), introduced in the colonial era, is one of the key ways in which Andean society is structured and organized. Fiesta sponsors (referred to in Northern Potosí Quechua as "alférez" (pronounced [alxiris]; *pasante* or *prioste* in Spanish) are usually a husband and wife pair; they take on the responsibility for hiring musicians and dancers, and overseeing the preparation of food and the brewing of chicha for all the members of the community or neighborhood group. Fiesta sponsorship involves capital outlay for those nominated; however, those who take on the role accrue prestige and enhance their social networks, which stands them in good stead in future years when they need to call on family and friends for assistance. Certain fiestas entail greater financial investment than others, leading anthropologists to talk of a "prestige hierarchy" through which people move progressively as they go from young adulthood to mature life.

Suggested reading: Isbell 1985; Paerregaard 1997.

Paykunaqa San Pedro llaqtaman fiesta ruwaq jamunku.

Ñawirina, yachakuna / Read and Learn

Tukuy imata ruwana tiyan.	We have to do everything.
Fiesta pasanapaq q'ipinay kachkan	I have to carry it [on my back] in order to be a fiesta sponsor.
Aqha aqhachina tiyan.	One must get someone to brew chicha.

Qallarina / Introduction

Boliviapi alférezkunaqa qhariwarmi kanku. Paykunaqa munaspa qullqinkuwan fiestata ruwanku. Paykunaqa ñawpaqmantapacha fiestapaq wakichinanku tiyan. Fiestamanqa tukuy runa allinta mikhunapaq, upyanapaq, tusunapaq ima rinku.

Kunanqa doña Primitiva fiestamanta parlachkan. Ñisqanmanjinaqa tukuy imata ruwana tiyan: aqhata aqhachina, mikhunata wayk'uchina. Wakin kutiqa wak llaqtaman purina. Sipas kaspaqa doña Primitiva Surumiman puriq; chayman fiesta pasaq riyta yachaq.

Qhawana / Video View ▶ DVD

Go to the following section in the *Kawsay Vida* multimedia program:

Bolivian Quechua > Fiesta > Qhawana > Fiesta ruwaymanta

Watch the video and listen to doña Primitiva talk about fiesta sponsorship obligations. Study the language of the text, using the lookup facilities on-screen.

Simi / Vocabulary

Ruway / Verbs

    akllay: to choose.
    casaray: to get married.
    chukuy: to sit, to squat.
    juntuy: to gather together.
    machay: to get drunk.
    mañay: to ask a favor; to contract someone.
    pasay: to sponsor (a fiesta).
    preparay: to prepare.
    rikuchiy: to show, to display.
    sawakuy: to get married.
    sayk'uy: to get tired.
    wakichiy: to prepare, to get something ready.

Ruway tikrachiq / Adverbs

    juk kuti: once.
    wakin kuti: sometimes, other times.

Suti / Nouns

    kuti: time, occasion.
    p'uyñu [p'uñu]: chicha jar.
    q'ipi: bundle.
    tata cura: priest.
    tatamama: parents.
    t'ika: flower.
    yatiri: shaman, ritual specialist.

Suti tikrachiq / Adjectives

    wak: another.

Expressions

    kikillantaq: "just the same."
    ñisqanman jina: "according to what s/he says."

Indefinite Pronoun

    tukuy: every.

Simip k'askaynin / Grammar

Ruway k'askaq / Verb Suffix

    -na

        (i) Verb nominalizer: futurative abstract noun

-na turns a verb root into a noun form referring to an abstract idea. **-na** conveys the idea of a future action, potentially to be performed.

| ruway | to do | >>> | ruwa-**na** | job, task |
| llamk'ay | to work | >>> | llamk'a-**na** | work |

Commonly this gives rise to nouns that refer to instruments, places where actions are performed, or general actions:

Instruments:

| away | to weave | >>> | awa-**na** | loom |
| pukllay | to play | >>> | puklla-**na** | toy |

Places:

| puñuy | to sleep | >>> | puñu-**na** | bed |
| chukuy | to sit | >>> | chuku-**na** | seat |

Actions:

| ruway | to do | >>> | ruwa-**na** | work |
| pukllay | to play | >>> | puklla-**na** | toy, game |

> (ii) Indicates encouragement to action

The -**na** form also acts as a verbal expression encouraging the listener(s) to shared action; there may be a sense of obligation in the action referred to:

| Ri-**na**. | Let's go; we ought to go. |
| Fiestapi tusu-**na**. | One has to dance at the fiesta. |

> -**na**- + -**paq**
> (iii) Indicates future purpose

The form of the verb ending in -**na** can combine with the benefactive suffix -**paq** to express the idea of future purpose:

Ima-**paq**-taq? Llamk'a-**na-paq**.	What is it for? It is for working.
Ima-**paq**-taq? Tarpu-**na-paq**.	What is it for? It is for planting.
Awa-**na-paq** phuchkanaraq.	In order to weave first one has to spin.
Kawsa-**na-paq** llamk'ana.	In order to live one has to work.

> -**na**- + possessive + auxiliary verb **tiyay/kay**
> (iv) Indicates future obligation

This construction indicates that the action of the verb remains to be done, giving a sense of *future obligation*. Person is marked by adding the possessive series of person suffixes. The auxiliaries **kay** or **tiyay** are used in the 3rd-person singular. The construction may be translated as "to have to."

Ñuqa llamk'a-**na-y tiyan**	I have to work	Ñuqayku llamk'a-**na-yku tiyan**	we (excl.) have to work
		Ñuqanchik llamk'a-**na-nchik tiyan**	we (incl.) have to work
Qam llamk'a-**na-yki tiyan**	you (sing.) have to work	Qamkuna llamk'a-**na-ykichik tiyan**	you (pl.) have to work
Pay llamk'a-**na-n tiyan**	he, she has to work	Paykuna llamk'a-**na-nku tiyan**	they have to work

In the present tense this construction is used with the auxiliary forms **tiyan** 'have to' and **kachkan** 'must'. The difference in meaning is shown below:

llamk'a-**na**-y **tiyan**	I have to work (it is my general obligation)
llamk'a-**na**-y **kachkan**	I must work (it is my planned obligation on a particular occasion).

To convey obligation in other tenses, the auxiliary **kay** is preferred:

llamk'a-**na**-y **karqa**	I had to work
llamk'a-**na**-y **kanqa**	I will have to work
llamk'a-**na**-y **kasqa**	I had to work (I just found out)

Ruwana / Exercises

1 Juk ⌘ Junt'achina / Video Exercise   ▶ DVD

Go to the following section in the *Kawsay Vida* multimedia program:

Bolivian Quechua > Fiesta > Junt'achina > Fiesta ruwaymanta

Follow the on-screen instructions, and do (i) the audio and (ii) the video gap-fill exercises. You can work through each text three times, gradually increasing the level of difficulty.

2 Iskay ⌘ Qillqana / Written Work

Make new sentences using the causative -**chi**, as shown in the model.

Wayk'uspa mikhuni.   >>>   Wayk'uspa payta mikhu-**chi**-ni.

1. Tususpa sayk'uni. _____
2. Mama Primitivaqa fiestapaq aqhan. _____
3. Qam chayamuspa p'achata t'aqsanki. _____
4. Llikllapi papata q'ipinku. _____
5. Fiestata ruwaspa sikuta pusamuyku. _____

3 Kimsa ⌘ Qillqana / Written Work

Talk about obligations using the "-**na** + possessive + auxiliary verb **tiyay/kay**" construction, as shown in the model.

Maymantaq rinayki tiyan? (llaqta)   >>>   Llaqtaman rinay tiyan.

1. Maymantaq rinayki kachkan? (Mamita Surumi)
_____

2. Imatataq apanayki tiyan? (t'ikas)
_____

3. Imatataq awananku tiyan? (lliklla)
_____

4. Maypitaq fiesta pasanaykichik kachkan? (San Pedro)
_____

5. Pipaqtaq aqhanayki tiyan? (fiesta riqkuna)
___

6. Imamantataq ch'arkita ruwanayki kachkan? (waka aycha)
___

7. Imapitaq jamunanku karqa? (chaki)
___

8. Maypitaq Juan llamk'anan kanqa? (qhuya)
___

4 Tawa ⌘ Qillqana / Written Work

Practice closing a list using **ima**, answering the questions as shown in the model; use the grammatical structures appropriate to the question.

Fiesta jamuqkunapaq imakunatataq wayk'uchina tiyan? (papa, ch'uñu, aycha)   >>>   Papata, ch'uñuta, aychata **ima** wayk'uchina tiyan.

Qhichwata yachakunapaq imatataq ruwanki? (ñawiriy, parlariy, qillqariy)   >>>   Nawirini, parlarini, qillqarini **ima**.

1. Sara rantikuq rinapaq imatataq valleman apachina tiyan? (ch'arki, kachi, llama millma)
___

2. Ayllupi casarachinapaq imatataq ruwana tiyan? (warmip tatamamanwan parlay, aqhachiy, iglesiaman riy)
___

3. Chay llaqta runakuna imatataq awachinku? (phullu, punchu, lliklla)
___

4. Fiestapaq imatataq ruwana tiyan. (p'acha rantiy, siku mañay, aqha aqhachiy)
___

5. Chay yachachiq imatataq yachakuqkunata ruwachin? (ñawichiy, qillqachiy, parlachiy, takichiy)
___

6. Chay patrones imatataq campo runata ruwachiq karqanku? (jallp'api llamk'achiy, mujuta tarpuchiy, papa allachiy)
___

5 Phichqa ⌘ Qillqana / Written Work

(i) Place in chronological order the preparations that have to be made for the fiesta, as given in the following list.

1. aqhachiy
2. alférezta akllay

3. mikhunata wayk'uchiy
4. tusuy, takiy
5. sikusta mañachiy
6. llikllakunata awachiy
7. llamt'a pallachimuy
8. machaykuy
9. fiestaman puriy
10. tullqata chinkita pusamuy
11. wallpa uchuta mikhuy
12. aqhata upyay

(ii) Using the "-**na** + auxiliary verb" construction, write a short paragraph answering the following question:

Fiestaman rinapaq, imakunatataq wakichina tiyan?

Mention in turn each of the preparations listed in part (i). You may link your sentences with conjunctions such as: **chaymanta** 'after that'; **chantá** 'then'; **ajinata** 'in that way.'
   Your paragraph can begin as follows:

Fiestaman rinapaqqa alféreztaraq akllana. Chaymanta _____

_____

_____

_____

_____

6 Suqta ⌘ Yuyarina / Review

Use what you know about the culture of fiestas in the Andes to answer the questions on the left by drawing a line to match them to the appropriate answer on the right:

Imatataq ruwana tiyan . . .
Tusunapaq takinapaqqa?   P'achataraq rantikuna.
Aqhata upyanapaqqa?   Alféreztaraq akllana.
Fiestaman rinapaqqa?   Aqhachinaraq.
Fiestata ruwanapaqqa?   Fiestamanraq rina.

7 Qanchis ⌘ Yachana / Practice   ▶ DVD

Go to the following section of the *Kawsay Vida* multimedia program:

Peruvian Quechua > Ayllu > Yachana

Do *Yachanapaq (3)* and *Yachanapaq (4)*. These exercises give you further practice with the benefactive suffix **-paq** 'for' and the "verb + **-na-** + **-paq**" construction "in order to." Make a note below of any new vocabulary you come across.

_____

_____

_____

_____

16 / Chunka suqtayuq

Unquy / Illness

In This Unit . . .

You revise and build on ways of talking about illness and symptoms, as introduced in Unit 8. You talk about the weather. You explore the use of impersonal verbs. You study the future tense; learn additional suffixes that mark the object of the verb; and use the conjectural suffix -**chá**.

KAWSAY / ANDEAN LIFE
Sickness and Cosmovision

In rural Andean communities the forces of nature are often seen as a source of illness, which can take many forms and is talked about in different ways. Any kind of shock, caused by a fall or an accident of some kind, may be referred to as susto (fright), and its symptoms include lethargy or paralysis and even deformity of the limbs. Where Western medical aid has not been called upon, viral causes of illness may go undiagnosed, and such conditions will be treated with herbal remedies rather than drugs and vaccines. The agents of sickness may be identified directly as natural forces: the wind and the hill god's anger, for instance, are often invoked. In some circumstances human agents are accused of malevolently causing illness by means of layqay (something akin to "casting a spell"). Nonhuman agents of illness are generically defined as khuru (worm), thought of as an alien body that physically invades the victim. Illness is also often attributed to "soul loss." In such cases the yatiri intervenes with the spirits of the natural world thought to be responsible, and coaxes the soul back into the body of the patient (a process referred to as aysay, or "dragging"). In Northern Potosí the saint Santiago is thought to help the yatiri in this healing ritual, a séance held in the dark and during which Santiago appears embodied as a condor flapping his wings.

Suggested reading: Platt 1997.

Kay yatiriqa urqusman mañaspa jampin.

Ñawirina, yachakuna / Read and Learn

Anchatachu chirisunki?	Are you very cold?
Arí, anchata chiriwan.	Yes, I am very cold.
Chirichá unquchisunki.	It was surely the cold that made you sick.
Rillasaqña.	I'll be going now.

Qallarina / Introduction

Kawsaypiqa mana kusiyllachu, llakiypis, unquypis tiyan. Runakunaqa imaymanata unqunku, wiksanku, umanku, k'iwichanku nanan. Wakintaq mancharisqa jap'iqasqa layqasqa kanku. Ajinata ayllukunapi wakin runa unquykunata jampiyta yachanku. Chay tukuy unquykunapaq jampikuna tiyan. Jampiriqa qhura jampiwan, makinwan, milluwan, wakkunawan ima jampiyta yachan.

Juk wayna, Rubén sutiyuq, tinkupi maqanakuspa chankanta nanachikun, p'akisqachá, punkisqa kachkan. «Q'ala q'uyu kachkan» ñin. Chayraykuchá jampiriqa «¿layqachisunkuchu, khuruykusunkuchu?» ñispa tapurin. Chantá kukata t'akarispa Rubénpa unquyninta qhawarin. Chaymanta Rubénqa qhura jampikunawan allinyanqa ñin.

Parlana / Dialogue

Jampiri (J): – Pitaq waqyachiwan?
Rubénpa maman: – Ñuqa qamta waqyachiyki. Waway unqusqa kachkan.
J: – Imayki nanasunki Rubén?
Rubén (R): – Chankay anchata nanawan, tatáy. Punkisqa kachkan. Mana puriyta atinichu.
J: – Imanakunkitaq?
R: – Tinkupi jayt'awanku.

J: – Jayt'asunkuchu?
R: – Arí, tatáy. Chiri chiri ima juqhariwan. Tullusniytaq nanachkawan.
J: – Jump'iwanchá kachkanki.
R: – Jinachá tatáy. Jump'ichkani, jampiriway!
J: – Tullu p'akisqapaq kinuwa kutasqata churasqayki. Punkisqapaqtaq qhurakunata churasqayki, chaykunawan allinyanki ari.
R: – Churaway, tatáy!
J: – Jina churachkani. Kunan rillasaqña. Q'aya juktawan kutimusaq.
R: – Q'ayakama tatáy.

Simi / Vocabulary

Ruway / Verbs

    gustay: to like.
    juqhariy: to rise, raise, pick up.
    t'akariy: to scatter.
    waqyay: to call.
    willay: to tell; relate.

    Unquy / Illness

    allinyay: to get better.
    imanay: to happen, to become of [someone].
    jap'iqay: to get grabbed (by forces of nature).
    jap'iy: to grab.
    jayt'ay: to kick.
    jump'iy: to sweat.
    kutay: to grind (grains, coffee, spices, herbs, etc.).
    khuruy: to infect (the body).
    layqay: to bewitch.
    manchariy: to get frightened.
    maqanakuy: to fight each other.
    maqay: to beat.
    punkiy: to swell.
    p'akiy: to break.
    q'iwiy: to twist.
    q'uñiy: to be hot.
    vacunay: to vaccinate.

    Pachamanta / Climate

    chikchiy: to hail.
    paray: to rain.
    pukatay: to be cloudy.
    qhasay: to freeze.
    rit'iy: to snow.
    wayray: to be windy.

Ruway tikrachiq / Adverb

    q'ala: totally (*colloquial*).

Suti / Nouns

  Unquy / Illness

    chiri chiri: fever.
    jampi: medicine.
    jampiri: traditional healer.
    kallpa: physical strength, moral courage.
    khuru: worm; bacteria.
    millu: sulphuric mineral (used in diagnosing illness).
    qhura: herb.
    q'uyu: bruise.
    unquy: illness.

  Pachamanta / Climate

    ch'aska: morning star.
    inti: sun.
    wayra: wind.

  Pacha / Periods of Time

    jamuq wata: next year.
    minchha: the day after tomorrow.
    paqarin: morning.
    q'aya: tomorrow.
    q'aya minchha: the day after the day after tomorrow.
    semana: week.

Suti tikrachiq / Adjectives

    sapa: each, every.
    sinchi: strong, physically tough.
    utqhay [usqhay]: fast.

Expressions

    chayrayku: "because of that."
    juktawan: "again," "another time."
    paqarinkama: "until tomorrow" (*S. Peru*).
    q'ayakama: "until tomorrow" (*Bolivia*).

Simip k'askaynin / Grammar

Rimay muyuchina / Verb Conjugation

  Future Tense

ñuqa ri-**saq**	I shall go	ñuqayku ri-**sqayku** *or* ri-**saqku**	we (excl.) shall go
		ñuqanchik ri-**sun**	we (incl.) shall go

	or ri-**sunchik**		
qam ri-**nki**	you (sing.) will go	qamkuna ri-**nkichik**	you (pl.) will go
pay ri-**nqa**	s/he will go	paykuna ri-**nqanku**	they will go

Notice that the future tense combines the tense and the person in the same suffix. Note also that the 2nd-person marker here is the same as the 2nd-person marker of the present tense (i.e., 2nd-person-singular -**nki**, 2nd-person-plural -**nkichik**). Meaning is determined by context.

Ruway k'askaq / Verb Suffixes

Person Object–Marking in the Verb: Rules

Both the person subject and the person object can be marked on the verb in Quechua. The suffixes we have studied so far have been subject suffixes. For example, in:

ñuqa qhawa-**ni**   I look

where -**ni** indicates the 1st-person-singular subject.

However, transitive verbs may contain an implicit 3rd-person object. For example:

ñuqa qhawa-**ni**   I look at him/her/it/them (object is understood)

If the object and the subject of the verb are the same person, the object is marked with the reflexive -**ku**-, for example:

qhawa-**ku**-ni   I look after myself
qhawa-**ku**-nki   you look after yourself

In other cases, where the person object is a first person the suffix -**wa**- occurs. Where the person object is a second person, usually the suffix -**su**- occurs. The marking of the person object in the verb form is one of the trickiest areas of Quechua grammar for the learner, not least because the system contains some irregularities. There are some rules which should be studied; the irregular cases need to be learned by heart.

The following rules apply to **object–subject combinations** in the **present tense**.

Rule 1: 1st-person-singular object ("me") -**wa**- + subject markers

Verb Root	Suffix	Object	Subject	Translation
riku-	wa-n	me	he/she	he/she/it sees me
riku-	wa-nki	me	you	you see me
riku-	wa-nkichik	me	you (pl.)	you all see me
riku-	wa-nku	me	they	they see me

The person object–marker precedes the person subject–marker as shown. This rule applies for all tenses.

Rule 2: 1st-person-plural object ("us") -**wayku**/-**wanchik**

Verb Root	Suffix	Object	Subject	Translation
riku-	wayku	us (*excl.*)	you/he/she/they	you/he/she/they see(s) us
riku-	wanchik	us (*incl.*)	he/she/they	he/she/they see(s) us

To apply this rule, first conjugate the verb normally with the person marker that corresponds to the subject in question, e.g., riku-**yku** 'we see,' then insert the object suffix -**wa**-, thus giving riku-**wayku** 'you/he/she/they see(s) **us**.' In interpreting meaning, the marking of the object takes priority over the marking of the subject. Interpretation of the subject in question depends on context.

Rule 3: 2nd-person-singular object ("you") -**su**- + subject markers

Verb Root	Suffix	Object	Subject	Translation
riku-	su-nku	you	they	they see you
riku-	su-yku	you (*sing./pl.*)	we (*excl.*)	we (*excl.*) see you

Rule 4: 2nd-person-singular object ("you") -**yki**/-**sunki**

Verb Root	Suffix	Object	Subject	Translation
riku-	yki	you (*sing.*)	I	I see you
riku-	ykichik	you (*pl.*)	I/we	I/we (*incl.*) see you all
riku-	sunki	you (*sing.*)	she/he	she/he sees you
riku-	sunkichik	you (*pl.*)	she/he	he/she sees you all

Person object–marking in the verb: Illustration

By way of illustration, here are some of the above rules as applied in use:

(4) Yanapa-**sunki**-chu? Does s/he help you?
(1) Arí, yanapa-**wa**-n. Yes, s/he helps me.

(4) Yatiri imatataq maña-**sunkichik**?   What does the healer ask you (all) for?
(2) Qhura jampita maña-**wayku**.   He asks us for herbal remedies.

(2) Ima mikhunatataq qu-**wanchik**?   What food does he/she give us?
(2) Wallpa uchuta qu-**wanchik**.   S/he gives us spicy chicken.

(3) Pikunataq jayt'a-**sunku**?   Who (all) has kicked you?
(1) Tinkuqkunaqa jayt'a-**wa**-nku.   The tinku fighters have kicked me.

(1) Waqya-**wankichu**?   Have you called me?
(4) Arí, waqya-**yki**.   Yes, I have called you.

We also give the following **future tense** form here, as it is particularly frequent in everyday speech:

Verb Root	Suffix	Object	Subject	Translation
riku-	sqayki	you	I	I shall see you
jukta tapuri-	sqayki	you	I	I'll ask you a question
cuentota willari-	sqayki	you	I	I'll tell you a story

Impersonal Verbs
 (**i**) Weather conditions

Verbs referring to weather conditions operate as "impersonal verbs" : **rit'iy** 'to snow', **paray** 'to rain', **qhasay** 'to freeze', **wayray** 'to be windy', **chiriy** 'to be cold', **ruphay** 'to be hot', and others. That is, they operate only in the 3rd-person singular:

Rit'i-chkan.   It is snowing.
Sinchita **para**-rqa.   It rained heavily.
Q'aya **qhasa**-nqachá.   It will probably freeze tomorrow.

The suffix -**mu**- is typically used with these verbs to indicate that the weather condition is affecting the place where the speaker is located:

Rit'i-**mu**-rqa.   It snowed here.
Wayra-**mu**-chkan.   It is windy here.
Para-**mu**-nqachu?   Will it rain here?

 (**ii**) Physical feelings

Some impersonal verbs can take person object-marking (as also seen in Unit 8):

Anchata chiri-**wan**.   I am very cold.
Yariqa-**sunkichik**-chu?   Are you (all) hungry?

Unquspaqa ukhuy rupha-**wan**.   Being ill, my insides feel hot.
Ruphaypi purispa sinchita ch'aki-**wayku**.   Walking in the heat has made us very thirsty.

This is the conjugation for impersonal verbs to talk about physical feelings in the present tense; as also noted in Unit 8, person object–marking is not needed in 3rd person:

(ñuqata) chiri-**wa**-n	I am cold	(ñuqanchikta) chiri-**wanchik**	we are cold (incl.)
		(ñuqaykuta) chiri-**wayku**	we are cold (excl.)
(qamta) chiri-**sunki**	you are cold	(qamkunata) chiri-**sunkichik**	you (pl.) are cold
(payta) chiri-**n**	he/she is cold	(paykunata) chiri-**n**	they are cold

If the object is named, it takes the direct-object marker **-ta** before an impersonal verb:

Qam-**ta** chiri-**sunki**-chu?   Are you cold?
Juan-**ta** chirin.   Juan is cold.

Wak k'askaq / Class-Free Suffix

    -**chá**

       Indicates conjecture, possibility, doubt; dubitative function

This suffix indicates possibility or doubt about the event or action referred to:

Qhipan wata tata Francisco-**chá** alférez kanqa.   Next year Francisco will probably be fiesta sponsor.
Atisaq-**chá**.   Perhaps I shall be able to do it.
Waqyamuchkayki-**chá**.   I shall probably call you.
Watapaq kutimusqayku-**chá**.   We shall probably come back next year.

Ruwana / Exercises

1 Juk ⌘ Qillqana / Written Work

Read the introductory dialogue again and answer the following questions in Quechua:

1. Pitaq unqun?
   _____

2. Pitaq jamun?
   _____

3. Imapaqtaq chay jampiri jamun?
   _____

4. Imantaq Rubénta nanan?
   _____

5. Maypitaq chankanta nanachikun?
   _____

6. Imaynataq kachkan?
   _____

7. Imatataq jampiri tullu p'akisqapaq churanqa?
   _____

8. Imatataq jampiri punkisqapaq churanqa?

9. Jayk'aqtaq chay jampiri kutimunqa ñin?

10. Qamrí, unqusqa kaspa imatataq ruwanki?

2 Iskay ⌘ Qillqana / Written Work

(i) Change the following sentences into the future tense as in the model:

Kunan p'unchaw jampiri jamun. (q'aya) >>> Q'aya p'unchaw jampiri jamunqa.
Today the doctor came. (tomorrow) >>> Tomorrow the doctor will come.

1. Qayna wata Francisco yachay wasiman rirqa (jamuq wata)

2. Kunan Rubén jampita upyan (q'aya)

3. Qam jampiq runata waqyanki (minchha)

4. Qayna p'unchaw Franciscowan tinkurqani (q'aya minchha)

5. Ñuqayku fiestapi macharqayku (jamuq wata)

(ii) Change the following sentences into the future tense as in the model:

Llaqtaman rinki. (ñuqa) >>> Ñuqapis llaqtaman rillasaqtaq.
You go to town. (I) >>> And I shall also go to town.

1. Jamuq wata Boliviaman risaq. (ñuqayku)

2. Minchha tusuq jamunqa. (qam)

3. Lunesta paykuna pukllanqanku. (ñuqanchik)

4. Q'aya tinkupi maqanakunqanku. (pay)

5. Jamuq semanata allquyta vacunachisaq. (qam)

3 Kimsa ⌘ Rikuna / Browse   ▶ DVD

(i) Go to the following section of the *Kawsay Vida* multimedia program:

Bolivian Quechua > Kawsay > Rikuna > Q'aya

Browse the exercise, noting the use of the future tense and any new vocabulary.

(ii) Go to the following section of the *Kawsay Vida* multimedia program:

Bolivian Quechua > Kawsay > Yachana > Q'aya imatataq ruwanqanku

Do the interactive exercise on-screen, noting the use of the future tense and any new vocabulary.

4 Tawa ⌘ Qillqana / Written Work

Answer the questions, using possessive markers and person object-marking in the verb where appropriate, as shown in the model:

Qamta imaykitaq nanasunki? (uma)	>>>	Ñuqata umay nanawan.
Rubénta imantaq nanan? (chanka)	>>>	Rubénta chankan nanan.
Qamta chirisunkichu?	>>>	Arí, chiriwan.

1. Qamta imaykitaq nanasunki? (kiru)   _____
2. Payta imantaq nanan? (wiksa)   _____
3. Qamta yariqasunkichu? (arí/mana)   _____
4. Qamkunata imaykichiktaq nanasunkichik? (uma)   _____
5. Paykunata ch'akichkanchu?   _____
6. Qamkunatarí ruphasunkichikchu?   _____

5 Phichqa ⌘ Yachana / Practice

Practice the use of object-marking in the verb. Match the Quechua sentences on the right with the English translations on the left:

1. He sees me.   A. Uyariwankichu?
2. Are you hungry?   B. Waqyayki.
3. I'm cold.   C. Yanapawayku.
4. They heal me.   D. Rikuwan.
5. Can you hear me?   E. Wayra unquchisunki.
6. She sees herself.   F. Yariqasunkichu?
7. He helps us.   G. Chiriwan.
8. Are you all hot?   H. Rikukun.
9. I call you.   I. Jampiwanku.
10. The wind has made you ill.   J. Q'uñisunkichikchu?

6 Suqta ⌘ Qillqana / Written Work

Describe weather conditions in different parts of the world, using the vocabulary suggested below. Follow the model and elaborate according to your own ideas:

puna; wayray   >>>   Punapi anchata wayran.

puna	chiriy
yunka	ruphay
valle	rit'iy
Amazonía ñisqa	paray
Inglaterra	chikchiy
Suecia	wayray
Africa	qhasay

1. _____
2. _____
3. _____
4. _____
5. _____
6. _____
7. _____

7 Qanchis ⌘ Parlana / Oral Work

Ask and answer questions with your classmates; use person object–marking in the verb where appropriate:

1. Chirisunkichu?
2. Helado gustasunkichu?
3. Ch'akisunkichikchu?
4. Yariqasunkichu?
5. Pitaq waqyasunkichik?
6. Payta q'uñichkanchu?
7. Waqyawankichu?
8. Imaykitaq nanasunki?
9. Imataq unquchisunki?
10. Pikunataq waqyawanku?

8 Pusaq ⌘ Parlana, qillqana / Oral and Written Work

Answer the questions using the conjectural suffix **-chá**, as in the model:

Imataq Rubénta unquchin? (chiri)	>>>	Chirichá unquchin.
What made Rubén ill?	>>>	The cold must have made him ill.

1. Imataq Maríata unquchin? (wayra) _____
2. Imataq Rubénta puñuchin? (jampi) _____
3. Imataq qamta machachisunki? (aqha) _____
4. Pitaq payta waqyachin? (fiesta ruwaq) _____
5. Juan, pipaqtaq jampita rantichkan? (tatan) _____
6. Maymantataq jamuchkanku? (Sucre) _____

9 Jisq'un ⌘ Junt'achina / Video Exercise   ▶ DVD

Go to the following section of the *Kawsay Vida* multimedia program:

Bolivian Quechua > Fiesta > Junt'achina > Tinkumanta jampiy

Do both the video and audio gap-fill exercises in this section. There are three levels of difficulty here; you can work through each text three times with different gaps to fill each time.

17 / Chunka qanchisniyuq

Feriaman riy / Going to Market

In This Unit...

You visit the market in San Pedro de Buenavista and learn how to negotiate a purchase. You study the imperative forms of the verb; and expressions of courtesy and respect. You meet person object-markers in imperative forms of the verb.

KAWSAY / ANDEAN LIFE
Trade and Markets

Traditionally, trade in the Andes takes the form of exchange and barter, a system that allows people to make the most of the diversity of crops available at different altitudes. The key economic strategy of the ayllu was to occupy land in different ecological zones, to ensure access to a full range of produce. In the Bolivian Andes a familiar sight, becoming rarer today, is a train of llamas carrying goods from the altiplano down to the warm valleys to trade with extended family members: for example, people barter salt and potatoes from the highlands for corn at the lower altitude. After the arrival of the Europeans, a capitalist economic system gradually took hold and market trading for money evolved. Even today, in provincial towns and villages, markets are not necessarily a weekly affair, but are associated with the festive season. In San Pedro de Buenavista, for example, the market appears at the feast of San Pedro and San Pablo (June 28 and 29); throughout the rest of the year people rely on small shop traders for industrially produced items, and subsistence farming for their main food needs.

Suggested reading: Larson and Harris 1995; Harris 2000.

Kay chumpita iskay chunkapi vendeni.

Ñawirina, yachakuna / Read and Learn

Kay pantita apakuy ari!	Take this red one!
Kayman tiyarikuychik!	Do sit down here (all of you)!
Machkhapitaq vendenki?	How much is it?
Kimsa chunkapi qusqayki.	I'll let you have it for 30 [pesos].

Qhawana / Video View ▶ DVD

Go to the following section in the *Kawsay Vida* multimedia program:

Bolivian Quechua > Kawsay > Qhawana > Berno kawsay ganaymanta

Watch the video and listen to don Berno talk about his life as a market trader. Then study the *Introduction* and *Dialogue* below, in which don Berno tries to sell his goods to some customers, with Rosaleen Howard looking on.

Qallarina / Introduction

Tata Franciscowan mama Consuelo warminwan San Pedro feriapi kachkanku. Paykunaqa pollerata mama Consuelopaq rantiyta munanku. Pollerasta akllachkanku. Pollerasqa imaymana llimp'iyuq t'ikasniyuq ima kanku. Paykunaqa machkhapitaq polleras kanku ñispa tapurinku. Don Berno ñin «Apakuy ari, kimsa chunkapi qusqayki,» ñispa panti pollerata rikuchin.

Parlana / Dialogue

Berno (B): – Tatáy, kayta treintapi qusqayki.

Consuelo (C): – Yanas achkha kan.

Francisco (F): – Mayqintataq munankiri?

C: – Ajina pantita munani.

B: – A, ya listo, apakuy ari.

F: – Rantisqayki, k'achitu ¿i?

B: – Apankichu?

F: – Apasaq.

C: – Machkhapi vendenki?

B: – Kimsa chunkapi.

Rosaleen (RH): – Pipaqtaqri?

F: – Señoraypaq.

RH: – Señoraykipaqchu?

F: – Señoraypaqpuni.

RH: – Kay, imataq sutin?

F: – Chay, pollera.

RH: – Kay dibujos, qhichwapi imatataq ñinki?

F: – Qhichwapi chayqa t'ikas.

RH: – T'ikas. Gustasunkichikchu?

F: – Gustawayku.

RH: – Qamta gustasunkichu mamáy?

C: – Gustawan.

Simi / Vocabulary

Ruway / Verbs

quy: to give.
rebajay: to give a discount.
yapay: to give an extra portion (in a sale).

Suti / Nouns

arus (Sp. *arroz*): rice.
arwija (Sp. *arveja*): peas.
jawas (Sp. *habas*): broad beans.
k'api: a handful.
latanu (Sp. *plátano*): bananas.
lichi (Sp. *leche*): milk.
luqutu: variety of hot pepper.
lurasnu (Sp. *durazno*): peaches.

misk'ichana: sugar.
qutu: pile.
sapa juk: each one.
siwulla (Sp. *cebolla*): onion.
tumati (Sp. *tomate*):[1] tomatoes.

Suti tikrachiq / Adjectives

astawan jatun: bigger.
astawan juch'uy: smaller.
bordadoyuq: embroidered.
k'acha : pretty.
llimp'iyuq: colored.
saltasniyuq: with decorative weave.

Tapuq suti ranti / Interrogative Pronouns

machkhapi?: how much for?
mayqin?: which one?

Rantinapaq / Shopping Expressions

caserito/caserita!: term of address between seller and customer.
qusqayki: "I shall give you."
Rantikuway!: "Buy it from me [for yourself]!"
Rantipuway!: "Buy it for me!"
rantisqayki : "I shall buy from you."
Rebajariway!: "Give me a discount!"
Wakta rikuchiway!: "Show me another!"
Yapariway!: "Give me a little extra!"

Simip k'askaynin / Grammar

Ruway k'askaq / Verb Suffixes

-y/-ychik

Assertive direct imperative marker

Regarding imperative forms, Quechua distinguishes between the direct imperative ("come here!") and the indirect form ("let him/her come!") and between the assertive and negative imperatives.

The assertive direct imperative forms are as follows:

Singular		Plural	
kayman jamu-**y**!	come here!	kayman jamu-**ychik**!	come here! (all of you)
kayta mikhuri-**y**!	eat this please!	kayta mikhuri-**ychik**!	eat this! (all of you)
kayta apaku-**y**!	take this for yourself!	kayta apaku-**ychik**!	take this for yourselves!
allinta uyari-**y**!	listen well!	allinta uyari-**ychik**!	listen well (all of you!)

---

1. The food terms in this list are in common use in the marketplace; they derive from Spanish but are pronounced according to Quechua sound rules, and are well assimilated into the language; for this reason we spell them in the "rephonologized" way.

In the singular form the imperative marker coincides with the form of the infinitive ending **-y**. Interpretation of this form is thus dependent on context.

ama ... -chu
Negative direct imperative construction

The negative direct imperative form (prohibition) is constructed by placing **ama** before the verb, and the negative particle **-chu** after the verb:

ñiway!	tell me!	**ama** ñiway-**chu**!	don't tell me!
ñiwaychik!	tell me (all of you)!	**ama** ñiwaychik-**chu**!	don't (you all) tell me!
qhaway!	look!	**ama** qhaway-**chu**!	don't look!
qhawaychik!	look (all of you)!	**ama** qhawaychik-**chu**!	don't (you all) look!

The particle **ama** may be combined with **–raq** to give the meaning of "don't ... yet":

ama riy-chu!	don't go!	**ama-raq** riy-**chu**!	don't go yet!
ama riychik-chu!	don't (you all) go	**ama-raq** riychik-**chu**!	don't (you all) go yet
ama parlay-chu!	don't speak!	**ama-raq** parlay-**chu**!	don't speak yet!
ama parlaychik-chu!	don't (you all) speak yet!	**ama-raq** parlaychik-**chu**!	don't (you all) speak yet!

Person object–marking in imperative forms

Person object–marking is placed before the imperative suffix in the verb:

rikurichiy!	show it!	>>>	rikurichi-**wa**-y!	show it to me!
uyariychik!	listen (you all)!	>>>	uyari-**wa**-ychik!	listen to me (you all)!

-ri-
Inceptive function

The verb suffix **-ri-** lends itself to a range of, probably interrelated, interpretations. It is used to indicate (**i**) that the action of the verb is just beginning (inceptive); (**ii**) that the action is just carried out a little bit; (**iii**) as a mark of courtesy in imperatives.

(i)	Fiestapi kusi-**ri**-kunku	They start to get happy in the fiesta.
(ii)	Kayta mikhu-**ri**-y mamáy!	Eat a little of this, ma'am!
(iii)	Kaypi tiya-**ri**-kuychik!	Please take a seat here (all of you)!
(iii)	Qullqita qu-**ri**-way!	Please give me some money!
(iii)	Rebaja-**ri**-way!	Please give me a discount!

-yku-
(**i**) Movement inward; (**ii**) movement downward; (**iii**) courtesy marker

The suffix **-yku-** indicates that an action (**i**) is taking place in an inward direction; (**ii**) involves a movement from up to down. (**iii**) On imperative forms it is used to mark courtesy. The three interpretations may be interrelated in some contexts.

(i)	Chay allquta wasiman apa-**yku**-y!	Take the dog into the house!
(ii)	Aqhata upya-**yku**-sqanku.	They drank down the chicha.
(iii)	Kay pollerata chura-**yku**-kuy!	Do try on this pollera!

Suti k'askaq / Noun Suffixes

-pi

Used in asking and giving prices

The suffix **-pi** is used in the following way to ask about and to express prices of goods:

| Kay ch'ulluta machkha-**pi**-taq vendenki? | How much is this ch'ullu? [lit. "In how much do you sell this ch'ullu?"] |
| Chunka phichqayuq-**pi**. | It's fifteen (pesos) [lit. "It's in fifteen."] |

Ruwana / Exercises

1 Juk ⌘ Parlana / Oral Work

(i) Read and study the following dialogue. Practice it with a partner.

Rantikuq (R): – Imaynalla caserito/caserita!
Vendeq (V): – Jamuy, jamuy caserito/caserita!
R: – Chay ch'ullu machkhapitaq?
V: – Iskay chunka phichqayuqpi qusqayki
R: – Rikurichiway!
V: – Kay, k'achitu!
R (umanman churaykuspa): – Ancha jatun kachkan, astawan juch'uyta munani
V: – Kayqa astawan juch'uy caserito
R: – Yanayuqta yuraqniyuqta munani, kanchu?
V: – Mana kanchu. Kay pukata aparikuy! Rebajarisqayki!
R: – Mana pukata munanichu. Jinaqa chay yana sombrerota apakusaq. Machkhapitaq?
V: – Sombreroqa phichqa chunkapi.
R: – Rebajariway caserita! Tawa chunkapi quway.
V: – Jina, tawa chunka phichqayuqpi apakuy!
R: – Kayqa, caserita.
V: – Kayqa cambioyki. Tinkunakama!
R: – Tinkunakama!

(ii) Based on the introductory text and the above dialogue, practice buying and selling items of clothing in the marketplace. In your conversation, use the imperative forms, object-marking in the verbs, and relevant expressions provided in this unit. Follow the suggestions below and/or use your own ideas.

Greet the salesperson.
S/he greets you and asks what you are looking for.
Say what you are looking for.
She shows you various items and asks which one you like.
Ask her to show you a particular item.
She hands it to you, saying it's nice.
You ask how much it is.
She tells you the price.
Say you want a different one (*in a different color, bigger, smaller*, etc.).
She does not have exactly what you want.
Decide on a different item and ask how much it is.

She tells you the price.
You ask for a discount and negotiate a price.
You pay her and say goodbye.

2 Iskay ⌘ Qillqana / Written Work

Practice the direct imperative forms.

(i) Convert the following negative statements into direct imperatives, as shown in the model:

Mana yachay wasiman rinkichu.   >>>   Yachay wasiman riy!
Mana radiota uyarinkichikchu.   >>>   Radiota uyariychik!

1. Mana wawaykita qhawankichu.   >>>   _____
2. Mana ch'ulluta rantikunkichu.   >>>   _____
3. Kay wata mana uqata tarpunkichikchu.   >>>   _____
4. Ñuqata mana uyariwankichikchu.   >>>   _____
5. Ñuqaqa mana lurasnuta rantikunichu.   >>>   _____

(ii) Convert the following assertions into negative imperatives, as shown in the model:

Aychata mikhunki.   >>>   Ama aychata mikhuychu!

1. Utqhayta parlanki.   >>>   _____
2. Aqhata upyaykunkichik.   >>>   _____
3. Wasi ukhupi tusunkichik.   >>>   _____
4. Anchata maqanakunki.   >>>   _____
5. Achkha papata qarawanki.   >>>   _____

3 Kimsa ⌘ Parlana / Oral Work

A note on these units of measurement:

Bs. = Bolivian pesos; bolivianos
cents. = céntimos (1/100 Bs.)
1 kilo = 2.2 lbs
1 arroba = 25 lbs (11.5 kg)

qutu = pile; a little pile of onions, garlic, etc., is set up on the market stall and given a unit price
k'api = price relates to a handful (of dry goods)
litro = 2.1 pints

(i) Look at the list of items and prices on the market stall. With a partner, ask and answer questions about the prices of food according to the model:

Machkhapitaq arroba papa?   >>>   Kimsa chunkapi arroba.
Machkhapitaq kilo wallpa aycha?   >>>   Chunka tawayuqpi kilo.

papa = 30 Bs./arroba (12 kilos)
wallpa aycha = 14 Bs./kilo
uqa = 6 Bs./cuartilla (¼ arroba; 3 kilos)
manzana = 2 Bs./sapa juk
queso [kisu] = 20 Bs./kilo
tumati = 8 Bs./qutu
luqutu = 12 Bs./qutu
jawas = 10 Bs./qutu
arwija = 6 Bs./qutu

t'anta = 5 cents/sapa juk
kachi = 2 Bs./kilo
lurasnu = 20 Bs./kilo
misk'ichana = 4 Bs./kilo
siwulla = 10 Bs./k'api
leche [lichi] = 5 Bs./litro
plátano [latanu] = 5 Bs./veinticinco
arroz [arus] = 8 Bs./kilo
kinwa = 10 Bs./kilo

(ii) Now practice talking about the food you plan to buy, following the model:

Qamrí, imakunatataq rantiyta munanki?   >>>   Kilo lurasnuta, iskay manzanata, k'api cebollata . . . ima rantisaq.

4 Tawa ⌘ Yachana / Browse   ▶ DVD

Go to the following section in the *Kawsay Vida* multimedia program:

Bolivian Quechua > Kawsay > Yachana > K'askarachinapaq (2)

Do the exercise, following the on-screen instructions.

5 Phichqa ⌘ Junt'achina / Video Exercise   ▶ DVD

Go to the following section in the *Kawsay Vida* multimedia program:

Bolivian Quechua > Kawsay > Junt'achina > Berno kawsay ganaymanta

Follow the on-screen instructions, and do (i) the audio and (ii) the video gap-fill exercises. You can work through each text three times, gradually increasing the level of difficulty.

18 / Chunka pusaqniyuq

Mikhunata ruway / Preparing Food

In This Unit...

You hear doña Roberta Villanueva describe the process of making pelado (peeled corn). You work on describing processes and forming complex sentences, using the suffixes of verbal subordination **-pti-** and **-spa-**. You practice verb suffixes **-ri-** and **-yku-**.

KAWSAY / ANDEAN LIFE
Foods

The Andean highlands are home to a vast range of food crops, which are indigenous to the region and have been cultivated here for millennia. The most famous of course is the potato, imported from the New World to Europe in the sixteenth century. The potato is a high-altitude crop in the Andean setting, grown above 9,000 feet above sea level; it exists in many varieties—all of which have names in Quechua—and these names vary from one region to another. The ancient Andeans developed technologies for conserving potatoes, to guard against crop failure in any year. Most well known is ch'uñu, prepared through a process of dehydration, whereby the potato is subjected to alternations of heat and cold in the dry summer months; ch'uñu can be conserved for years, and needs thorough rehydration before it is consumed in soups or as a side dish. Corn, a warm valley crop grown at altitudes between 6,000 and 9,000 feet above sea level, similarly grows in many varieties and colors, and is put to a multitude of different uses as a foodstuff. Corn is also ground and brewed to produce an alcoholic beer known as chicha ("aqha" in Quechua), most prized by the Incas, and an essential feature of the Andean fiestas today.
  Suggested reading: Weismantel 1998; Krögel 2012.

Jatun paylapi yaku timpuchispa papasta chayachinku.

Ñawirina, yachakuna / Read and Learn

Yaku t'impuriptin uchphata churanchik.	When the water starts to boil, we put in the ash.
Sarata mayllakuspataq ch'akichinchik.	And when we have washed the corn, we dry it.

Qallarina / Introduction

Doña Roberta yuraq sarata lluch'unanpaq pelado ñisqapaq wakichichkan, chaypaq sarata muchhachkan. Peladopaq ñawpaqta yakuta paylaman churan. Chantá uchphatawan churaykun. Chay uchpha t'impuptintaq sarata jich'aykun. Chaymanta qaywin. Qaywiptintaq sarap qaran ch'utaran. Allinta ch'utaraptintaq sarata paylamanta jurqhupun. Jurqhuspataq ch'uya yakuwan mayllan. Mayllaspataq ch'akichin. Pelado ch'akiptintaq chayachispa mikhunchik. Chayqa sara lluch'usqa mut'i.

Parlana / Dialogue

Rosaleen (RH): – Chay yuraq sara . . .
Roberta (R): – Yuraq sara . . .
RH: – Arí. Imapaqtaq?
R: – Peladopaq.
RH: – Imaynataq peladota ruwankichik?
R: – Primerota churanchik perolman, paylaman, yakuta.
RH: – Arí.
R: – Chay jawataq uchphata t'impuriptin . . .
RH: – A, uchphawanchu?
R: – Uchphata churanchik.

RH: – Chantá?
R: – Chay uchpha t'impuriptintaq sarata jich'aykunchik, muchhaspa. Arí.
RH: – Chantá?
R: – Chaymantaqa qaywinchik qaywinchik, ch'utaran qarasnin.
RH: – Qarasninchu?
R: – Qarasnin ch'utaran. Allillanlla kaptintaq jinarispaqa jurqhupunchik. Arí.
RH: – Chantarí?
R: – Jurqhuspataq mayllanchik yakuwan. Arí. Mayllakuspataq ch'akichinchik.
RH: – A, ch'akichinkichik.
R: – Ch'akichinchik. Ajinata peladota ruwanchik.
RH: – Hmm. Chantarí listoñachu?
R: – Chaywanqa listo a. Ch'akillanña. Ch'akiptintaq chayachispa mikhullanchikña.
RH: – Ajinata ruwankichik.
R: – Ajinata ruwayku.

(Adapted from a conversation between Roberta Villanueva and Rosaleen Howard, San Pedro de Buenavista, Northern Potosí, Bolivia, summer 1989)

Simi / Vocabulary

Ruway / Verbs

    chayachiy: to cook (*trans.*).
    ch'akichiy: to dry (*trans.*).
    ch'utaray: to peel off (multiple items).
    ch'utay: to peel off; to displace outward by pressure.
    jich'ay: to pour (liquids, grains).
    jinay: to do thus.
    jurqhupuy: to take out at once.
    lluch'uy: to peel off.
    muchhay: to strip corn from the cob.
    puquy: to grow, to mature; to ferment.
    qaywiy: to stir.
    qhatay: to cover over.
    tantakuy: to meet up, to gather together (*trans.*).
    t'impuchiy: to boil (*trans.*).
    t'impuy: to boil (*intrans.*).

Suti / Nouns

    jilanqu: traditional political leader.
    payla: large cooking vessel.
    pelado [peladu]: peeled corn.
    uchpha: ash.

Suti tikrachiq / Adjectives

    ch'uya [ch'uwa]: clear, translucent.

Simip k'askaynin / Grammar
Ruway k'askaq / Verb Suffixes

-**pti**- [-qti-]

Subordinate verb marker in complex sentences

In Unit 12 we saw how -**spa** marks the subordinate verb in complex sentences where the subjects of the main verb and the subordinate verb are the same. Here we look at how -**pti**- (pronounced [-qti-]) is used to construct complex sentences where the subjects of the main verb and the subordinate verb are different.

In the case of -**pti**- the meanings of such complex sentences may be rendered in English through the use of temporal or causal clauses, for example:

"When you get here, I'll tell you."
"When he saw me, I ran away."
"When their father died, the children went to live with their grandparents."
"If you come, we'll go for a walk."
"As it was raining, we stayed at home."

-**pti**- is used when the main verb in the sentence has a different subject from that of the subordinate verb(s). The subordinate verb form with -**pti**- is also marked for person.

Sara puqu-**pti**-**n** sumaqta mikhusunchik.   When the corn ripens, we shall eat well.

In 'puqu-**pti**-**n**' the 3rd-person singular is marked with -**n**.

By contrast, -**spa** is used when the subject of the main verb and the subordinate verb(s) is one and the same.

Boliviaman rispa sara lluch'usqa mut'ita mikhusaq.   When I go to Bolivia, I shall eat peeled corn.

In the case of -**pti**- there may be a relationship (i) of cause or (ii) of condition, between the main verb and the subordinate verb:

(i) Indicates causal relationship

Kay wata mana paramu-**pti**-n sara mana puqunchu.   This year, as it didn't rain, the corn didn't grow.
Qullqiy ka-**pti**-n p'achata rantikuni.   As I have some money, I buy myself some clothes.
Qam muna-**pti**-yki Boliviaman jamunchik.   As you wanted to, we have come to Bolivia.

(ii) Indicates conditional relationship

Paramu-**pti**-n-**qa** sara puqunqa.   If it rains here, the corn will grow.
Qullqiyki ka-**pti**-n-**qa** p'achata rantikuy!   If you have some money, buy yourself some clothes!
Qam muna-**pti**-yki-**qa** Boliviaman risunchik.   If you want to, we shall go to Bolivia.

Note the use of the topic marker -**qa** in the conditional examples; this prevents any ambiguity in certain contexts.

-**pti**- + person suffixes

Used in formation of subordinate clauses

The subject of the subordinate verb is marked by a person suffix. Formally speaking, the person markers correspond to the possessive series of person suffixes:

chaya-**pti**-y fiesta qallarikurqa	when I arrived the party began	chaya-**pti**-yku	when we (excl.) arrived...
		chaya-**pti**-nchik	when we (incl.) arrived...
chaya-**pti**-yki	when you arrived...	chaya-**pti**-ykichik	when you (pl.) arrived...
chaya-**pti**-n	when she/he arrived...	chaya-**pti**-nku	when they arrived...

The -**pti**- form of the verb is not marked for tense; tense marking is found in the main verb phrase, as in the above conjugation where the past tense is marked on "qallariku-**rqa**."

-ra-

Indicates action with dispersed subject or object

(i) The suffix -**ra**- indicates that the action of the verb is performed "in many pieces" or is distributed to different recipients:

p'akiy	to break (solids)	>>>	p'aki-**ra**-y	to break into pieces
watay	to tie	>>>	wata-**ra**-y	to tie lots of things up together

-**ra**- may lend a negative idiomatic connotation to some verbs:

qhaway	to look at something	>>> qhawa-**ra**-y	to criticize

(ii) -**ra**- may indicate that the action of the verb is reversed or undone.

watay	to tie	>>>	wata-**ra**-y	to untie
qhatay	to cover	>>>	qhata-**ra**-y	to uncover

Ruwaykuna / Exercises

1 Juk ⌘ Qillqana / Written Work

Answer the questions about the introductory text, in Quechua:

1. Imatataq doña Roberta wakichichkan?

_____

2. Peladota ruwanapaq ñawpaqta paylaman imatataq churan?

_____

3. Uchpha t'impuptin imatataq paylaman jich'aykun?

_____

4. Sarap qarasnin allinta ch'utaraptin imatataq ruwan?

_____

5. Ch'akichisparí peladota mikhunapaq imatataq ruwana?

_____

2 Iskay ⌘ Qillqana / Written Work

Answer the following questions to practice the use of **-pti-**.

Q'uñimuptin imatataq ruwankichik? (yakuta upyay)   >>>   Q'uñimuptin yakuta upyayku.

1. Paramuptin, sara imanantaq? (puquy)
_____

2. Wayramuptin, imanasunkitaq? (chiriy)
_____

3. Jilanqu chayamuptin, imatataq ruwarqankichik? (tantakuy)
_____

4. Yariqasuptin, imanarqankitaq? (mikhuy)
_____

5. Chayaptiyki, tatayki imatataq ruwanqa? (llamk'aq lluqsiy)
_____

6. Warmikuna mayupi t'aqsaptinku, imapitaq yanaparqanki (p'achankuta ch'akichiy)
_____

3 Kimsa ⌘ Qillqana / Written Work

The following sentences describe the process of making pelado, according to doña Roberta. List them in the correct chronological order.

A. Qarasnin allinta ch'utaraptin paylamanta jurqhupunku.
B. Ch'akiptintaq sarata chayachinku.
C. Paylaman yakuta t'impunanpaq churanku.
D. Sara chayaptintaq mikhurikunku.
E. Yaku t'impuriptin uchphata churanku.
F. Munaptinkuqa uchuwanpis peladota mikhullankutaq.
G. Mayllaspataq ch'akichinku.
H. Sarata qaywiptintaq qarasnin ch'utaran.
I. Jurqhuspataq yakuwan mayllanku.
J. Uchpha t'impuriptintaq sarata jich'aykunku.

4 Tawa ⌘ Junt'achina / Video Exercise   ▶ DVD

Go to the following section in the *Kawsay Vida* multimedia program:

Bolivian Quechua > Fiesta > Junt'achina > Aqhaymanta

Do both the video and audio gap-fill exercises in this section. There are three levels of difficulty here; you can work through each text three times with different gaps to fill each time.

19 / Chunka jisq'unniyuq

Inkamanta / About the Incas

In This Unit...

You meet don Celestino Fernández, who speaks about the curse of the Inca. This text comes from the play entitled *Tragedia del fin de Atahuallpa* (Lara 1989), which portrays the death of the Inca emperor Atahuallpa at the Spaniards' hands. You learn to talk about socioeconomic differences and natural resources. You study the imperative forms of verbs and the contrastive use of the verb suffixes **-mu-**, **-ku-**, and **-pu-**.

KAWSAY / ANDEAN LIFE
The Conquest of the Incas

The arrival of a small band of Spaniards in northern Peru in the early part of the sixteenth century, and its devastating consequences for the indigenous populations of the Andes, including the Incas, left a lasting mark in the cultural memory of Andean people. This memory is expressed, among other ways, in a popular theatrical tradition whereby, on certain festive occasions, townspeople perform a reenactment of the critical encounter at Cajamarca in November 1532. The play, which depicts the Incas and the Spaniards attempting to understand each others' languages and each others' motives, takes a number of different forms: in some locations the script is in Quechua and Spanish, in other places the play is more of a dance drama without words, and, in the case of the version that was written down in Bolivia by the indigenist writer Jesús Lara, the communication breakdown between the two parties is expressed by the Incas speaking in Quechua to the Spaniards, while when the latter speak only their lips move and no words can be heard. The exchanges between the two parties are interpreted by a character called Felipillo, an actual historical personage who, according to eyewitness accounts, was present on the fateful day at Cajamarca. The play was still performed in San Pedro de Buenavista up until the early 1980s. Don Celestino Fernández, an old man at the time we interviewed him in 1989, remembered taking part.

Suggested reading: Beyersdorff 1998; Howard 2002.

Sapa wataqa Orurollaqtapi Inka jina lluqsimunku.

Ñawirina, yachakuna / Read and Learn

Yaykupuy qhapaq kay!	Wealth, go away inside!
Lluqsimuy wakcha kay!	Poverty, come out here!
Sapa jukpis yawarninkuwan kawsayta yachachunku.	Let each one learn to live by their (own) blood.
Pipaqtaq apapuchkan?	Whom is s/he carrying it for?
Mamanpaq apapuchkan.	S/he is carrying it for his/her mother.
Tata Jasintu apapuchun.	Let don Jacinto take it for her/him.

Qallarina / Introduction

Unay pacha, waranqa phichqa pachak kimsa chunka iskayniyuq watapi, españa awqa runa kay chhiqaman, América ñisqaman, chayamusqanku ñin. Paykunaqa kay jallp'akunapi, qhapaq kayninta, runakunamanta qichusqanku. Chaymantapacha colonización ñisqa kay jallp'api qallarisqa.

San Pedro de Buenavistapi, Norte de Potosípi, sapa wata Inkakunata yuyariq kanku. Fiestapi wakin runaqa Inka Atawallpamanta parlaq kanku. Kay Inkaqa españa awqa runap makinpi wañusqa. Wañuy patapi kachkaspataq payqa kay jinata rimasqa: 'Yaykupuy qhapaq kay, lluqsimuy wakcha kay. Sapa jukpis yawarninkuwan kawsayta yachachunku' ñispa.

Chaymantapacha españoles ñisqa urqu ukhupi, sach'a sach'a ukhupi ima, qurita qullqita mask'aspa indio runakunawan jurqhuchisqanku. Ajinamanta Qhapaq Urqu ukhupi qhuyakunata kicharispa mitayu runata llamk'achisqanku.[1]

[1]. "Qhapaq Urqu" is the Quechua term for "Cerro Rico," the name of the mountain that dominates the skyline of the city of Potosí, where silver mining in the Americas was at its height in the colonial period, and where many thousands of *mitayos* perished.

Simi / Vocabulary

Ruway / Verbs

    apapuy: to carry for someone.
    ch'allay: to spill; to sprinkle liquid in ritual offering.
    kichariy: to open.
    lluqsimuy: to come out here (*toward speaker*).
    puchuy: to be left over.
    qichuy: to take something away from someone; to pillage.
    rimay: to declare, to pronounce.
    ripuy: to go away; depart.
    ruwapuy: to do for another person.
    sayk'upuy: to get tired out.
    tariy: to find.
    tukukuy: to become.
    tukupuy: to turn into something else.
    urmay: to fall.
    yaykupuy: to go inside for good.

Suti / Nouns

    anta: copper.
    awqa: enemy.
    awqa sunkha: bearded enemy.
    españa [ispaña]: Spaniard.
    jump'i: sweat.
    kachipampa: salt lake.
    kawsay: life.
    kay: being, existence.
    mitayu: enforced laborer.
    qhapaq kay: riches, wealth.
    qhatu: marketplace.
    q'illay: iron.
    quri: gold.
    rimay: commandment, declaration.
    rumi: stone; rock.
    rumip sunqun: heart of the rock.
    sach'a: tree; wood, forest.
    sach'a sach'a: forest, jungle.
    sunkha: beard.
    titi: lead (mineral).
    wakcha kay: poverty, destitution.
    wañuy: death.

Suti tikrachiq / Adjectives

    qhapaq: rich.
    wakcha: poor, orphan.

Expression
kaqkamapas: "whatever exists."

Conjunction
chaypis: even if.

Simip k'askaynin / Grammar
Ruway k'askaq / Verb Suffixes

-chun/-chunku

Indirect imperative; "let him/her/them . . ."

The indirect imperatives operate in the 3rd-person singular and plural as follows:

pay takin	he/she sings	pay taki-**chun**	let him, her sing
paykuna takinku	they sing	paykuna taki-**chunku**	let them sing

-na/-nachik

Dual or collective imperatives; "let's . . ."

The dual imperatives exhort to action the 1st person and one other person (-**na**), or the 1st person as part of a collective "we" (-**nachik**):

qamwan ñuqawan taki-**na**	let's (both) sing
ñuqanchik taki-**nachik**	let's (all) sing

-pu-

(i) Benefactive; "for another person"

In this function, -**pu**- indicates that the action is performed for the benefit of another person. The beneficiary is the object of the verb. -**pu**- may occur with the noun suffix -**paq** 'for' in the same sentence; the purposive sense of -**paq** is thus reinforced. There is a sense of pleasure, affection, or obligation in this use of -**pu**-.

Warmin-**paq** ruwa-**pu**-rqa.	He did it for his wife.
Ñañay wawayta qhawa-**pu**-wan.	My sister takes care of my child for me.
Feriapi qam-**paq** pollerata ranti-**pu**-yki.	I bought a skirt for you at the market.
Masiyki chay llikllaykita qu-**pu**-sunki.	Your friend gave you your awayo.

In this function -**pu**- can be contrasted with -**ku**-. While -**pu**- shows that the action is for the benefit of the person-object, -**ku**- shows that the action is for the benefit of the person-subject. Compare the following:

llamt'ata apa-**pu**-chka-n	she/he is taking firewood (for someone else)
llamt'ata apa-**ku**-chka-n	s/he is taking firewood (for him/herself)

(ii) Indicates centrifugal direction; movement away from speaker

With verbs of movement -**pu**- indicates movement away from the speaker, for example:

Wasinman ri-**pu**-n.	S/he goes home.
Kanchamanta uwijas lluqsi-**pu**-nku.	The sheep get out of the corral here.

In this function -**pu**- can be contrasted with -**mu**-. While -**mu**- indicates movement toward the speaker (Unit 6), -**pu**- indicates movement away from the speaker. This distinction depends on the orientation of the speaker either in reality or in his/her mind's eye:

yayku-**mu**-n	s/he comes in (toward speaker)
yayku-**pu**-n	s/he goes in (away from speaker)
lluqsi-**mu**-n	s/he comes out (speaker is outside)
lluqsi-**pu**-n	s/he goes out (speaker is inside)

(**iii**) Indicates sudden or definitive action

In other contexts, -**pu**- indicates that the subject of the verb has finally made a decision, or something definitive and/or sudden has occurred, for example:

Wasinman ri-**pu**-n	S/he decided to go home.
Juch'uy llaman wañu-**pu**-n.	Her/his small llama died suddenly.
Inkaqa rimayninwan qurita ukhuman yaykuchi-**pu**-n, ñin.	At his command the Inca made the gold go inside (the ground) forever, it is said.

In this function, -**pu**- may combine with -**ku**-, giving -**kapu**-:

Lawata mikhu-**ku**-n.	He ate the broth with pleasure.
Lawata mikhu-**kapu**-n.	He finally ate up the broth.
Pampapi puñu-**kapu**-n.	He fell asleep on the ground.
Awqa runa qurita apa-**kapu**-n.	The enemies carried off the gold.
Mitayu runapaq kawsay tuku-**kapu**-n.	They ended up living as slaves.

-**y**
  Infinitive: formation of abstract nouns

The suffix -**y**, attached to the verb root to form the infinitive, can give rise to abstract nouns such as:

paqari-**y**	birth; dawn
kawsa-**y**	life
wañu-**y**	death
llaki-**y**	sorrow
kusi-**y**	happiness

The abstract noun **kay** 'existence, being' may be qualified by an adjective to give rise to further concepts:

kay	existence	>>>	qhapaq **kay**	riches; wealth
		>>>	wakcha **kay**	poverty; orphanhood
		>>>	juch'uy **kay**	smallness
		>>>	warmi **kay**	womanhood

As nouns (i.e., verb roots which have been nominalized by the suffix -**y**), these forms take noun suffixes:

kawsay-**ta** munani	I want to live (+ direct-object marker)
Inkap wañuy-ni-**n**	the Inca's death (+ 3rd-person-sing. possessive)
wakcha kay-ni-**nku**	their poverty (+ 3rd-person-pl. possessive)
Patiñop qhapaq kay-ni-**n**	Patiño's wealth (+ 3rd-person-sing. possessive)

Ruwana / Exercises

1 Juk ⌘ Waturikuna / Analysis

Interpret the location of the speaker in relation to the following utterance. What is the cultural significance of the phrase in the context of the conquest of the Incas?

Yaykupuy qhapaq kay, lluqsimuy wakcha kay.

2 Iskay ⌘ Parlana, qillqana / Oral and Written Work

Ask and answer questions according to the example, using the suffix **-pu-** in your answers.

Pipaqtaq chayta ruwachkanki? (tatay)   >>>   Tataypaq ruwapuchkani.

1. Pipaqtaq wallpa uchuta wayk'uchkanki? (wawasniy)
___

2. Pipaqtaq mochilata masiyki qhawachkan? (ñuqa)
___

3. Pipaqtaq cigarrosta rantirqanki? (tata Mariano)
___

4. Pipaqtaq chakrata llamk'achkankichik? (yachachiq)
___

5. Pipaqtaq qhuyamanta qurita jurqhusqanku? (españa runa)
___

3 Kimsa ⌘ Qillqana / Written Work

Add **-pu** to the verbs **boldfaced** in the sentences below. How does this suffix change the meaning of the verb so modified?

tususpa sayk'uni (I got tired dancing)   >>>   tususpa sayk'upuni (I suddenly got tired dancing)

1. Paykunaqa llaqtankuman **rinku**.
___

2. Mamaypaq qullqita **apan**.
___

3. Uwijan qhatupi **wañun**.
___

4. Wawakunaqa wasiman **yaykurqanku**.
___

5. Qhuyapi patronespaq **llamk'aq** kanku.
___

6. T'impusqa sara ruphaywan **ch'akin**.
___

4 Tawa ⌘ Qillqana / Written Work

Change the person orientation of the following sentences by making the necessary grammatical changes, as shown in the model:

Ñuqaqa llamk'akuni. (pay)   >>>   Paypaq llamk'apuni.
I work for myself.   >>>   I work for him/her.

1. Imillaqa papata q'ipikun. (maman)
_____

2. Payqa qullqita apakusqa. (runa)
_____

3. Ayllu runa papata tarpukunqanku. (wak runa)
_____

4. Chay urqupi qurita mask'akurqa. (paykuna)
_____

5. Papallata wayk'ukunku. (tatanku)
_____

6. Llamt'ata apakunku. (wasinku)
_____

5 Phichqa ⌘ Qillqana / Written Work

Fill in the blanks with the suffixes **-mu**-, **-pu**-, or **-ku**- as appropriate:

1. Maymantataq chaya____chkanku?
2. Wasinkuman chaya____chkanku.
3. Kaypi p'achata ranti____yku.
4. Wawaykipaqchu ranti____chkanki?
5. Payqa kayman kuti____n.
6. Wasinman yayku____n.
7. Qamkuna chaymanta lluqsi____ychik!
8. Qamchu llamata qhatiri____rqanki?
9. Tatanpaq kay ch'uspata apa____chkan.
10. Paykuna quri qhuyaman llamk'a____nku.

6 Suqta ⌘ Qillqana / Written Work

Change the following statements into direct or indirect imperatives, as appropriate.

purinki	>>>	puriy!
purinkichik	>>>	puriychik!
purin	>>>	purichun!
purinku	>>>	purichunku!
purinchik	>>>	purina! / purinachik!

1. Qam qurita mask'amunki. _____
2. Paykuna kachita apamunku. _____
3. Tata Juan chakranpi papata tarpun. _____
4. Ñuqanchik wasiman ripunchik. _____
5. Qamkuna llaqtapi llamk'amunkichik. _____
6. Ñuqa qamwan purini. _____
7. Qam ñuqawan purinki. _____
8. Qam llikllata apamunki. _____
9. Pay qhatuman rin. _____

7 Qanchis ⌘ Ñawirinapaqpis, qillqanapaqpis

Read the following speech by Inka Atawallpa from Jesús Lara's play *Tragedia del fin de Atawallpa*. Identify (i) the imperative forms and (ii) the abstract nouns in the text.

Atawallpa parlan:
Awqa sunkha runakuna,
kunanqa, kunanqa
jallp'ataraq pallankichik;
quri qullqi kaqkamapis
rumip sunqunman yaykupuchun.
Chaymanta puchunman chaypis
uchphamanraqtaq tukupuchun.
Yaykupuy qhapaq kay!
Lluqsimuy wakcha kay!
Sapa jukpis qurita munaspa
kallpankuwan tarichunku
yana jump'ita ch'allachispa.

(Lara 1989)

8 Pusaq ⌘ Parlana, qillqana / Oral and Written Work

Use the following vocabulary to answer the questions about where different natural resources are to be found in Bolivia:

qhuya	puna
kachipampa	yunka
mayu	valle
sach'a sach'a	qucha

1. Chay quri qullqi kaq maypitaq mask'amunku?

_____

2. Chay kachita maymantataq q'ipimunki?

_____

3. Yaku maypitaq tarikun?

_____

4. Maypitaq llamt'ata pallakunku?

___

5. Maypitaq tata Andrés wawasninpaq naranjata mask'apun?

___

6. Maypitaq ayllu runa papa puquchinku?

___

7. Maymantataq mama Juana kukata vendeq apakamun?

___

9 Jisq'un ⌘ Qhawana / Video View   ▶ DVD

Go to the following section in the *Kawsay Vida* multimedia program:

Peruvian Quechua > Hampikuy > Qhawana > Hampiqta waturina

Watch the video, and note below the imperative forms that you find in the text.

___

___

___

___

___

___

20 / Iskay chunka

Kamachiqmanta / About the President

In This Unit

We describe the current social and political situation in Bolivia since January 2006, when the indigenous leader Evo Morales was inaugurated as president. You study use of the verb suffix -**sqa**; the verb suffix -**naku**-; and the noun suffixes -**kama** and -**pura**.

KAWSAY / ANDEAN LIFE
Indigenous Political Revival

Bolivia has been undergoing a cultural and political revolution since the election to the presidency of Evo Morales (formerly leader of the tropical lowland coca growers' union yet of highland Aymara origin). Indigenous social movements had been gathering strength in the Andean countries since the late 1970s, reaching a symbolic turning point in 1992 with the quincentennial of the "discovery" of America by Columbus. The decade of the 1990s, with the relaxing of State power in favor of NGO intervention in social programs and policy making, favored the further empowerment of many indigenous organizations. With the turn of the millennium, Bolivians began to mobilize against the neoliberal economic policies of the previous decade, and the path was laid for Morales's victory on an indigenous electoral platform. One of the first actions taken by the government, led by Morales and his Movimiento al Socialismo (MAS) party, was to convene a Constituent Assembly in Sucre for the redrafting of the State Constitution. The document was approved in 2009 and in 2010 the Bolivian Republic was redesignated the Plurinational State of Bolivia, with many indigenous people occupying key posts in government.
Suggested reading: Canessa 2006; Crabtree 2005; Howard 2010.

Sucre llaqtapiqa Asamblea Constituyente ñisqapi tukuy runakuna qutucharqanku.

Ñawirina, yachakuna / Read and Learn

Ayllu runaqa qutuchasqa Sucrekama chayanku.	Grouped together, the people from the ayllus reach Sucre.
Warmikunaqa parlanakuspa llamk'arqanku.	Talking to each other, the women worked.
Runapura jatarisqanku.	The people rose up together.

Qallarina / Introduction

Boliviap kawsayninmanta parlarispa

Estado boliviano ñisqa kay qhipa pachapi pisimanta pisi musuq kawsayman yaykuchkan. Kay suyupiqa unaymantapacha ayllu runa tantanakuspa tukuypis runa jina qhawasqa kayta munaspa, maqanakusqanku. Colonización ñisqamantapacha wakin ayllu runa qunqasqa, karunchasqa, chiqnisqa ima karqanku.

Chayrayku iskay waranqa suqtayuq watapi Sucre llaqtapi Asamblea Constituyente ñisqata wakichinku. Chaypi imaymana runa, tukuy ayllumanta, organizaciones sociales ñisqapi qutuchasqa Sucrekama chayaspa Asambleaman yaykunku. Chaymanta Comisiones ñisqapi rimanakuspa yanapanakuspa ima sinchita llamk'arqanku, Nueva Constitución Política del Estado (NCPE) ñisqata qillqarqanku.

Chaymantataq tata Evo Morales jatun kamachiqwan iskay waranqa chunkayuq watapi Estado Plurinacional de Bolivia ñisqa jatarimun. Kay musuq Estado ñisqapi runakunaqa democracia ukhupi, equidad ukhupi tukuypis allinta kawsayta munanku.

Simi / Vocabulary

Ruway / Verbs

    chiqniy: to despise; to hate.
    jatariy: to rise up.
    karunchay: to marginalize.
    puquchiy: to cultivate.
    phiñakuy: to get angry.

qutuchay: to group together.
thatkiy [thaskiy]: to move forward, to progress.
yuyay: to think.

Past Participles

jurqhusqa: extracted, taken out.
machasqa: drunk.
puqusqa: grown, matured; fermented.
wañusqa: dead.

Suti / Nouns

jatun kamachiq: president.
kamachiq: authority, leader.
kamachiy: law.
phutiy: sorrow.
yura: plant.

Suti tikrachiq / Adjectives

jasa: easy.
kikin: same.
kusa: good.
misk'i: sweet.
sasa: difficult, hard.

Expressions

pachi: "thank you."

Simip k'askaynin / Grammar

Ruway k'askaq / Verb Suffixes

-**sqa**

Nominalizer: past participle

In Unit 11 we saw how -**sqa** is used to construct the indirect past tense. Here we see that it is also a marker of the past participle. Attached to the verb root, it turns the verb into a nominalized form, which then acts as a noun or an adjective.

wañuy	to die	>>>	wañu-**sqa**	dead
unquy	to be ill	>>>	unqu-**sqa**	ill
kusiy	to be happy	>>>	kusi-**sqa**	happy
qutuchay	to group together	>>>	qutucha-**sqa**	grouped together

These examples show the -**sqa** participle in its adjectival function:

Macha-**sqa** kani.	I am drunk.
Kusi-**sqa** kachkanku.	They are happy.
Wañu-**sqa** runaqa aya wasipi kanku.	The dead people are in the cemetery.
Phuchka-**sqa** millmata munankichu.	Do you want the spun wool?

Constituciónqa qillqa-**sqa** kamachiy.	The Constitution is a written law.
Qutucha-**sqa** runa jatarisqanku.	Grouped together, the people rose up.

These examples show the -**sqa** participle in its noun function. The -**sqa** forms may take noun class suffixes such as -**ta**, -**man**, -**manta**, and so on:

Wañu-**sqa**-ta rikuni.	I saw the dead person.
Unqu-**sqa**-ta jampin.	S/he cured the sick person.

In the following examples note the use of the person marker after -**sqa**-. The translation of such forms may require a relative clause in English.

Wañu-**sqa-n**-ta willawarqanku.	They told me that s/he had died.
Chinka-**sqa-y**-ta tarini.	I found what I had lost.

-naku-
Indicates reciprocal action; "each other"

The suffix -**naku**- marks reciprocal action between two or more parties:

Qutuchasqa runa parla-**naku**-nku.	Grouped together, the people talk to each other.
Tinkupi sinchita maqa-**naku**-nku.	In the tinku they fight each other hard.

Noun Suffixes
-kama
Terminative; "until," "as far as"

-**kama** marks the point up to which a movement or action takes place; it marks a limit in space and time:

Jayk'aq-**kama**-taq kakunki?	How long will you be here?
Martes-**kama** kakusaq.	I shall be here until Tuesday.
May-**kama**-taq purirqanku?	How far did they walk?
Urqu pata-**kama** purirqanku.	They walked as far as the top of the mountain.

-pura
"Among"

This suffix is added to a noun root to express the idea of a group or class of the same kind as the subject of the verb:

Warmi-**pura** sinchita llamk'anku.	They work very hard among the women.
Runa-**pura** jatarirqanku.	They rose up among the indigenous people.

Ruwana / Exercises
1 Juk ⌘ Qillqana / Written Work

Turn the verbs into participle forms, using -**sqa**. Add the verb **kay** as in the examples:

Qamkuna machankichik.	>>>	Machasqa kachkankichik.
Ñuqa puñurqani.	>>>	Puñusqa karqani.

1. Mama Elisaqa unqun.   _____
2. Tata Pablo chinkan.   _____
3. Llamaqa wañun.   _____
4. Aqha puqun.   _____
5. Wawakuna puñurqanku.   _____
6. Ayllu runaqa qutuchakusqanku. _____

2 Iskay ⌘ Watuykuna / Analysis

In the following text you will find various different uses of the suffix **-sqa**. Identify them and explain their function in each case.

Chiru Q'asa runas fiestaman risqanku. Achkha aqhata chaypi upyasqanku. Ayllupi ruwasqa aqhata upyasqanku. Puqusqa aqhaqa sumaq kasqa, misk'i kasqa. Wakin runaqa anchatapuni machasqanku. Machasqa runaqa maqanakusqanku. Chaymanta pampallapi puñusqanku. Manaña wasikama chayasqankuchu. Warmisninku machasqankurayku phiñasqa kasqanku ñin.

3 Kimsa ⌘ Parlanakuy / Conversation

Study this imagined conversation between a journalist and a woman delegate to the Constituent Assembly in Bolivia in 2006. Then answer the questions below in English.

Journalist (J): – Imaynalla doña Cristina. Jukta tapurisqayki. Qam Constituyente jina imaynatataq kay llamk'ayta rikunki?
Constituyente (C): – Ñawpaqtaqa pitaq kanki? Imataq sutiyki?
J: – Ñuqaqa TV Canal 7manta kani. Sutiyqa Raúl Cárdenas.
C: – Waliqpacha. Tapurillay!
J: – Ima Comisiónpi kanki doña Cristina?
C: – Ñuqaqa Comisión de Género ñisqapi llamk'achkani. Warmisqa kunankama mana sociedad ñisqapi allintaraqchu uyariwayku.
J: – Imatataq warmikuna mañankichik?
C: – Warmisqa qhariwan khuska llamk'ayku, mana wawasnillaykutachu uywayku, chakrapipis llamk'allaykutaq, chantapis ayllu tantanakuypi rimayta munayku.
J: – Llaqtapi, campopi warmikuna kikillanchu kanku?
C: – Kikillanpuni ari. Llaqtapitaq campopitaq warmiqa llamk'ayku, yanapayku.
J: – Chaypaqrí, imatataq ruwachkankichik?
C: – Mana jasachu, warmipurapis mana kikintachu yuyayku.
J: – Pachi doña Cristina, tinkunakama.
C: – Tinkunakama señor Raúl.

1. Who are the participants in this conversation?
   _____

2. What role does Cristina play in the Constituent Assembly?
   _____

3. What particular demands do the women in the Gender Commission have and why?
_____

4. What makes arguing for equality for women difficult, according to Cristina?
_____

4 Tawa ⌘ Qillqana / Written Work

Ask and answer an initial question in the future tense according to the cue provided; ask a follow-up question to double check the answer, as shown in the model:

| Jayk'aqtaq Sucreman rinki? (tomorrow) | >>> | Q'aya Sucreman risaq. |
| Q'ayachu rinki? | >>> | Q'ayapuni risaq. |

1. Jayk'aqtaq Asambleaman rinkichik? (tomorrow)
_____

2. Jayk'aqtaq yachachiq jamunqa? (this evening)
_____

3. Jayk'aqtaq ayllu runa tantakunkichik? (day after tomorrow)
_____

4. Jayk'aqtaq fiestaman rinqanku? (on Monday)
_____

5. Jayk'aqtaq kay wawayki yachaywasiman rinqa? (next year)
_____

5 Phichqa ⌘ Junt'achina / Video Exercise   ▶ DVD

Go to the following section in the *Kawsay Vida* multimedia program:

Bolivian Quechua > Kawsay > Junt'achina > Vitalio jallp'a tiyaymanta

Do both the video and audio gap-fill exercises in this section. There are three levels of difficulty here; you can work through each text three times with different gaps to fill each time.

21 / Iskay chunka jukniyuq

Yuyarina / Review

A Look Back

Ima k'askaqkunatawantaq kaykama yachakuspa kanchik? What further suffixes have we studied so far?

Verb Conjugation Suffixes

-nki	future tense, 2nd-person singular (Unit 16)
-nkichik	future tense, 2nd-person plural (Unit 16)
-nqa	future tense, 3rd-person singular (Unit 16)
-nqanku	future tense, 3rd-person plural (Unit 16)
-saq	future tense, 1st-person singular (Unit 16)
-sqayku; -saqku	future tense, 1st-person plural, exclusive (Unit 16)
-sun; -sunchik	future tense, 1st-person plural, inclusive (Unit 16)

Verb Suffixes

-chun	indirect imperative, plural (Unit 19)
-chunku	indirect imperative, singular (Unit 19)
-na	futurative nominalizer; encouragement to action (Unit 15)
-na	dual imperative (Unit 19)
-nachik	collective imperative (Unit 19)
-naku-	indicates reciprocal action (Unit 20)
-pti- [-qti]	subordinate verb marker; different subject (Unit 18)
-pu-	benefactive; centrifugal action; definitive action (Unit 19)
-ra-	distributive; action with dispersed subject or object (Unit 18)
-ri-	inceptive action (Unit 17)
-sqa-	past participle (Unit 20)
-sqayki	2nd-person-singular object/1st-person-singular subject (Unit 16)
-sunki	2nd-person-singular object/3rd-person subject (Unit 16)
-sunkichik	2nd-person-plural object/3rd-person subject (Unit 16)

-wanchik	1st-person plural, inclusive, object marker (Unit 16)
-wayku	1st-person plural, exclusive, object marker (Unit 16)
-y	infinitive marker (Units 14, 19); direct imperative, singular (Unit 17)
-ychik	indirect imperative, singular (Unit 17)
-yki	2nd-person-singular object/1st-person subject (Unit 16)
-ykichik	2nd-person-plural object/1st-person subject (Unit 16)
-yku-	movement inward, downward, courtesy marker (Unit 17)

Noun Suffixes

-itu/-ita	diminutive (Unit 14)
-kama	terminative; "as far as" (Unit 20)
-paq	benefactive (Unit 14)
-pi	question tag regarding price
-pura	"among members of a group" (Unit 20)
-situ	diminutive (Unit 14)

Class-Free Suffixes

-chá	dubitative (Unit 16)
-pacha	temporal emphatic (Unit 14)
-raq	imperfective aspect (Unit 14)
-spataqri	conjunctive compound (Unit 14)

Simi / Vocabulary

Ruway / Verbs

   jap'ikapuy: to take on body (*in reference to a plant as it grows*).
   llamp'uchay: to soften (*trans.*).
   mallkiy: to plant seedlings.
   sembray: to hill (plants in a furrow).[1]
   surk'ay: to dig a furrow.
   wanuchay: to fertilize.
   yakuta pusay: to channel water along the irrigation ditches.

Ruway tikrachiq / Adverb

   qaylla: near; nearby.

Suti / Nouns

   liwk'ana: digging implement with curved blade.

---

1. The word "sembray" has taken on a different meaning in Quechua from Spanish sembrar 'to sow'; the Quechua word is "jallmay" (Sp. aporcar). Quechua speakers may use Spanish words when Quechua words are still available; semantic changes in the hispanisms may then occur, as in this case.

Ruwana / Exercises

1 Juk ⌘ Qillqana / Written Work

Ñawirinapis kutichinapis / Read and answer the questions below in Quechua.

Tata Vitalioqa aylluntin chakrapi cebollata mallkichkan. Chaymanta parlachkan. Siminta sumaqta ñawirispa tapuykunata kutichiy.

Tata Vitalio: – Kay chakrapi ñawpaqta puquchirqani papata. Allaraytawantaq kunanqa cebollata mallkiykuchkayku. Kay jallp'ata mana samarichiykuchu. Puquchiyku, cosechayku, chaymanta watiqmanta puquchichkallaykutaq. Jinamanta venderanapaq, mikhunapaq ima. Mana tarpusunman chayqa mana mikhunapaq kanmanchu. Kaypiqa chantapis tukuy ima puqun: papa, trigo, sara, jinataq hortaliza cosaspis puqun. Cebolla, chaymanta zanahoria, beterraga, repollo, tukuy ima puqun kaypiqa. Arí. Chay jina, puquptinqa mikhunapaq tiyan, mana llaqtamantaraqchu juqharimuna. Kayllapi puqun.

1. Imatataq tata Vitalio ñawpaqta chakranpi puquchirqa?
_____

2. Kunan imatataq mallkichkanku?
_____

3. Kay jallp'ata samarichiyta yachankuchu?
_____

4. Imakunatataq kay jallp'api puquchinku?
_____

5. Imapaqtaq chay hortalizasta puquchinku?
_____

6. Qamrí maymantataq puquykunata mikhunaykipaq juqharinki?
_____

2 Iskay ⌘ Qillqana / Written Work

Ñawirispa riqsisqa k'askaqkunata tarina / Read and identify the suffixes you know in the text.

Group the suffixes in the tables below according to their type. Make a note of their meaning and/or function, an example of how they are used, and a translation of the example. List each different suffix only once. If you come across suffixes you don't know, just ignore them for now. You can come back to them in your more advanced learning.

Mama Rosaleen (*indicating a digging implement*): – Kaypata imataq sutin?
Tata Vitalio: – Kaypataqa liwk'ana sutin. Kaywan ñawpaqtaqa jallp'ataqa wakichina, kay plantata churaykunapaq, mallkiykunapaqqa. Allarquna, sumaqta llamp'ucharquna entonces chayta llamp'ucharquytawan kay liwk'anawan surk'aykuna. Chay jawataqmin plantata mallkiykuna. Chay jawataq sembraykuna chay jawa patanpi yakuwan qarpaykuna mana ch'akirichkananpaq. Chayqa plantitaqa jap'ikapun, mana ch'akikunchu.

Verb Suffixes	Meaning and/or Function	Example of Use from the Text
-chi-	causative	wakichina 'one has to prepare'

Noun Suffixes	Meaning and/or Function	Example of Use from the Text
-n-	3rd-person-singular possessive	sutin 'its name'

Class-Free Suffixes	Meaning and/or Function	Example of Use from the Text
-taq-	Question tag	imataq 'what?'

3 Kimsa ⌘ Qillqana / Written Work

Ñawirispa rimaykunata tarina, inglés simiman tikrana / Identify the verbal forms in the text and translate into English.

Enter the verbal forms you identify in the table below, following the example. Enter each different form only once. A "verbal form" should be taken as a verb root plus verb suffixes and person markers. Verb roots that have been nominalized (e.g., llamk'ay, mallkisqa) should be disregarded for the sake of this exercise.

Tata Vitalio: – Ñuqaqa surk'ani. Wawasniytaq mallkinku plantitasta. Ususiyqa sembraykamun. Kay llamk'aypiqa ajinata organisakuspa llamk'ayku: wakin surk'ayku, wakin mallkiyku, wakin sembrayku, wakintaq yakuta pusayku. Yakutataq pay qarpaykuchkantaq, mana ch'akinanpaq. Ajina llamk'ana kachkan.

    Kay mallkisqaykuqa puqunqa tawa killamanta. Puqunqa allin umasniyuq, chaytataq recién mikhunapaq. Waliqña kanqa jinataq vendenapaqpis. Chantapis kay llaqtaykuqa ancha qaylla kay San Pedro llaqtaman. Chaymanta jamunku rantirakuq kay verdurastaqa. Tukuy imata apakunku mikhunankupaq.

Verbal Form	Translation into English
surk'ani	I open the furrow

4 Tawa ⌘ Parlana / Oral Presentation

As tata Vitalio talks, he is a participant in his own activity. He uses the 1st-person singular and plural (*excl.*) as he speaks. Imagine that you are making a television program on Andean agricultural techniques. You film tata Vitalio and his family at work, and provide the commentary on what you film. Drawing on the texts in Exercises 1, 2, and 3 above, describe the activities of tata Vitalio and his family in the field. Write at least six sentences of commentary, this time in the 3rd-person singular and plural as appropriate.

Kunan p'unchawqa tata Vitalio chakrapi cebollata mallkiykuchkan. . . . (*you continue*)

22 / Iskay chunka iskayniyuq

Jallp'amanta Parlarisun / Let's Talk about the Earth

Ñawirina / Reading Practice

According to Andean ways of thinking, neglect of appropriate rituals to the earth can cause harm not only to the human body, animals, and plants, but also to the very land itself. The Andean vision seems to be vindicated today, with the worldwide realization that excessive exploitation of natural resources may cause irreversible environmental damage, such as erosion, climate change, damage to the ozone layer, and pollution of the air and waterways. Perhaps it could be said that people everywhere cause the earth to "fall ill," as Andean people say. The conversation in this unit reveals how Andean people think about land erosion and death of livestock, and the way to address the problem.

Kay warmi wasi kanchapi pachamamamanta mañarikuchkan.

The following is a conversation between Fanny and Marco about the time that Marco's family had to call in a traditional medicine man to perform a ritual to stop the erosion of their land and related deaths of their sheep.

Fanny (F): – Jukta tapurisqayki, juk kuti jallp'aykichikta llunch'ikuchkaptin jampichirqankichik. Imaynataq chayta ruwarqankichik? Ñuqa jampichiyta munani kikinta, jaqay chimpapi jallp'ay llunch'iykukuchkan. Chayta willariway.

Marco (M): – Ñuqayku jampichirqayku juk yatiriwan, Luis sutinqa, juk jallp'aykupi tiyakun, paywan. Chaymanta mañawarqayku: «Yariqaywan kachkan jallp'aykichik, ni kay qanchis wataña mana ni imata qarankichikchu. Chantá jinalla llunch'iykuchkan» ñiwarqayku.

F: – Chantá imastawan astawan mañasurqankichik?

M: – Juk yuraq uwijata mañawarqayku iskay watayuqta. Chaymanta chay uwija aychata parichirqanku laq'apachata ni mikhuna jinata. Chaymanta aychata partirawarqayku ñuqaykuman, laq'allata. Chaymanta tullusnintataq qupurqayku.

F: – Chayllatachu mañasurqankichik o wak cosastawanchu?

M: – Chayllata, misk'i cosastawan. Chantá mañariwarqayku chaymantaqa.

F: – Chantá kay tapuris ñichkarqayki:[1] anchata qampata uwijasniyki wañupun, imamantataq chhikata wañuqri?

M: – Mana qarachiqchu kayku jallp'ata chaymanta ñiwayku yatiriqa kay atuq ñisqa chay khuruqa allquwan ñinakun ñin chaymanta allqutaq apamun ñin, aychata kawrasta uwijasta chaytataq aychantataq, allqu mikhun, chay atuq ñisqa, chaymanta yawarnintataq pampa ch'unqan ñin jallp'a.

F: – Chaymantachu wañuq kasqa?

M: – Arí.

F: – Entonces jallp'ayki yariqasqa kaptin?

M: – Arí, chay, jinallamanta.

(Adapted from a conversation between Fanny Murillo Villanueva and Marco recorded by Rosaleen Howard, San Pedro de Buenavista, Northern Potosí, Bolivia, summer 1989)

Simi / Vocabulary

Ruway / Verbs

    ch'unqay: to suck.
    llunch'iy: to slide down.
    ñinakuy: to resemble each other.
    parichiy: to bake on hot stones.
    qupuy: to pile up, heap up.

Suti / Nouns

    atuq: fox.

---

1. "Tapurisaq ñichkarqayki" ("I was wanting to ask you") translates literally as "I shall ask you I was saying." Note how the 2nd-person object marker appears on the verb "ñiy"; another example of this construction could be "waturisaq ñichkarqayki" "I was wanting to visit you."

Suti Tikrachiq / Adjectives
  laq'a: unsalted (food).

Ruway tikrachiq / Adverbs
  chhikata: a lot.

Ruwana / Exercise

Read and study the text. Then: (i) give an interpretation in English of the belief system that is being expressed here; (ii) do some further reading on beliefs about the relationship between humans and the earth in the Andes. With more knowledge of the cultural belief system, you will develop a contextual understanding of Quechua discourse.
  Suggested reading: Harris 2000; Allen 2002.

VOCABULARY CHECKLIST

[ ] = *pronounced form*
adj. = adjective
adv. = adverb
conj. = conjunction
dem. = demonstrative
excl. = exclusive
incl. = inclusive
indef. = indefinite
inter. pn. = interrogative pronoun
intrans. = intransitive
n. = noun
past part. = past participle
pers. pn. = personal pronoun
pn. = pronoun
pl. = plural
poss. = possessive
sing. = singular
Sp. = Spanish [word is]
trans. = transitive
v. = verb

achkha (*adj.*): many (Unit 11).
ajina (*adv.*): so; like this; thus (Unit 14).
akllay (*v.*): to choose (Unit 15).
akulliy (*v.*): to chew coca leaves (Unit 5).
alférez [alxiris] (*n.*): fiesta sponsor (ritual role) (Unit 6).
allay (*v.*): to dig up, harvest (tubers) (Unit 4).
allchhi (*n.*): grandson, granddaughter (Unit 1).
allin (*adj.*): well, good, fine (Unit 1).
allinyay (*v.*): to get better (Unit 16).
allpaqa (*n.*): alpaca (Unit 4).
allqu (*n.*): dog (Unit 4).
almilla (*n.*): plainwoven woolen dress (Unit 3).
ancha (*adv.*): very (Unit 11).
anchata (*adv.*): a lot, very much (Unit 11).
anqas (*adj.*): blue (Unit 10).
anta (*n.*): copper (Unit 19).
apakamuy (*v.*): to bring for oneself (Unit 9).

apamuy (*v.*): to bring (Unit 6).
apapuy (*v.*): to carry for someone (Unit 19).
apay (*v.*): to carry (Unit 6).
aqsu (*n.*): handwoven overskirt (Unit 3).
aqha (*n.*): chicha, corn beer (Unit 4).
aqha wasi (*n.*): bar where chicha is sold (Unit 6).
aqhay (*v.*): to make chicha (Unit 10).
arí (expression): yes (Unit 2).
arus (Sp. *arroz*) (*n.*): rice (Unit 4).
arwija (Sp. *arveja*) (*n.*): peas (Unit 17).
astawan (*adv.*): more (Unit 11).
astawan jatun (*adj.*): bigger (Unit 17).
astawan juch'uy (*adj.*): smaller (Unit 17).
astay (*v.*): to fetch and carry (Unit 14).
atiy (*v.*): to be able (Unit 9).
atuq (*n.*): fox (Unit 22).
auto [awtu] (*n.*): car (Unit 5).
avión (*n.*): plane (Unit 5).

awana (*n.*): loom (Unit 10).
away (*v.*): to weave (Unit 4).
awicha (*n.*): grandmother (Unit 1).
awichu (*n.*): grandfather (Unit 1).
awqa (*n.*): enemy (Unit 19).
awqa sunkha (*n.*): bearded enemy (Unit 19).
aya wasi (*n.*): cemetery (Unit 6).
aycha (*n.*): meat (Unit 4).
ayllu (*n.*): social group, extended family (Unit 1).
ayllu masi (*n.*): fellow ayllu member (Unit 1).
ayllu runa (*n.*): member of an ayllu (Unit 2).
ayqiy (*v.*): to escape (Unit 6).

bayeta (*n.*): plain-woven cloth (Unit 4).
blusa (*n.*): blouse (Unit 3).
bordadoyuq (*adj.*): embroidered (Unit 17).
bufanda [wuhanta] (*n.*): sash worn around waist (Unit 3).

campo [kampu] (*n.*): countryside (Unit 2).
campo runa (*n.*): rural-dwelling person (Unit 2).
carro [karu] (*n.*): bus (Unit 5).
casaray (*v.*): to get married (Unit 15).
caserito/caserita!: *term of address between seller and customer* (Unit 17).
cebada [siwara] (*n.*): barley (Unit 4).
cuñada (*n.*): sister-in-law (Unit 1).

chaki (*n.*): foot (Unit 5).
chakra (*n.*): field (Unit 4).
chanka (*n.*): leg (Unit 8).
chantá (*conj.*): then (Unit 11).
chaqueta [chakita] (*n.*): embroidered jacket (Unit 3).
charanku (*n.*): charango (Unit 9).
chawpi (*positional particle*).: center, middle (Unit 9).
chay (*dem.*): that (Unit 3).
chayachiy (*v.*): to cook (*trans.*) (Unit 18).
chayamuy (*v.*): to arrive (in the direction of the speaker) (Unit 5).
chayay (*v.*): to arrive (Unit 5).
chay jawa (*conj.*): then, after that, on top of that (Unit 12).
chaymanta (*conj.*): then; after that; from there (Unit 9).
chaypis (*conj*): even if (Unit 19).
chayrayku: because of that (Unit 16).
chikchiy (*v.*): to hail (Unit 16).

chimpay (*v.*): to approach; to cross over (river, street) (Unit 6).
chinkachiy (*v.*): to lose (Unit 11).
chinkakuy (*v.*): to get lost (Unit 11).
chinkapuy (*v.*): to disappear completely (Unit 11).
chinkay (*v.*): to be lost; to disappear (Unit 11).
chinki (*n.*): fiesta sponsor's sister (ritual role); small drum played by fiesta sponsor's sister in ritual (Unit 6).
chipaya (*n.*): Chipaya language (Unit 11).
chiqniy (*v.*): to despise; to hate (Unit 20).
chiri (*n.*): cold (Unit 8).
chiri chiri (*n.*): fever (Unit 16).
chiriy (*v.*): to be cold (Unit 8).
chukcha (*n.*): hair (Unit 8).
chukuy (*v.*): to sit, to squat (Unit 15).
chumpa (*n.*): pullover (Unit 12).
chumpi (*n.*): woven belt (Unit 3).
chunka (*n.*): ten (Unit 5).
chuqllu (*n.*): *choclo* (corn on the cob) (Unit 4).
churay (*v.*): to put, to place (Unit 12).
churakuy (*v.*): to put on (clothes) (Unit 12).
churi (*n.*): son (*man speaking*) (Unit 1).
chuwa (*n.*): wooden dish (Unit 10).

chharara (*n.*): stovepipe straw hat (worn by women) (Unit 3).
chhikata (*adv.*): a lot (Unit 22).
chhiqa (*n.*): place (Unit 6).

ch'akichiy (*v.*): to dry (*trans.*) (Unit 18).
ch'akiy (*v.*): to be thirsty; to dry (*intrans.*) (Unit 8).
ch'allay (*v.*): to spill; to sprinkle liquid in ritual offering (Unit 19).
ch'arki (*n.*): sun-dried meat (Unit 4).
ch'aska (*n.*): morning star (Unit 16).
ch'in (*adj.*): silent (Unit 9).
ch'iqchi (*adj.*): pale gray (Unit 10).
ch'ullu (*var.* lluch'u) (*n.*): knitted cap with earflaps (Unit 3).
ch'umpi (*adj.*): brown (Unit 10).
ch'unqay (*v.*): to suck (Unit 22).
ch'uñu (*n.*): freeze-dried potato (Unit 4).
ch'uspa (*n.*): coca pouch (Unit 3).
ch'utaray (*v.*): to peel off (multiple items) (Unit 18).
ch'utay (*v.*): to peel off, displace outward by pressure (Unit 18).

ch'uya [ch'uwa] (*adj.*): clear, translucent (Unit 18).

día [diya] (*n.*): day (Unit 5).

escuela [iskwila] (*n.*): school (Unit 6).
españa [España] (*n.*): Spaniard (Unit 19).
estandarte [istantarti] (*n.*): pennant (religious icon) (Unit 6).

feria (*n.*): market (Unit 6).
fideos [firiyus] (*n.*): pasta (Unit 4).
fiesta [hista] (*n.*): religious festival (Unit 6).
fiesta ruwaq (*n.*): fiesta sponsor (Unit 6).

guaraní (*n.*): Guaraní language (Unit 11).
gustay (*v.*): to like (Unit 16).

habas [jawas] (*n.*): broad beans (Unit 4).

iglesia [inlisya] (*n.*): church (Unit 6).
ima (*conj*): and (closes a list) (Unit 9).
ima? (*inter. pn.*): what? (Unit 1).
imanay (*v.*): to happen, to become of [someone] (Unit 16).
imapaq? (*inter. pn.*): what for? (Unit 14).
imapi?: how/by what means of transport? (*lit.* "in what?") (Unit 5).
imatawan? (*inter. pn.*): what else? (Unit 12).
imawan? (*inter. pn.*): what with? (Unit 10).
imaymana (*n.*): all sorts of things (Unit 11).
imayna? (*inter. pn.*): how? (Unit 1).
imaynata? (*inter. pn.*): how, in what way? (Unit 11).
imayuq? (*inter. pn.*): with what attributes? (Unit 12).
imilla (*n.*): young girl (Unit 2).
inkuña (*n.*): small cloth for carrying coca leaves (Unit 14).
inti (*n.*): sun (Unit 16).
iñiy wasi (*n.*): church (Unit 6).
iskay (*n.*): two (Unit 5).

jaku!: "let's go!" (Unit 7).
jallp'a (*var.* allpa) (*n.*): earth, land (Unit 9).
jamk'a [jank'a] (*n.*): grilled cereal or pulses (Unit 4).
jamk'ay [jank'ay] (*v.*): to grill, to toast (in frying pan) (Unit 4).
jampi (*n.*): medicine (Unit 16).
jampiq (*n.*): doctor (Unit 8).

jampiri (*n.*): traditional healer (Unit 16).
jampiy (*v.*): to cure, heal (Unit 8).
jampiy wasi (*n.*): hospital (Unit 6).
jamuq wata (*n.*): next year (Unit 16).
jamuy (*v.*): to come (Unit 5).
jap'ikapuy (*v.*): to take on body (*in reference to a plant as it grows*) (Unit 21).
jap'iqay (*v.*): to get grabbed (by forces of nature) (Unit 16).
jap'iy (*v.*): to grab (Unit 16).
jaqay (*dem.*): that over there (Unit 3).
jasa (*adj.*): easy (Unit 20).
jatariy (*v.*): to rise up (Unit 20).
jatun (*adj.*): big (Unit 10).
jatun kamachiq (*n.*): president (Unit 20).
jatun mama (*n.*): grandmother (Unit 1).
jatun tata (*n.*): grandfather (Unit 1).
jatun yachay wasi (*n.*): university (Unit 6).
jawa (positional particle): outside (Unit 9).
jawa runa (*n.*): outsider, foreigner (Unit 2).
jawas (Sp. *habas*) (*n.*): broad beans (Unit 17).
jayk'aq? (*inter. pn.*): when? (Unit 14).
jayk'aqmanta? (*inter. pn.*): since when? (Unit 14).
jayt'ay (*v.*): to kick (Unit 16).
jich'ay (*v.*): to pour (liquids, grains) (Unit 18).
jilanqu (*n.*): traditional political leader (Unit 18).
jina (*adv.*): thus, in that way (Unit 12); like (Unit 14).
jinay (*v.*): to do thus (Unit 18).
jisq'un (*n.*): nine (Unit 5).
juch'uy (*adj.*): small (Unit 10).
juk (*n.*): one (Unit 5).
juk kuti (*adv.*): once (Unit 15).
juktawan: "again," "another time" (Unit 16).
juk'uta (*n.*): rubber sandal (Unit 3).
jump'i (*n.*): sweat (Unit 19).
jump'iy (*v.*): to sweat (Unit 16).
juntuy (*v.*): to gather together (Unit 15).
juqhariy (*v.*): to rise, raise, pick up (Unit 16).
jurqhupuy (*v.*): to take out at once (Unit 18).
jurqhusqa (*past part.*): extracted, taken out (Unit 20).
jurqhuy [orqhoy]: to extract; to take something out of an inner space (Unit 9).

kachi (*n.*): salt (Unit 12).
kachipampa (*n.*): salt lake (Unit 19).
kalsuna (*n.*): man's trousers of homespun cloth (Unit 12).

kallpa (*n.*): physical strength, moral courage (Unit 16).
kamachiq (*n.*): authority, leader (Unit 20).
kamachiy (*n.*): law (Unit 20).
kancha (*n.*): corral; houseyard; sports ground; football pitch (Unit 6).
kaqkamapas: "whatever exists" (Unit 19).
karu (*adj.*): far (Unit 5).
karuna (*n.*): horse blanket (Unit 10).
karunchay (*v.*): to marginalize (Unit 20).
karwa (*n.*): goat (Unit 4).
kastilla simi (*n.*): Spanish language (Unit 11).
kawallu (*n.*): horse (Unit 4).
kawsay (*v.*): to live (be alive) (Unit 9).
kawsay (*n.*): life (Unit 2).
kay (*v.*): to be (Unit 1).
kay (*n.*): being, existence (Unit 19).
kay (*dem.*): this (Unit 3).
kichariy (*v.*): to open (Unit 19).
kichwa (*n.*): Ecuadorian Quechua (Unit 11).
kikillantaq: "just the same" (Unit 15).
kikin (*adj.*): same (Unit 20).
killa (*n.*): month; moon (Unit 14).
kimsa (*n.*): three (Unit 5).
kinwa (*n.*): quinoa (Unit 4).
kiru (*n.*): teeth (Unit 8).
kulli (*adj.*): purple (Unit 10).
kunan (*adv.*): now (Unit 5).
kunan p'unchaw (*adv.*): today (Unit 12).
kunitan (*adv.*): right now (Unit 12).
kunka (*n.*): neck (Unit 8).
kurku (*n.*): body (Unit 8).
kusa (*adj.*): good (Unit 20).
kusisqa (*adj.*): happy (Unit 8).
kusiy (*v.*): to be happy (Unit 9).
kustala (*n.*): sack (Unit 4).
kutay (*v.*): to grind (grains, coffee, spices, herbs, etc.) (Unit 16).
kuti (*adv.*): time, occasion (Unit 15).
kutichiy (*v.*): to respond, to answer (Unit 7).
kutimuy (*v.*): to come back (Unit 9).
kutiy (*v.*): to return, to go back (Unit 9).

khuchi (*n.*): pig (Unit 4).
khuru (*n.*): worm; bacteria (Unit 16).
khuruy (*v.*): to infect (the body) (Unit 16).
khuska (*adv.*): together (Unit 7).

k'acha (*adj.*): pretty (Unit 17).
k'ajay (*v.*): to have a temperature (Unit 8).
k'anka (*n.*): rooster (Unit 4).
k'anti (*n.*): spindle for twisting yarn (Unit 10).
k'antiy (*v.*): to twist, ply yarn (Unit 10).
k'api (*n.*): a handful (Unit 17).
k'aspi (*n.*): stick (Unit 10).
k'iwicha (*n.*): liver (Unit 8).
k'uychi (*n.*): rainbow (Unit 10).

laq'a (*adj.*): unsalted food (Unit 22).
larqha (*var.* rarqha, larq'a) (*n.*): irrigation canal (Unit 6).
latanu (Sp. *plátano*) (*n.*): banana (Unit 17).
lat'ay (*v.*): to crawl (Unit 14).
lawa (*n.*): broth (grain-based soup) (Unit 4).
layqay (*v.*): to bewitch (Unit 16).
lichi (Sp. *leche*) (*n.*): milk (Unit 17).
liwk'ana (*n.*): digging implement with curved blade (Unit 21).
lomas (*n.*): hills (Unit 9).
luqutu (*n.*): variety of hot pepper (Unit 17).
luq'u (*n.*): floppy felt hat (Unit 3).
lurasnu (Sp. *durazno*) (*n.*): peaches (Unit 17).

llakisqa (*adj.*): sad (Unit 8).
llakiy (*v.*): to be sad (Unit 9).
llama (*n.*): llama (Unit 4).
llamk'ay [llank'ay] (*v.*): to work (Unit 4).
llamp'uchay (*v.*): to soften (*trans.*) (Unit 21).
llamt'a (*n.*): firewood (Unit 4).
llaqta (*n.*): town (Unit 2).
llaqta runa (*n.*): town-dwelling person (Unit 2).
lliklla (*n.*): handwoven carrying cloth (Unit 3).
llimp'i (*n.*): color (Unit 10).
llimp'iyuq (*adj.*): colored (Unit 17).
lluch'uy (*v.*): to peel off (Unit 18).
llunch'iy (*v.*): to slide down (Unit 22).
lluqalla [lloqalla]: young boy (Unit 2).
lluqsimuy (*v.*): to come out here (toward speaker) (Unit 19).
lluqsiy (*v.*): to go out (Unit 9).

machasqa (*past part.*): drunk (Unit 20).
machay (*v.*): to get drunk (Unit 15).
machay (*n.*): cave, rock overhang (Unit 9).

machkha? (*inter. pn.*): how much, how many? (Unit 5).
machkhapi? (*inter. pn.*): how much for? (Unit 17).
machu runa (*n.*): old man (Unit 2).
maki (*n.*): hand (Unit 8).
mallkiy (*v.*): to plant seedlings (Unit 21).
mama (*n.*): mother (Unit 1).
mama simi (*n.*): mother tongue (Unit 11).
mamáy! (*n.*): "Mother!," "ma'am"; *term of address for married woman* (Unit 1).
manaña (*adv.*): no more, not any more (Unit 11).
mañay (*v.*): to ask a favor; to contract someone (Unit 15).
manchariy (*v.*): to get frightened (Unit 16).
manka (*n.*): clay cooking pot (Unit 10).
manta (*n.*): factory-made shawl (Unit 3).
mapudungun (*n.*): Mapuche language (Unit 11).
maqanakuy (*v.*): to fight each other (Unit 16).
maqay (*v.*): to beat (Unit 16).
masi (*n.*): coparticipant in a group or activity (Unit 1).
mask'ay (*v.*): to look for something (Unit 9).
mast'ay (*v.*): to spread out on a surface (Unit 9).
mathi (*n.*): gourd (*used as recipient for liquids*) (Unit 10).
may? (*inter. pn*): where? (Unit 1).
mayllay (*v.*): to wash (one's face, hands, body; food) (Unit 8).
maymanta? (*inter. pn*): where from? (Unit 5).
maypi? (*inter. pn.*): where? (Unit 11).
mayqin (*inter. pn.*): which one? (Unit 17).
mayu (*n.*): river (Unit 5).
michiy (*v.*): to graze animals (Unit 4).
mikhuna (*n.*): food (Unit 4).
mikhuy (*v.*): to eat (Unit 4).
millma (*n.*): wool (Unit 4).
millu (*n.*): sulphuric mineral (*used in diagnosing illness*) (Unit 16).
minchha (*n.*): the day after tomorrow (Unit 16).
misi (*n.*): cat (Unit 4).
misk'i (*adj.*): sweet (Unit 20).
misk'ichana (*n.*): sugar (Unit 17).
mitayu (*n.*): enforced laborer (Unit 19).
molino [mulinu] (*n.*): mill (Unit 6).
monte [munti] (*n.*): bush; hilly woodland (Unit 6).
montera [muntira] (*n.*): cowhide helmet worn in *tinku* fighting (Unit 3).
mozo [musu] (*n.*): town-dwelling *mestizo* (Unit 2).

muchhay (*v.*): to strip corn from the cob (Unit 18).
muju (*n.*): seed (Unit 6).
mullu (*adj.*): pink (shell-colored) (Unit 10).
munakuy (*v.*): to love (Unit 9).
munay (*v.*): to want, to like (Unit 9).
musuq (*adj.*): new (Unit 12).
mut'i (*n.*): *mote* (*grilled or boiled grains or pulses eaten as side dish or snack*) (Unit 4).

nanay (*v.*): to hurt (Unit 8).
napaykuy (*v.*): to greet (Unit 1).

ña (*adv.*): already (Unit 11).
ñan (*n.*): road, path (Unit 6).
ñaña (*n.*): sister of a woman (Unit 1).
ñañu (*adj.*): thin (*referring to yarn*) (Unit 14).
ñawi (*n.*): eye (Unit 8).
ñawiriy (*v.*): to read (Unit 1).
ñawpaqta (*var.* ñampaqta) (*adv.*): before, firstly (*time*); in front (*space*) (Unit 11).
ñin (expression): he/she says (Unit 5).
ñinakuy (*v.*): to resemble each other (Unit 22).
ñisqa (*past part.*): so-called (Unit 6).
ñisqanman jina: "according to what s/he says" (Unit 15).
ñiy (*v.*): to say (Unit 6).
ñuñu (*n.*): breast (Unit 8).
ñuqa [noqa] (*pers. pn.*): I, me (Unit 1).
ñuqanchik (*pers. pn.*): we, us (*incl.*) (Unit 5).
ñuqayku (*pers. pn.*): we, us (*excl.*) (Unit 5).

pacha (*n.*): period of time, world, space (Unit 11).
pachamama (*n.*): female earth deity; mother earth (Unit 8).
pachan (*adv.*): unchanged; remains the same (Unit 14).
pachi: "thank you" (Unit 20).
pallay (*v.*): to gather; to collect; to pick threads in weaving design (Unit 4).
pana (*n.*): sister of a man (Unit 1).
pantalon [pantalun] (*n.*): trousers (Unit 3).
panti (*adj.*): dark red (Unit 10).
papa (*n.*): potato (Unit 4).
papa lisa (*n.*): *melloco* (*Andean tuber*) (Unit 4).
paqarin (*n.*): morning (Unit 16).
paqarinkama: "until tomorrow" (*S. Peru*) (Unit 16).
paray (*v.*): to rain (Unit 16).

parichiy (*v.*): to bake on hot stones (Unit 22).
parlay (*v.*): to speak (Unit 1).
pasay (*v.*): to sponsor (a fiesta) (Unit 15).
pata (*positional particle*): above (Unit 9).
pay (*pers. pn.*): he, him; she, her (Unit 1).
paya (*n.*): old woman (Unit 2).
paykuna (*pers. pn.*): they, them (Unit 5).
payla (*n.*): large cooking vessel (Unit 18).
paypata (*poss. pn.*): his/hers (Unit 1).
pelado [peladu] (*n.*): peeled corn (Unit 18).
pi? (*inter. pn.*): who? (Unit 2).
pichay (*v.*): to sweep (Unit 4).
pili (*n.*): duck (Unit 4).
pipaq? (*inter. pn.*): who for? (Unit 14).
pipta? (*inter. pn.*): whose? (Unit 10).
pisi (*adv.*): a little (Unit 11).
pisimanta pisi (*adv.*): little by little (Unit 14).
pisita (*adv.*): a little (Unit 11).
polera (*n.*): t-shirt (Unit 3).
pollera [pullira] (*n.*): dirndl skirt (Unit 3).
preparay (*v.*): to prepare (Unit 15).
puchuy (*v.*): to be left over (Unit 19).
puka (*adj.*): red (Unit 10).
pukatay (*v.*): to be cloudy (Unit 16).
pukllay (*v.*): to play (Unit 6).
pukyu (*n.*): spring (of water) (Unit 6).
puna (*n.*): high moorland (Unit 6).
punchu (*n.*): poncho (Unit 3).
punkiy (*v.*): to swell (Unit 16).
punku (*n.*): door, doorway (Unit 9).
puñuna (*n.*): bed (Unit 8).
puñuy (*v.*): to sleep (Unit 8).
puquchiy (*v.*): to cultivate (Unit 20).
puqusqa (*past part.*): grown, matured; fermented (Unit 20).
puquy (*v.*): to grow, to mature; to ferment (Unit 18).
puriy (*v.*): to walk, to move, to work (machinery) (Unit 5).
pusaq (*n.*): eight (Unit 5).
pusay (*v.*): to bring, lead, guide (a person) (Unit 6).

phaway (*v.*): to fly, run (Unit 6).
phichqa (*n.*): five (Unit 5).
phiñakuy (*v.*): to get angry (Unit 20).
phuchka (*n.*): spindle for spinning (Unit 10).
phuchkay (*v.*): to spin (Unit 4).
phukuy (*v.*): to blow (Unit 9).

phullu (*n.*): blanket (Unit 4).
phusa (*n.*): lungs (Unit 8).
phutiy (*n.*): sorrow (Unit 20).

p'acha (*n.*): clothing (Unit 3).
p'akiy (*v.*): to break (Unit 16).
p'inqay (*v.*): to be ashamed (Unit 11).
p'unchaw [p'unchay] (*n.*): day, daylight (Unit 5).
p'uyñu [p'uñu] (*n.*): chicha jar (Unit 15).

qallariy (*v.*): to begin (Unit 14).
qallpa (*n.*): uncultivated plot of land (Unit 9).
qallu (*n.*): tongue (Unit 8).
qam [qan] (*pers. pn.*): you (Unit 1).
qamkuna (*pers. pn.*): you (*pl.*) (Unit 5).
qampata (*poss. pn.*): yours (Unit 1).
qanchis (*n.*): seven (Unit 5).
qaqa (*n.*): rock, boulder (Unit 9).
qara (*n.*): skin (Unit 8).
qarpay (*v.*): to irrigate (Unit 4).
qaylla (*adv.*): near; nearby (Unit 21).
qayna (*adv.*): yesterday (Unit 12).
qayna p'unchaw (*adv.*): yesterday (Unit 14).
qayna wata (*adv.*): last year (Unit 14).
qaywiy (*v.*): to stir (Unit 18).
qichuy (*v.*): to take something away from someone; to pillage (Unit 19).
qillqay (*v.*): to write (Unit 14).
qucha (*n.*): lake (Unit 9).
qullqi (*n.*): silver; money (Unit 10).
qunqapuy (*v.*): to forget completely (Unit 11).
qunqay (*v.*): to forget (Unit 11).
qunqur (*n.*): knee (Unit 8).
quñiy (*v.*): to be hot; to be on heat (animals) (Unit 8).
qupuy (*v.*): to pile up, heap up (Unit 22).
quri (*n.*): gold (Unit 19).
qusqayki: "I shall give you" (Unit 17).
qutu (*n.*): pile (Unit 17).
qutuchay (*v.*): to group together (Unit 20).
quwi (*n.*): guinea pig (Unit 4).
quy (*v.*): to give (Unit 17).

qhapaq (*adj.*): rich (Unit 19).
qhapaq kay (*n.*): riches, wealth (Unit 19).
qhari (*n.*): man; male human being (Unit 2).
qhariwarmi (*n.*): male and female couple, married couple (Unit 12).

qhasay (*v.*): to freeze (Unit 16).
qhatay (*v.*): to cover over (Unit 18).
qhatiy (*v.*): to herd animals, to follow (Unit 9).
qhatu (*n.*): marketplace (Unit 19).
qhawakuy (*v.*): to watch (Unit 9).
qhaway (*v.*): to look at (Unit 9).
qhichwa (*n.*): Quechua language (*central Peru, Bolivia*); warm valley region (Units 9, 11).
qhipa (*adv.*): later, recent (Unit 11).
qhipata (*adv.*): afterward, later, nowadays (*time*); behind (*space*) (Unit 11).
qhura (*n.*): herb (Unit 16).
qhuya (*n.*): mine (Unit 6).

q'ala (*adv.*): totally (*colloquial*) (Unit 16).
q'ara (*n.*): outsider (Unit 2).
q'aya (*n.*): tomorrow (Unit 16).
q'ayakama: "until tomorrow" (*Bolivia*) (Unit 16).
q'aya minchha (*n.*): the day after the day after tomorrow (Unit 16).
q'aytu (*n.*): thread, yarn (Unit 10).
q'illay (*n.*): iron (Unit 19).
q'illu (*adj.*): yellow (Unit 10).
q'ipi (*n.*): bundle (Unit 15).
q'ipimuy (*v.*): to bring on one's back (Unit 6).
q'ipiy (*v.*): to load onto one's back (Unit 6).
q'iwiy (*v.*): to twist (Unit 16).
q'umir (*adj.*): green (Unit 10).
q'uñiy (*v.*): to be hot; to be on heat (*referring to animals*) (Unit 16).
q'uyu (*n.*): bruise (Unit 16).

rakhu (*adj.*): thick (*referring to solid objects*) (Unit 14).
Rantikuway!: "Buy it from me (for yourself)!" (Unit 17).
rantina (*n.*): merchandise (Unit 10).
Rantipuway!: "Buy it for me!" (Unit 17).
rantisqayki: "I shall buy from you" (Unit 17).
rantiy (*v.*): to buy, to barter (Unit 6).
raymi (*n.*): religious festival (Unit 6).
Rebajariway!: "Give me a discount!" (Unit 17).
rebajay (*v.*): to give a discount (Unit 17).
rikra (*var.* likra): arm (Unit 8).
rikuchiy (*v.*): to show, to display (Unit 15).
rikuy (*n.*): to see (Unit 9).
rikhuriy (*v.*): to appear (Unit 11).
rimay (*v.*): to declare, to pronounce (Unit 19).

rimay (*n.*): commandment, declaration (Unit 19).
rinri (*var.* ninri) (*n.*): ear (Unit 8).
ripuy (*v.*): to go away; depart (Unit 19).
riqsiy (*v.*): to know (*a place, person*); to recognize (Unit 14).
rit'iy (*v.*): to snow (Unit 16).
riy (*v.*): to go (Unit 6).
rosado [rusadu] (*adj.*): pink (Unit 10).
rumi (*n.*): stone; rock (Unit 19).
rumip sunqun (*n.*): heart of the rock (Unit 19).
runa (*n.*): person (Unit 2).
runakuna (*var.* runas) (*n.*): people (Unit 2).
runa simi (*n.*): Quechua language (*southern Peru*) (Unit 11).
ruphay (*v.*): to burn; to be sunny (Unit 8).
rurun (*v.*): kidney (Unit 8).
ruwana (*n.*): task, activity (Unit 4).
ruwapuy (*v.*): to do for another person (Unit 19).
ruway (*v.*): to do, to make (Unit 1).

sach'a (*n.*): tree; wood, forest (Unit 19).
sach'a sach'a (*n.*): forest, jungle (Unit 19).
saltasniyuq (*adj.*): with decorative weave (Unit 17).
samariy (*v.*): to rest (Unit 14).
sapa (*adj.*): each, every (Unit 16).
sapa juk (*n.*): each one (Unit 17).
saqiy (*v.*): to leave something (Unit 9).
sara (*n.*): maize, corn (Unit 4).
sara jamk'a (*n.*): grilled corn (Unit 4).
sasa (*adj.*): difficult, hard (Unit 20).
sawakuy (*v.*): to get married (Unit 15).
sayay (*v.*): to stand (Unit 9).
sayk'upuy (*v.*): to get tired out (Unit 19).
sayk'uy (*v.*): to get tired (Unit 15).
semana (*n.*): week (Unit 16).
sembray (*v.*): to hill (plants in a furrow) (Unit 21).
siku (*n.*): panpipe player; panpipe (Unit 6).
sillu (*n.*): fingernail (Unit 8).
simi (*n.*): mouth; language; word (Unit 1).
simp'ay (*v.*): to braid, to plait (Unit 12).
simp'ay (*n.*): plait, braid (Unit 12).
sinchi (*adj.*): strong, physically tough (Unit 16).
sinqa (*n.*): nose (Unit 8).
sipas (*n.*): young woman (Unit 2).
sirinu (*n.*): female water spirit (Unit 9).
siwulla (Sp. *cebolla*) (*n.*): onion (Unit 17).
sombrero [sumiru] (*n.*): hat (Unit 3).

sumaq (*adj.*): well, good, fine, virtuous (Unit 1).
sumaqta (*adv.*): well, good-heartedly (Unit 11).
sunkha (*n.*): beard (Unit 19).
sunqu (*n.*): heart (Unit 8).
suqta (*n.*): six (Unit 5).
surk'ay (*v.*): to dig a furrow (Unit 21).
sut'iyay (*v.*): to dawn, to get light (Unit 9).
sut'iyay (*n.*): dawn (Unit 9).
suti (*n.*): name; noun (Unit 1).
suyay (*v.*): to wait for (Unit 7).
suyu (*n.*): territory, region (Unit 11).

takiy (*v.*): to sing (Unit 6).
takiy (*n.*): song (Unit 9).
tantakuy (*v.*): to meet up, to gather together (Unit 18).
tapuy (*v.*): to ask (Unit 8).
tariy (*v.*): to find (Unit 19).
tarpuy (*v.*): to sow (seeds and tubers) (Unit 6).
tata (*n.*): father (Unit 1).
tata cura (*n.*): priest (Unit 15).
tatamama (*n.*): parents (Unit 15).
tatáy! (*n.*): "Father!"; "sir!"; *term of address for married man* (Unit 1).
tawa (*n.*): four (Unit 5).
tinku (*n.*): ritual battle between two halves of a community (Unit 9).
Tinkunakama! (*Bol.*): "See you later!" "Until the next meeting!" (Unit 1).
tinkuq (*n.*): participant in ritual battle (Unit 12).
tinkuy (*v; Bol.*): to meet (Unit 1).
titi (*n.*): lead (mineral) (Unit 19).
tiyakuy (*v.*): to live, to reside (Unit 6).
tiyay (*v.*): to be (located in space) (Unit 10).
tocay [tukay] (*v.*): to play (a musical instrument) (Unit 9).
trigo [riwu] (*n.*): wheat (Unit 4).
tukukuy (*v.*): to become (Unit 19).
tukupuy (*v.*): to turn into something else (Unit 19).
tukuy (*v.*): to finish; to pretend (to be) (Unit 14).
tukuy (*indef.*): every (Unit 15).
tullma (*n.*): hair tie (for plaited hair) (Unit 12).
tullqa (*n.*): son-in-law, brother-in-law (Unit 1); fiesta sponsor's brother-in-law (ritual role) (Unit 6).
tullu (*n.*): bone (Unit 8).
tumati (Sp. *tomate*): tomatoes (Unit 17).
Tupananchikkama! [tupananchiskama] (*Peru*): "See you later!" "Until we meet again!" (Unit 1).

tupay (*v; S. Peru*): to meet (Unit 1).
tura (*n.*): brother of a woman (Unit 1).
tusuy (*v.*): to dance (Unit 6).
tusuy wasi (*n.*): nightclub, discotheque (Unit 6).
tuta (*n.*): night (Unit 9).
tutantin (*adv.*): all night (Unit 9).

thanta (*adj.*): old (*referring to clothes*) (Unit 12).
thatkiy [thaskiy] (*v.*): to move forward, to progress (Unit 20).

t'akariy (*v.*): to scatter (Unit 16).
t'anta (*n.*): bread (Unit 4).
t'aqsay (*v.*): to wash clothes (Unit 4).
t'ika (*n.*): flower (Unit 15).
t'impuchiy (*v.*): to boil (*trans.*) (Unit 18).
t'impuy (*v.*): to boil (*intrans.*) (Unit 18).
t'ipay (*v.*): to knit (Unit 14).
t'iyu (*n.*): sand (Unit 9).
t'uru (*n.*): clay (Unit 10).

uchpha (*n.*): ash (Unit 18).
uchu (*n.*): chili pepper; chili-based dish eaten on festive occasions (Unit 4).
ukhu (*n.*): insides; interior space (Unit 8).
ukhu (*positional particle*): inside (Unit 9).
uma (*n.*): head (Unit 8).
uña (*n.*): newborn offspring (Unit 14).
unku (*n.*): short poncho (Unit 3).
unqusqa (*adj.*): ill, sick (Unit 8).
unquy (*v.*): to be ill (Unit 8).
unquy (*n.*): illness (Unit 16).
upyay [ukyay] (*v.*): to drink (Unit 4).
uqa (*n.*): *oca* (Andean root vegetable) (Unit 4).
uqi (*adj.*): lead gray (Unit 10).
ura (*positional particle*): below (Unit 9).
urmay (*v.*): to fall (Unit 19).
urpi (*n.*): dove (Unit 9).
urqu (*n.*): hill, mountain (Unit 6).
ususi (*n.*): daughter (Unit 1).
utqhay [usqhay] (*adv.*): fast (Unit 16).
uwija (*n.*): sheep (Unit 4).
uya (*n.*): face (Unit 8).
uyarikuy (*v.*): to listen attentively; to obey (Unit 9).
uyariy (*v.*): to hear; to listen (Unit 9).
uywa (*n.*): animal (Unit 4).
uyway (*v.*): to nurture (children, animals) (Unit 14).

vacunay (*v.*): to vaccinate (Unit 16).
valle [walli] (*n.*): warm valley region (Unit 6).
vara [wara] (*n.*): staff of authority (Unit 12).
verso [wirsu] (*n.*): tune (Unit 9).

wak (*adj.*): another (Unit 15).
waka (*n.*): cow (Unit 4).
wakcha (*adj.*): poor, orphan (Unit 19).
wakcha kay (*n.*): poverty, destitution (Unit 19).
wakichiy (*v.*): to prepare, to get something ready (Unit 15).
wakin (*partitive*): some (Unit 9).
wakin kuti (*adv.*): sometimes, other times (Unit 15).
Wakta rikuchiway!: "Show me another!" (Unit 17).
waliq [walex] (*adj.*): fine, well (Unit 1).
wallpa (*n.*): hen (Unit 4).
wallpa uchu (*n.*): spicy chicken (Unit 14).
wanuchay (*v.*): to fertilize (Unit 21).
wañupuy (*v.*): to die out (Unit 11).
wañusqa (*past part.*): dead (Unit 20).
wañuy (*v.*): to die (Unit 11).
wañuy (*n.*): death (Unit 19).
waqyay (*v.*): to call (Unit 16).
wara (*n.*): calf-length trousers (Unit 3).
warmi (*n.*): woman; wife; female human being (Unit 2).
wasa (*n.*): back (Unit 8).
wasa (*positional particle*): behind (Unit 9).
wasi (*n.*): house (Unit 4).
wata (*n.*): year (Unit 14).
watay (*v.*): to tie up (Unit 14).
watuy (*v.*): to visit (Unit 22).
watuykuy (*v.*): to analyze, to inquire; to visit (Unit 1).
wawa (*n.*): child, son (*woman speaking*) (Unit 1).
wawqi (*n.*): brother of a man (Unit 1).
wayaqa (*n.*): woven bag used for carrying food or coca (Unit 4).
wayk'uy (*v.*): to cook (Unit 4).
wayna (*n.*): young man (Unit 2).
wayñu (*n.*): Andean song and dance style (Unit 4).

wayq'u (*n.*): small river, gully (Unit 9).
wayra (*n.*): wind (Unit 16).
wayray (*v.*): to be windy (Unit 16).
wich'uña (*n.*): weaving pick (Unit 10).
wich'uy (*v.*): to beat threads down with the weaving pick (Unit 10).
wiksa [wisa] (*n.*): stomach (Unit 8).
willay (*v.*): to tell; relate (Unit 16).
wiñay (*v.*): to grow, to grow up (children, animals) (Unit 14).
wiphala (*n.*): rainbow flag of the indigenous organizations (Unit 10).
wislla (*n.*): spoon (Unit 10).
wuru (*n.*): donkey (Unit 4).

yachachiy (*v.*): to teach (Unit 9).
yachakuy (*v.*): to learn (Unit 1).
yachay (*v.*): to know (Unit 9).
yachay wasi (*n.*): school (Unit 6).
yaku (*n.*): water (Unit 4).
yakuta pusay (*v.*): to lead the water along the irrigation channels (Unit 21).
yana (*adj.*): black (Unit 10).
yanapay (*v.*): to help (Unit 12).
Yapariway!: "Give me a little extra!" (Unit 17).
yapay (*v.*): to give an extra portion (in a sale) (Unit 17).
yariqay (*var.* yarqhay) (*v.*): to be hungry (Unit 8).
yatiri (*n.*): shaman, ritual specialist (Unit 15).
yawar (*n.*): blood (Unit 8).
yawar masi (*n.*): blood kin (Unit 1).
yaykupuy (*v.*): to go inside for good (Unit 19).
yaykuy (*v.*): to enter, to go in (Unit 9).
yunka (*n.*): tropical lowlands; Andean foothills (Unit 6).
yupay (*v.*): to count (Unit 5).
yupay (*n.*): number (Unit 5).
yuqch'a (*var.* ñuqch'a) (*n.*): daughter-in-law (Unit 1).
yura (*n.*): plant (Unit 20).
yuraq (*adj.*): white (Unit 10).
yuyay (*v.*): to think (Unit 20).

REFERENCES

Adelaar, Willem, and Pieter Muysken. 2004. *The Languages of the Andes*. Cambridge: Cambridge University Press.

Albó, Xavier. 1974. *Los mil rostros del quechua: Sociolingüística de Cochabamba*. Lima: Instituto de Estudios Peruanos.

Allen, Catherine J. 2002. *The Hold Life Has: Coca and Cultural Identity in an Andean Community*. 2nd ed. Washington, D.C.: Smithsonian Institution Press.

Anderson, Roger. 2005–2011. *Ucuchi: Quechua Live and in Color*. Digital Resources for the Study of Quechua: http://quechua.ucla.edu/. University of California, Los Angeles.

Arnold, Denise Y. 1997. Making men in her own image. In R. Howard-Malverde, ed., *Creating Context in Andean Cultures*, 99–131. Oxford: Oxford University Press.

Beyersdorff, Margot. 1998. *Historia y drama ritual en los Andes bolivianos (siglos XVI–XX)*. La Paz: Plural Editores/UMSA.

Bills, Garland D., Bernardo Vallejo C., and Rudolph C. Troike. 1971. *An Introduction to Spoken Bolivian Quechua*. Austin: University of Texas Press.

Brush, Stephen B. 1977. *Mountain, Field, and Family: The Economy and Human Ecology of an Andean Valley*. Philadelphia: University of Pennsylvania Press.

Canessa, Andrew. 2006. Todos somos indígenas: Towards a new language of political identity. *Bulletin of Latin American Research* 25.2:241–263.

Cerrón Palomino. 1987. *Lingüística quechua*. Cuzco: Centro de Estudios Rurales Andinos "Bartolomé de las Casas."

Crabtree, John. 2005. *Patterns of Protest: Politics and Social Movements in Bolivia*. London: Latin American Bureau.

Crandon-Malamud, Libbet. 1993. *From the Fat of Our Souls: Social Change, Political Process, and Medical Pluralism in Bolivia*. Berkeley: University of California Press.

Crevels, Mily, and Pieter Muysken, eds. 2009. *Lenguas de Bolivia*, 1: *Ámbito andino*. La Paz: Plural Editores.

Cusihuamán, Antonio. 2001. *Gramática quechua Cuzco-Collao*. 2nd ed. Cuzco: Centro de Estudios Rurales Andinos "Bartolomé de las Casas."

Femenías, Blenda. 2005. *Gender and the Boundaries of Dress in the Peruvian Andes*. Austin: University of Texas Press.

Gade, Daniel. 1999. *Nature and Culture in the Andes*. Madison: University of Wisconsin Press.
González de Holguín, Diego. 1993 [1608]. *Vocabulario de la lengua quichua*. 2 vols. Quito: PEIB/Corporación Editora Nacional.
Grondín N., Marcelo. 1971. *Método de Quechua: Runa simi*. Oruro.
Harris, Olivia. 2000. *To Make the Earth Bear Fruit: Essays on Fertility, Work, and Gender in Highland Bolivia*. London: Institute of Latin American Studies.
Healy, Kevin. 2001. *Llamas, Weavings, and Organic Chocolate: Multicultural Grassroots Development in the Andes and Amazon of Bolivia*. Notre Dame, Ind.: University of Notre Dame.
Howard, Rosaleen. 2002. Yachay: The *Tragedia del fin de Atahuallpa* as evidence of the colonisation of knowledge in the Andes. In H. Stobart and R. Howard, eds., *Knowledge and Learning in the Andes: Ethnographic Perspectives*, 17–39. Liverpool: Liverpool University Press.
———. 2007. *Por los linderos de la lengua: Ideologías lingüísticas en los Andes*. Lima: Instituto de Estudios Peruanos/Instituto Francés de Estudios Andinos/PUCP.
———. 2009. Beyond the lexicon of difference: Discursive performance of identity in the Andes. *Latin American and Caribbean Ethnic Studies* 4.1:17–46.
———. 2010. Language, signs, and the performance of power: The discursive struggle over decolonization in the Bolivia of Evo Morales. *Latin American Perspectives* 37.3:176–194.
———. 2011. The Quechua language in the Andes today: Between statistics, the state, and daily life. In Paul Heggarty and Adrian Pearce, eds., *History and Language in the Andes*, 185–213. Basingstoke: Palgrave.
Isbell, Billie Jean. 1985. *To Defend Ourselves: Ecology and Ritual in an Andean Village*. 2nd ed. Austin: University of Texas Press.
Krögel, Alison. 2012. *Food, Power, and Resistance in the Andes: Exploring Quechua Verbal and Visual Narratives*. Lanham, Md.: Lexington Books.
Lara, Jesús. 1989. *La tragedia del fin de Atahuallpa*. Cochabamba: Los Amigos del Libro.
Larson, Brooke, and Olivia Harris. 1995. *Ethnicity, Markets, and Migration in the Andes: At the Crossroads of History and Anthropology*. Durham, N.C.: Duke University Press.
Lastra, Yolanda. 1968. *Cochabamba Quechua Syntax*. The Hague: Mouton.
Mannheim, Bruce. 1991. *The Language of the Inka since the European Invasion*. Austin: University of Texas Press.
Meyerson, Julia. 1990. *Tambo: Life in an Andean Village*. Austin: University of Texas Press.
Morató Peña, Luis, and Luis Morató Lara. 1994. *Quechua boliviano trilingüe: Qheshwa/English/castellano: Curso intermedio*. La Paz: Los Amigos del Libro.
Paerregaard, Karsten. 1997. *Linking Separate Worlds: Urban Migrants and Rural Lives in Peru*. Oxford: Berg.
Parker, Gary. 1963. La classificación genética de los dialectos quechuas. *Revista del Museo Nacional* 32:241–252.
———. 1969. *Ayacucho Quechua Grammar and Dictionary*. The Hague: Mouton.
Platt, Tristan. 1997. The sound of light: Emergent communication through Quechua shamanic dialogue. In R. Howard-Malverde, ed., *Creating Context in Andean Cultures*, 196–226. Oxford: Oxford University Press.
Plaza, Pedro. 2009. Quechua. In Mily Crevels and Pieter Muysken, eds., *Lenguas de Bolivia*, 1: *Ámbito andino*, 215–284. La Paz: Plural Editores.
———. 2010. *Qallarinapaq: Curso básico de quechua boliviano*. Cochabamba: Funproeib Andes.
Rasnake, Roger. 1988. *Domination and Cultural Resistance: Authority and Power among an Andean People*. Durham, N.C.: Duke University Press.

Sallnow, Michael. 1987. *Pilgrims of the Andes: Regional Cults in Cusco*. Washington, D.C.: Smithsonian Institution Press.

Solá, Donald. 1970. *Spoken Cuzco Quechua*. Lima: Yachay Wasi Academy.

Soto Ruíz, Clodoaldo. 1976. *Gramática quechua: Ayacucho-Chanca*. Lima: Instituto de Estudios Peruanos.

Stobart, Henry. 2006. *Music and the Poetics of Production in the Bolivian Andes*. Burlington, Vt.: Ashgate.

Stobart, Henry, and R. Howard, eds. 2002. *Knowledge and Learning in the Andes: Ethnographic Perspectives*. Liverpool: Liverpool University Press.

Torero, Alfredo. 1964. Los dialectos quechuas. *Anales Científicos de la Universidad Agraria* 2:446–478.

———. 1974. *El quechua y la historia social andina*. Lima: Universidad Ricardo Palma.

Turino, Thomas. 1993. *Moving Away from Silence: Music of the Peruvian Altiplano and the Experience of Migration*. Chicago: University of Chicago Press.

van Vleet, Krista E. 2008. *Performing Kinship: Narrative, Gender, and the Intimacies of Power in the Andes*. Austin: University of Texas Press.

Weismantel, Mary. 1998. *Food, Gender, and Poverty in the Ecuadorian Andes*. Prospect Heights, Ill.: Waveland Press.

Zorn, Elayne. 2004. *Weaving a Future: Tourism, Cloth, and Culture on an Andean Island*. Iowa City, Iowa: University of Iowa Press.